The Sopranos and Philosophy

Popular Culture and Philosophy™
Series Editor: William Irwin

The Sopranos and Philosophy

I Kill Therefore I Am

Edited by
RICHARD GREENE
and
PETER VERNEZZE

OPEN COURT
Chicago and La Salle, Illinois

Volume 7 in the series, Popular Culture and Philosophy[TM]

To order books from Open Court, call toll free 1-800-815-2280, or visit our website at www.opencourtbooks.com.

Open Court Publishing Company is a division of Carus Publishing Company.

First printing 2004

Printed and bound in the United States of America

Library of Congress Cataloging-in-Publication Data

The Sopranos and philosophy : I kill therefore I am / edited by Richard Greene and Peter Vernezze.
    p. cm. — (Popular culture and philosophy ; v.7)
    Includes bibliographical references and index.
    ISBN 0-8126-9558-5 (pbk. : alk. paper)
    1. Sopranos (Television program) — Miscellanea. I. Greene, Richard, 1961– II. Vernezze, Peter, 1959– III. Series.
PN1992.77.S66S67 2004
791.45'72—dc22
                                                            2004002571

To Nancy and Pam

Contents

Contorno

Dolce

Vino

Foreword: Forewarned

Need more Sopranos?

Can't wait for the next season. And/or will the next be the last?

During your Down Time, the In Between, the Empty Void, you should read this book—or else!

It's got Bada-Bing! all over it—

The Inside and the Out—

"The Sopranos and Philosophy"—

Who would have thought?

Forget about it!

So now when I get sad and blue, and think about "the Boys," I just pick up The Sopranos and Philosophy.

And remember—

Remember when times were good. And "Big Pussy" wasn't sleeping with the fishes.

Not yet!

Vincent Pastore
(Sal "Big Pussy" Bonpensiero)

Stop. We're Grateful to You. We Are.

Much of the joy that comes from working on a collection such as this one can be attributed to the fine people that help the project along. First, we are very grateful for the generous support we've received from Bill Irwin and David Ramsay Steele at Open Court. Throughout the process they were there to meet our editorial needs while offering consistently insightful advice and guidance. Carolyn Madia Gray deserves kudos for her work on the publicity for this book.

An inestimable debt of gratitude is owed to the contributors to this volume. We were extremely fortunate to find so many talented philosophers who shared our love for the show and were willing to impart their insights to a general audience. Without their enthusiasm, commitment, and effort, there would be no book. *Grazie. Molto grazie.*

Special thanks are due to Nancy Balmert, Dawn Bergin, Luke Fernandez, Dan Fox, Paul Goggi, Leo Greiner, Kris Greene, Pam Hall, Roxanne Hinds, Jaynie Hirschi, Thom Kuehls, Paul Lulewicz, Troy Marzziotti (who independently suggested to Open Court that a volume on *The Sopranos* would be worthwhile), Susan Matt, Leah Murray, Abigail Myers, and Richard Vernezze each of whom provided helpful comments on drafts of the essays. Their insights led to a number of improvements in the collection.

Special thanks are also due to Skye Brimley, Jock Glidden, Frank Guliuzza, Caril Jennings, Hubbell King, Greg Lewis, Warren Pettey, Carl Porter, Michael Schumacher, and Sally Taylor for providing inspiration, technical help, and/or useful feedback at critical stages in the development of this manuscript.

Finally, we'd like to thank our colleagues in the Department of Political Science and Philosophy (many of whom have been mentioned above) and Weber State University for creating the sort of environment where projects of this type are not only allowed, but are encouraged.

This Book of Ours

We never had any doubt that *The Sopranos* would make for a great book in the Open Court "Popular Culture and Philosophy" series. A show the *New York Times* had dubbed possibly "the greatest work of American popular culture in the last quarter century" seemed tailor-made for inclusion in a series whose declared mission was to apply philosophical analysis and clarity to significant contemporary movements, entertainment, and the arts. So when we discovered the *Sopranos* project was available, we didn't hesitate to offer our services (and, though we were prepared to, we didn't have to kill anyone to get the contract. Sure we made threats and came heavy, but that's just business—nothing personal).

We were big fans of Open Court even before we edited this volume. With books on *The Simpsons*, *Seinfeld*, *The Matrix*, *Buffy the Vampire Slayer*, and *Lord of the Rings*, the "Popular Culture" series has done more than anything we can think of to get philosophy back to where Socrates had it, on the streets and available to everyone. We both have stories about students who've turned up in an Introduction to Philosophy class inspired by one of these books, queries from colleagues, and interactions with complete strangers who rattle off a title or two when we tell them that we teach philosophy.

We suspect that we are not alone in noticing this trend towards the popularization of philosophy that Open Court has done so much to bring about. Anyone who visits the philosophy section of a local bookstore will probably witness the same phenomenon we have, namely, that a disproportionate number of browsers will pick up one of the titles in this series. In fact, this may well be where you are right now, deciding whether to purchase this book.

We have one thing to say to you: If you don't buy this book, we genuinely don't think there's anything to gain by keeping you around.

Okay, perhaps we've identified a bit too much with the show in the course of doing this project. But we think you are going to enjoy this book. Like gabagool, philosophy is a bit strange at first. But try it. You'll like it. You always knew *The Sopranos* was more than a show about gangsters. As Al Gini says in our first essay, "*The Sopranos* may not be high art, but neither is it a cheap action thriller or a murderous melodrama. It is a mass media, action-packed, X-rated version of *Waiting for Godot*. A story of both existential despair, and, in the words of Victor Frankl, 'man's search for meaning'." As this book demonstrates, there's a lot of philosophy in it as well.

There are of obvious nods to philosophy within the show: A.J.'s bout with Existentialism; Tony's familiarity with Sun Tzu and Machiavelli; Ralph's heart to heart with Father Phil concerning the problem of evil; Meadow's enrollment in an ethics course. You can be sure that we've dealt with these moments. But the glaring examples only scratch the surface of the philosophical content of *The Sopranos*. The essays in this book cover everything from God to Greek tragedy, ancient ethics to modern morality, the purpose of art to the possibility of self-knowledge, and bring into play the entire spectrum of philosophy: aesthetics, religion, politics, value theory, metaphysics, epistemology, feminism, and philosophy of language.

For this thing of ours we've gathered a very knowledgeable and talented group of folks who love *The Sopranos* as much as you do. We like to think of them as our family. Even if *this* family doesn't quite come before everything else, we believe that you'll still be quite impressed with their work. Combining a close analysis of the show with a thorough knowledge of their discipline, the contributors to this volume have created a work that explores and analyzes the great ideas that drive the series (and our lives): love and death, good and evil, crime and punishment. Our sincere hope is that this book exemplifies the symmetrical and mutually supporting relationship that exists between philosophy and popular culture: pop-culture provides a rich background for philosophical investigation, while important philosophical concepts serve to make-up part of the complex tapestry that is pop-culture.

Aristotle said that philosophy begins in wonder. We marvel at the world and then we try to understand it. The same drive that causes the scientist to probe beneath the surface of nature and attempt to discern its true laws compels philosophers to undertake a similar task with respect to religious claims, political institutions, moral behavior, and yes, television shows. Like digging a grave at the Pine Barrens, it's a dirty job, but somebody's got to do it.

Antipasto

Prolegomenon

1

Bada-Being and Nothingness: Murderous Melodrama or Morality Play?

AL GINI

We are, says media critic Susan Sontag, a video-addicted, media-saturated society. We live in a turned on, tuned in world. According to a recent report in the *New York Times*, ninety-eight percent of American households own at least one television, and forty percent own three or more TVs. Moreover, private ownership of TVs is not limited to our living rooms. Car, cab, and SUV manufacturers started offering backseat TVs in 1999, and according to the Consumer Electronics Association, more than 400,000 "mobile video units" were installed in 2002. TVs have now taken over our public lives as well. Banks and super-markets have installed them in cashier and checkout lines. Airports, railway, and bus stations have them prominently dis-played everywhere. Restaurants, bars, but not coffee-houses (they are reserved for low platform information systems—music, books, magazines, and newspapers) have TVs strategically placed to better keep their customers entertained, informed, or at least distracted while they wait. And let's not forget, no mat-ter where we are or what we're doing, we can always access our favorite TV show or movie on our laptops or by using portable DVD players.

Media maven and author of *Amusing Ourselves to Death*, Neil Postman, believes that watching television is the most com-monly shared cultural experience in America. Household televi-sions are turned on, even if not closely watched, an average of 7.8 hours per day, and the average American attentively watches more than four hours of TV every day. Television, suggests Postman, is the primary medium by which most of us seek entertainment, gain information, or just relax.

What was it that Marshall McLuhan said, "the medium is the message" or "the medium is the massage"? Either way, the fact is we get the bulk of our messages from the media. (The French philosopher André Glucksman goes much further than McLuhan. For Glucksman, the media is "mediatique"—the focus of reality, that which frames and delimits reality, and, due to its all pervasiveness, the only reality we really know.) The media brings us the sights and sounds of the world. The media and its messages insinuates itself into our consciousness by virtue of its omnipresence and repetition. Like it or not, from *Mr. Roger's Neighborhood* to *Dan Rather* to *Seinfeld* to *Friends* to *Sex and the City*, TV bombards us with messages, manners, metaphors, and models of reality.

My thesis is a simple one. In the past, many of us learned some of our first lessons in manners and morals by watching *Sesame Street*: cooperate, play fair, share things, don't hit people, say you're sorry when you hurt somebody. Today, in watching *The Sopranos*, about eleven million viewers an episode are taking an advanced course (one containing adult language, violence, nudity, and explicit sex scenes) about the self-defined universe of Mafia ethics: What is *Duty*? What is *Honor*? What is *Omertà*? But more than just a curious and titillating analysis of an aberrant ethical code—the tribal or warrior justification of murder, mendacity, prostitution, infidelity, extortion, and usury—it is, in some sense, a traditional morality play. *The Sopranos* may not be high art, but neither is it a cheap action thriller or a murderous melodrama. I believe it is a mass media, action-packed, X-rated version of *Waiting for Godot*, a story of both existential despair and, in the words of Victor Frankl, "man's search for meaning."

Bad Boys and Pirate Kings

In one magic movie moment, Francis Ford Coppola completely transformed the semi-slapstick antics of gangster flicks into serious films that gave mythic, metaphysical, and moral status to Italian mobsters and wise guys. This transformation was, of course, cemented into permanent place (pun intended) with the works of Martin Scorsese. Before *The Godfather*, mob films were predominately, but not exclusively, about non-Italian, urban, bad guys. Gangsters with Irish, German, English, and "everyman" caucasian faces. And the stars of these films, different from most of the casts of *The Sopranos, Godfather I, II, III,* and *Goodfellas*, were anything but Italian, for instance James Cagney, Humphrey Bogart, Edward G. Robinson, and Pat O'Brian. Perhaps these early mob films were urban updates of the American love affair with the wild, wild west, and our infatuation with the action packed but laconic cowboy lifestyle.

The American cinema has depicted the life of the cowboy in many different ways. He has been portrayed as a loner, the drifter, always on the move, living without commitments or roots; as the strong, silent type that rides into town and gets rid of all the bad guys, marries the schoolmarm, and lives happily ever after; as the drunken, bar-brawling saddle hand, who works hard and plays even harder; as the single and seemingly celibate circuit-riding marshal whose exclusive quest is to pacify any and all hostiles in the territory. And then, there are the exploits of the marshals' opposite number, the outlaw heroes: Jesse James, Butch Cassidy and the Sundance Kid, Billy the Kid. Their stories, too, have filled our screens and captured our hearts.

We have long loved the roughneck, the rascal, the bad boy— in both our films and our literature. We seem to be drawn to their sense of rugged individualism, their resourcefulness, their eagerness to take risks, their need to be experimental, push the envelope, be different. We wonder at their daring, their cheek, their flair for the outrageous. We are, I think, envious of their ability to break with convention and, to paraphrase Frank Sinatra, do it their way.

Of course, our infatuation with these "bad boys" and "pirate kings" has its limits. We do not want nor are we easily drawn, in fiction or in fact, to anti-heroes who were sadists, serial killers, or ghouls. Jeffrey Dahmer and John Wayne Gacy may evoke our curiosity, but their conduct and behavior is too ghastly and writ-too-large to qualify as "loveable rascals" or even as "rascals we love to hate." Anti-heroes need to be both scary and lovable, need to find a balance between being naughty and nice, tough and soft, strong and yet compassionate. The creator of *The Sopranos*, David Chase, has intentionally fashioned just such an anti-hero in his main character, Anthony "Tony" Soprano.

In his mid-forties, Tony Soprano is a second-generation wise guy. Although he tells his neighbors, his children's teachers, and the IRS that he is in waste management, in fact he is the acting boss of the most powerful criminal organization in New Jersey. Tony likes his work and occasionally loves his life, both professionally and personally—at least, when he can keep them all properly separated, balanced, and under control. Tony is a big, powerful, physical man with even bigger appetites for good wine, good food, good cigars, and good sex—whether with his Russian *goomah*, her amputee best friend and cousin, his local Mercedes sales-nymphet, Ralph's new *goomah*, a quickie at the Bada Bing!, or, on occasion, even with his wife. In his interactions with his family, friends, and associates, he is by turns benign or brutal, selfish or sensitive, lecherous or loving, overwhelmingly physical or psychologically insightful. Like the heroine in Erica Jong's *Fear of Flying*, Tony's general outlook on life is that of an alpha warrior-hunter—"the world is a predatory place, take big bites, eat faster!"

A major piece of the dramatic tension of *The Sopranos* comes out of just how much Tony likes the life of being a wise guy, a made man, a *capo di capi*. Paulie Walnuts, Big Pussy, Christopher, Silvio, and Furio aren't just his employees or even his fellow workers. They are his crew, his tribe, his truest family. As Tony said, "This family comes before everything else . . . *everything*. Before your wife or your children and your mother and your father" ("Fortunate Son"). These are the guys he plays with, fights and argues with, steals with, makes war and kills with—and, if needs be, would die with. These are the men with whom he shares his real life—life on the street, life on the hustle. Tony likes his gang and he likes the games they play to get by—gambling, racketeering, union scams, stolen property, loan sharking. He likes the dreaming, the scheming, the game playing, the con, the heist. He likes the risks and the dangers. He likes the chances they take to "put food on the table," and, most importantly in their eyes, prove their manhood.

As a second-generation mob guy, Tony chose "the life" because he wanted it. Although he regularly preaches the line that Italians were forced into "the life" because they had no other choice, neither he nor his daughter Meadow are entirely convinced. "Right, Dad! Italians had no other choice. Just like Mario Cuomo, huh Dad?" ("University"). Nor is his therapist convinced. When Tony attempted to explain his entrance into the mob in terms of the fact that the Carnegies were crooks and killers and that early Italian immigrants just wanted a piece of the action, Melfi responded, "What do poor Italian immigrants have to do with you?" ("From Where to Eternity"). Nevertheless, Tony wants to rationalize his choices and actions by saying he is a man of honor, doing his job. As far as he's concerned, he's fulfilling his duty. In his mind, he's just a businessman trying "to get by" and do well for his family. But protestations aside, Tony's claims of "honor, duty, and family" simply do not pass the litmus test for the code of honor or described by Mario Puzo in *The Godfather*.

According to Puzo, Vito Corleone was an accidental if not a reluctant Don. He was not a man who sought the title, and only embraced it when circumstances and necessity forced it upon him. As a child, Vito came to this country as an orphan and on the run from a blood-feud in Sicily. As he grew into adulthood, his hopes and aspirations were modest—a wife, a family, and an honest job. Only when a local member of the "Black Hand" forced him out of his job and began to harass his friends did the young Corleone take action. He killed this "Black Hand," this "fellow Italian who stole from other Italians," out of a sense of duty and justice and not for personal gain or in an attempt to establish a reputation. Vito Corleone became a "man of honor"—*un uomo d'onore*—because he acted on principle and not on impulse. Even at the end of his life, sitting in his garden talking to his son Michael, Vito Corleone felt he had only done what was necessary to do. "I make no apologies for my life. What I did, I had to do. I did it for my family." No such motives can be associated with Tony Soprano's career choice. His selection of a vocation came from the adrenaline rush he got out of watching the strong arm and bully boy tactics of his father "Johnny Boy" and his uncle "Junior" Soprano. Honor and ethnic pride aside, Tony sought out, chose, and eagerly embraced "the life" because it looked like fun. For him, it was all about the thrill of the game—the hunt, the chase, and the kill.

Avoiding the Regularness of Life

Perhaps the central issue and overriding existential tension of the entire series is best captured in the lamentation of Tony's nephew, Christopher Moltisanti: "The fuckin' regularness of life is too fuckin' hard for me" ("The Legend of Tennessee Moltisanti"). Christopher, at the time, is just a soldier and not yet a "made guy," and he desperately wants to be somebody. He wants recognition. He wants to be a player. He wants to overcome the "nothingness" of being an average guy, a working-stiff, a nobody. He wants what Tony wants, what Uncle Junior wants, what Silvio, Paulie, Bobby Bacala, Richie Aprile want—recognition, "stugots" (balls)! Christopher wants to be "*igualio*," "a man among men," one of the boys, one of the crew, a member of the tribe.[1]

Psychiatrist Glen O. Gabbard perfectly captures the collective psyche of Tony's mob by referring to them as a "band of lost boys" suffering from a sense of existential meaninglessness and fearing being doomed to an unheralded and unobserved life. Doomed to a mediocre, middle-class existence. Doomed to being a pawn and not a player. So, they individually and collectively seek meaning and seek self through boisterous activity, violence, criminal behavior, and murder. In breaking the rules, says Gabbard, in their almost total disregard for the rights of others, they achieve status, stuff, and success, and thereby overcome the numbing sense of absurdity and boredom that pervades their lives.[2]

Both Jean-Paul Sartre and Ernest Becker have argued that the human condition is burdened with two unavoidable realities—our gnawing sense of purposelessness and the inevitability and absurdity of death. Like Tony's son A.J., Sartre holds that life is "dumb to us." There is no God, no menu or logical set of directions from which we may seek advice and select options. We are on our own and left to our own devices. For Sartre, our only alternative is to thrash out, to act. For Sartre, to be is to act. Whether the outcome be right or wrong, "the act is everything."

---

[1] E. Anthony Rotundo, "Wonderbread and Stugots," in *A Sitdown with the Sopranos*, edited by Regina Barreca (New York: Palgrave, 2002), p. 47.

[2] Glen O. Gabbard, *The Psychology of the Sopranos* (New York: Basic Books, 2002), pp.15, 16, 157, 158, 159.

It is only in choosing to act that we assert our "Being" and, at least temporarily, overcome "Nothingness."

In *The Denial of Death*, Becker argues that our innate drive is not the pursuit of sex as Freud proposed. Rather, it is the fear of death and "no-thing-ness" that drives us to attempt to overcome death through both culturally sanctioned heroic acts as well as outrageous acts of violence and evil. Like Livia Soprano, Tony's mother, Becker believes we all view life as "a big nothing." For Becker, all humanly caused evil or heroic acts are nothing more than attempts to deny our creatureliness (mortality) and overcome our insignificance (meaninglessness). For Becker and Sartre, it can be argued, to act, to be bold, to achieve hero or anti-hero status is to achieve at least a modicum of immortality. In so doing, we overcome our humdrum lives and, at least for a while, put away our fears of dying and being forgotten. Like the "lost boys" of William Golding's *Lord of the Flies*, Tony's "band of boys," with more "stugots than savvy," pursue a lifestyle that, while destructive and dysfunctional, distracts them from the dread of dwelling on their own personal sense of insignificance and eventual demise.

A Janus-faced Mobster

George Anastasia, organized crime reporter for the *Philadelphia Inquirer*, is right: "If Shakespeare were alive today, he'd be writing for *The Sopranos*."[3] *The Sopranos* is not your standard mob show. It's not just about bad guys. It's not just about good guys chasing bad guys. It's not just about being an Italian gangster. It's not even just about the Mafia. It's a drama. It's a story. It's about a group of guys trying to get by, no matter how unusual and unorthodox their line of work. Yes, it's a show full of clichés and stereotypes about Italians and food, the number of times the "F--" word can be used in the same sentence, New Jersey accents, cheating on your wife, and D.A. (duck-ass) hair cuts with pompadours. It is also a show that explores the "big picture problems" writ-large each week—problems and issues that each of us face in our private lives, but hopefully in a much less dramatic and dangerous context. It's a show interlaced with comedy,

---

[3] George Anastasia, "If Shakespeare Were Alive Today, He'd Be Writing for the Sopranos," in *A Sitdown with the Sopranos*, pp. 149–166.

chaos, complexity, and confusion. As a cover story in *Newsweek* put it: "F. Scott Fitzgerald said the mark of a first-rate mind is the ability to hold two opposing ideas at once. It is also the mark of a first-rate TV show." *The Sopranos* is just such a show.

Tony Soprano is a perfect example of this point. Tony is not just another bad guy. True, he has proven to be a horrible, gruesome thug. He is a *capo di capi* who has earned his rank by being ruthless, exploitative, and corrupt. At the same time, he is a man who desperately wants to be loved, and a "made man" who risks his life and reputation by secretively seeking the help and advice of a psychiatrist.

The dramatic and human point here seems obvious. Tony is interesting because he is clever, complicated, and conflicted. He wants to be brutally Machiavellian during the day, but at night he wants to come home and be Alan Alda (I mean Alan Alda the real person, the do-gooder, the political activist and feminist, not the womanizing schemer that Alan Alda played in *M*A*S*H*.) so he can bond with his wife and help the kids do their homework. Tony's dilemma, and perhaps the central dramatic tension of the series, is that he cannot sustain the dysfunctional dichotomy of being "Janus-faced in New Jersey."[4] With each episode Tony continues to lose control of his life, his wife, and his empire. And we are fascinated by his dichotomous efforts and his slow demise.

In the end, I believe that *The Sopranos* is a show rich in Freudian themes, Shakespearean character development, Byzantine political plots, and philosophical reflection. On the other hand, you may not agree and feel that my thesis is absolutely *assurdità*. If that is the case, . . . FUGHEDDA-BOUTIT!!![5]

---

[4] For further discussion of the dichotomous nature of Tony's psyche, see Chapter 3 of this volume.

[5] The title of this chapter and many of the ideas contained herein were inspired by the research and insights of Glen O. Gabbard, M.D. Dr. Gabbard's book, *The Psychology of The Sopranos*, as well as his *Sopranos* chatroom on the internet magazine *Slate*, are worthy of serious attention.

Primo Piatto

History of Philosophy: Tony and the Philosophers

2

Tony Soprano and the Art of War: New Jersey Meets the East

STEVEN C. COMBS

> TONY: Well I am improving. You have to joyfully participate in the suffering of the world.
> DR. MELFI: Your thoughts have a kind of Eastern flavor to them.
> TONY: Well, I've lived in Jersey my whole life. ("The Telltale Moozadell")

Tony Soprano is one of the most complex and interesting characters on television. His life is burdened with tremendous responsibilities and plagued by powerful conflicts. Tony's woes lead him to a psychiatrist, Dr. Melfi, who engages him in psychotherapy in order to alleviate his panic attacks and blackouts, which are in large part triggered by the burdens and demons of his criminal world. At one point in his treatment, Dr. Melfi suggests sarcastically that Tony seems more interested in being a successful crime boss than in improving his mental health: "You want to be a better mob boss, read *The Art of War*" ("Big Girls Don't Cry"). Later, in another therapy session, Tony mentions that he is reading *The Art of War*, and has implemented some of its ideas in his own life and work ("He Is Risen").

The references to Chinese philosophy are interesting because Tony's world resembles, in significant ways, the seminal period in classical China when Sun Tzu[1] wrote his masterpiece on

---

[1] According to J.H. Huang, "Sun-tzu is the original title of the book, and it was

strategy. The social structure of organized crime parallels the feudalism of the Spring-Autumn and Warring States periods. Furthermore, many of Tony's tactics are found in *The Art of War.* Still, despite these superficial similarities, and Tony's allusions to Sun Tzu's ideas, Tony misappropriates Sun Tzu's advice because he fails to incorporate the core philosophical aspects of the work. By looking more closely at *The Sopranos* and *The Art of War* we can begin to understand the social and political world in ancient China that spawned tremendous philosophical insight as well as some of the significant differences that characterize Eastern and Western thought. Furthermore, analysis of *The Art of War* reveals insights on strategy and suggests new possibilities for managing conflict. Ultimately, through Tony, we can glimpse some of the potential challenges and opportunities in incorporating classical Eastern thought in the contemporary Western world.

Organizational Structure

TONY: Over the next couple of years, more and more, I'm gonna be givin' my orders through you. And then finally . . . only through you.

CHRISTOPHER: Well what about Sil? You got that with him, and Paulie.

TONY: Those other guys, Sil, Paulie . . . one thing they're not my blood. You hear what I'm sayin' to you? It's a matter of trust. ("Everybody Hurts")

While there are enduring questions about the authorship of *The Art of War,* the core text was probably written during the Chou dynasty, toward the end of the Spring-Autumn period (around 770–481 B.C.E.) or during the early Warring States period (around 403–221 B.C.E.). These historic periods are characterized by constant and brutal warfare between the various states in China. The chaos and cruelty of the Spring-Autumn and Warring States

---

renamed Sunzi bingfas (bingfa means 'the principles for using forces') at a much later date. This is generally translated in English as 'The Art of War,' which actually is an emulation of the titles of books written by Machiavelli and Baron de Jomini. Sun-tzu in the pinyin system is spelled Sunzi, but Sun-tzu is the broadly accepted English rendering." In J.H. Huang, *Sun Tzu: The New Translation* (New York: Morrow, 1993), p. 25.

periods inspired many of Asia's most profound thinkers, writers, and artists, including Confucius, Lao Tzu, and Zhuang Tzu.

The Chou dynasty was formed around 1100 B.C.E. The early years of Chou rule were often thought of as a time that unified and enriched the world. The Chou created a ruling structure based on kinship ties. Familial relatives and their kin were appointed as rulers to oversee the vast territory, which was guarded by a system of outposts manned by Chou warriors. All rulers, even those with no direct biological connection, were viewed as members of the royal family. By connecting family with power, the Chou were able to inspire loyalty. The system was structured so that rulers were independent of one another, but nonetheless beholden to the emperor or central authority. The rulers of each territory or state were, in turn, supported by a strict hierarchy composed of ministers and officers of various ranks.[2]

Like the Chou empire, Tony's criminal world is organized according to a feudal, familial structure. Tony, as his uncle's proxy, runs the Soprano family business, which controls the northern New Jersey territory. He and the heads of other families on the East coast operate independently of one another, separated by their respective territories. As long as they respect the territory of the other families, they have sovereignty over illegal activities such as gambling, prostitution, and extortion. They earn a percentage of the profits from the activities of their underbosses and their soldiers. Tony explains: "This thing is a pyramid, since time immemorial. Shit runs downhill, money goes up. It's that simple" ("For All Debts Public and Private"). Furthermore, the crime groups have a familial organizational structure, much like the Chou. Interestingly, the criminal family can be more important than the biological unit. In one scene, Christopher and Eugene are initiated as "made" men, meaning they enjoy extra status and protection in the organization. Tony tells them solemnly: "once you enter this family there's no getting out. This family comes before everything else, . . . *every-thing*. Before your wife and children and your mother and your father" ("Fortunate Son"). Thus the crime family is a superior structure that functions to secure the well-being of its members'

---

[2] Cho-yun Hsu, *Ancient China in Transition: An Analysis of Social Mobility, 722–222 B.C.* (Stanford: Stanford University Press, 1965), pp. 2–7.

subordinate, nuclear families. This is not meant to suggest that blood relations are not important in the hierarchy. When it comes to leadership, the most powerful figures tend to be chosen from bloodlines because relatives are thought to be more trustworthy than others.

Decentralization of Power

LARRY BOY: Why don't we run this thing like a council?
JIMMY: Larry, the old guy set this up as a paramilitary organization. We need a supreme commander at the top, not the fuckin' Dave Clark Five. ("Meadowlands")

The Chou eventually found it impossible to control the vast empire and the incursions of barbarians into far-flung territories. The kings countered these threats by granting fiefs and monetary rewards to feudal lords in return for their support and pledges of loyalty to the Chou. As the feudal lords became more powerful, the central government became impoverished. In 770 B.C.E., the western capital was lost, allowing the feudal lords to further exert their power. Central authority continued to disintegrate to the point where city-states operated independently, with little or no deference to the house of Chou. Feudal lords were eager to fill the power vacuum left by the weak central government, but no city-state was strong enough to control all the rest. Consequently, China endured continual battles for conquest and survival that lasted for hundreds of years.

Tony Soprano is also involved in constant warfare, as was his father before him, and almost certainly as will be those who replace him. This is in part because there is no central authority that is able to control all criminals in the region. Tony's family regularly challenges his authority, as witnessed by Junior's attempt to have Tony whacked, Richie Aprile's efforts to stir up a coup, and the betrayal of Big Pussy. There are other threats to Tony's authority, as evidenced in Tony's uneasy alliances with Russian mobsters who launder his money, and the attempts by law-enforcement to decapitate the crime syndicate. Tony's life is rife with violent preemptive strikes and paybacks designed to maintain a semblance of order in a chaotic world.

Strategic Precepts

TONY: Been readin' that book you told me about. *The Art of War* by Sun Tzu. Here's this guy, a Chinese general. Wrote this thing twenty-four hundred years ago. And most of it still applies today. Balk the enemy's power. Force him to reveal himself. ("He Is Risen")

Given the prevalence of warfare in ancient China, it is not surprising that the finest thinkers wrote about military strategy. Sun Tzu's book stands apart from the rest. Ralph Sawyer maintains that the book eclipses "all the other military strategy books combined."[3] Roger Ames calls the book "the world's foremost classic on military strategy."[4] J.H. Huang declares it "the most brilliant and widely applied strategic book ever written."[5]

Tony Soprano has seized on significant precepts of Sun Tzu—most notably deception and surprise. Sun Tzu advocates being formless, which involves using deception to mask one's appearance or create disastrous miscalculations through false perceptions. He says:

> The ultimate skill in taking up strategic position (*hsing*) is to have no form (*hsing*). If your position is formless (*hsing*), the most carefully concealed spies will not be able to get a look at it, and the wisest counselors will not be able to lay plans against it.[6]

One can also appear formless by keeping secret the place where the battle will be fought.

> The place we have chosen to give the enemy battle must be kept from him. If he cannot anticipate us, the positions the enemy must prepare to defend will be many. And if the positions he must prepare to defend are many, then any unit we engage in battle will be few in number.[7]

---

[3] Ralph D. Sawyer, *Sun-Tzu: The Art of War* (New York: Barnes and Noble, 1994), p. 16.

[4] Roger Ames, *Sun-Tzu: The Art of Warfare* (New York: Ballantine, 1993), p. 35.

[5] Huang, *Sun-Tzu*, p. 15.

[6] Ames, *Sun-Tzu*, Chapter 6, p. 126.

[7] *Ibid*, Chapter 6, p. 125.

Finally, if one can force the enemy to reveal itself, that is to manifest its form, one can analyze the situation and respond with the most effective battle plan.

Water provides an excellent metaphor for Sun Tzu's notion of formlessness and strategic positioning. Water takes no form and the nature and timing of its attack is virtually impossible to predict. It is also tremendously powerful. After all, water created the Grand Canyon, and the concentrated force of water can dislodge huge boulders and knock an army off of its feet. Tony uses Sun Tzu's advice—to deceive the enemy, attack indirectly, remain flexible, and move decisively—to improve the efficacy of his criminality.

Philosophical Principles

DR. MELFI: You can't control everything that happens.

TONY: But you can get pissed off.

DR. MELFI: And then what? Lose control?

TONY: Who said anything about that? You direct your anger where it belongs.

DR. MELFI: You have panic attacks. Panic occurs when feelings of anger, revenge, whatever, overwhelm you. That's where behavioral therapy comes in. It can teach you to control those triggers.

TONY: Then how do you get people to do what you want? ("Employee of the Month")

While Sun Tzu focuses on the topic of warfare, and the strategic approach to battle, his view is undergirded by a significant philosophical stance. According to Ames, "Almost every one of the early Chinese philosophers took warfare to be an area of sustained philosophical reflection."[8] Chinese military texts are considered to be applied philosophy. Sun Tzu was not content simply to elaborate on battlefield strategies and tactics, but strove to develop a systematic approach to strategy that was consistent with his worldview and morality. Sun Tzu, like all classical Chinese philosophers, held a monistic worldview that

---

[8] Ames, *Sun-Tzu*, p. 7.

is distinct from the dualism that pervades Western culture. His approach emphasizes the unity and connectedness of all things, and harmony and minimization of turmoil. He demands that the commander understand the workings of the world, and maintain personal unity, balance, and harmony. The perspective on warfare emphasizes the importance of strategy as a way of deterring war and achieving victory without doing battle. War, or conflict, is to be avoided and, if used at all, must be kept to a minimum. The purpose of war is to restore harmony and balance in the universe for the well being of all.

Classical Chinese cosmology espouses a monistic, or "one-world," view that stands in sharp contrast with a dualist, or "two-world," theory we have inherited from the Greeks. The Greek Plato believed that humans dwell in a false reality of perception and sensory experience. Humans have deluded themselves into thinking that this world is real. According to Plato, there is a true reality, another world where the perfect form of all things and concepts exists in a permanent, ideal state. Even Aristotle, who does not accept Plato's theory, believes that there is a difference between the way something appears and the way it actually is. He maintains that there is an underlying order to the world that stands behind or apart from our experience and perception. The Greek two-world view is also integral to Christianity, which pervades Tony's family environment. In fact, Tony maintains a clear separation between the human world and God's world in order to convince himself that his crimes will not lead to eternal damnation, believing that as a "soldier" he will not be held morally blameworthy for his actions ("From Where to Eternity").

In classical China, philosophers held that there is one world, and it alone constitutes reality. There is nothing else, no outside agent such as a god, to order and give life to the world. Instead, order results from the intermingling of opposite forces—*yin* and *yang*. *Yin* is likened to the feminine. It is represented by darkness, water, and stillness. *Yang* is masculine. It is light, fiery, and active. These two forces alternately rise and fall, interacting to constantly produce novel moments in their ceaseless combinations. The order of the world comes from the interaction of everything else. Hence, the world exists as a consequence of the dynamic interaction of all things.

Because things exist or are meaningful as a consequence of their interaction with everything else, classical Chinese philosophy emphasizes the interdependence of everything in the world. Everything is connected, and all actions ripple through everything else. Hence, there is great value placed on balance and harmony. When things are balanced with one another, everything is enriched and sustained. But when someone suffers, everyone suffers. Harmony is valued because it is a reflection of a balanced system. When things are in balance, they are harmonious and healthy.

It is clear that Tony's life lacks harmony, which results in the panic attacks that first send him to a psychiatrist. His unhappiness stems from his inability to see the connections between all things. It becomes clear to the audience that Tony is affected by his parents, and he in turn is affecting his own children. Through his therapy, the audience learns that Tony's father was a brutal mobster who, one day, chopped off the butcher's pinkie to "inspire" him to pay off a debt. The experience traumatizes young Tony, who disobeyed his father and witnessed the bloody event. Later, Tony's father brings home packages of fresh meat from the butcher, much to the delight of his mother. Tony's mother is pleased that dad "brought home the bacon" even though he had to mutilate a man to do it. Tony realizes that some day he will be called upon to bring home the bacon. Consequently, as an adult, he experiences panic attacks and passes out when he grills sausages and eats cold cuts from the refrigerator. Later, his son (Anthony Jr.) is named "defensive captain" of his high school football team. Anthony Jr. is overwhelmed with the responsibility and proceeds to faint ("Fortunate Son").

Instead of recognizing the connections between his criminality and psychological problems, his adultery and marital failure, and his objectification of women and emotional distance from his mother, wife, and daughter, Tony compartmentalizes his life as a coping mechanism. He distances his emotional and spiritual self from his consciousness in order to cope with his racism, sexism, and inhumanity. Unless he recognizes the connectedness of all things, the imbalances in his life, and his role in promoting unhappiness in others, Tony's entire life, let alone his therapy, will fail to promote harmony.

Character and Command

TONY: Why am I telling you? You know all this. You're a captain. Chain of command is very important in our thing.
("Army of One")

Sun Tzu believes that war is a regrettable event that damages
even the victors. Regardless of the outcome, war is always a
"loss" for all sides in the short term because of the expenditure
of resources, the loss of life and property, and the shattering of
harmony. The goal of strategy is to avoid war by defeating the
enemy before the battle with overwhelming superiority, prompt-
ing surrender: "So, to win a hundred victories in a hundred battles is not the highest excellence; the highest excellence is to
subdue the enemy's army without fighting at all."[9] Thus, "the
expert in using the military subdues the enemy's forces without
going to battle, takes the enemy's walled cities without launch-
ing an attack, and crushes the enemy's state without a protracted
war."[10] Military action is the last resort when all other efforts to
restore harmony have failed.

Because military action is designed as an attunement of the
balance of the world, Sun Tzu places heavy emphasis on the
leader and his or her ability to discern the necessity for and
appropriate measures to be taken in conflict. He demands that
the military commander be of superior character, because of the
tremendous responsibility one must hold and the need for
exquisite discernment not only of the battle, but the long-term
and far reaching consequences of engagement. The leader is not
one who can win battles, but one who is capable of achieving
harmony.

Harmony is a difficult enterprise, because harmony stems
from a state of equilibrium throughout the world. To be able to
harmonize the world requires a tremendous amount of knowledge and wisdom. One must be able to look to the particular
conditions of the conflict—the army, the opponent, the terrain—
and determine the optimal response.

---

[9] Ames, Chapter 3, p. 111.
[10] *Ibid.*, p. 111.

> He who knows the enemy and himself
> Will never in a hundred battles be at risk;
> He who does not know the enemy but knows himself
> Will sometimes win and sometimes lose;
> He who knows neither the enemy nor himself
> Will be at risk in every battle.[11]

One must also understand the *tao*, or "way" of all things. One must be able to detect the ongoing process of transformation of *yin* and *yang* that makes the world an ever-changing swirl. One must be able to understand the rhythmic connections between things in order to predict their flow. One must know how to win without fighting, and fight at the most economical level needed to restore the balance of the world. If one has the ability to see and act with exemplary character, one can even send soldiers to their deaths, knowing that the loss, while regrettable, is justified by the benefit it brings to the entire world.

It should be obvious by now that when Tony goes to war he does so without the philosophical foundation or leadership skills that Sun Tzu demands of military commanders. His character is suspect, lacking the harmony and integrity needed to make vital decisions of life and death. His interests extend, if beyond himself at all, only to his family and their economic well-being.[12] Tony is openly confrontational, and his ability to create discipline with his troops comes not from his integrity and inner spirituality but from fear of his ever-present rage. Perhaps the most telling indictment of Tony's military prowess is found in his own words, where he identifies himself as a soldier: "We're soldiers. You know, soldiers don't go to hell. It's war. Soldiers, they kill other soldiers" ("From Where to Eternity"). Sun Tzu makes it clear that the commander stands above the rest as a person of exemplary character. While every military commander is also a soldier, not every soldier is a commander. Tony is just a soldier. A soldier with overwhelming responsibilities.

---

[11] *Ibid.*, p. 113.

[12] For an examination of the limited nature of Tony's commitments see Chapter 8 of this volume.

A Life Without Balance

This examination of Tony Soprano and his world has taken us back thousands of years and across thousands of miles, and given a glimpse of the chaotic world in classical China that spurred philosophical perspectives contrasting sharply with our European inheritance. We have explored the ingenious and comprehensive response Sun Tzu offers to conflict. Through Tony, we have seen that being acquainted with a message without understanding its full meaning can be unrewarding.

In many ways, Tony's misappropriation of Chinese thought is no different from that of other Westerners who practice martial arts, feng shui, and Chinese medicine without understanding the cultural and philosophical underpinnings of these activities. Our examination of Tony's conflicts brings out a key difference between implementing philosophical precepts in a goal-oriented perspective designed to achieve narrowly defined objectives, and instead, attempting to perfect the individual in the social world, thus creating not only efficacy but also balance and harmony for the individual and the society.

3

The Unhappiness of Tony Soprano: An Ancient Analysis

JENNIFER BAKER

TONY: I got the world by the balls and I can't stop feelin' like I'm a fuckin' loser. ("The Happy Wanderer")

Fans of *The Sopranos* acknowledge, with glee, that Tony Soprano has the above-described grip on the world. When Tony is crossed—if someone owes him money, attempts to hold him to a contract, or harms something he cares about (be it a person or a racehorse)—the audience is primed to think, "don't they know who they are dealing with? This is *Tony Soprano*."

Tony's reactions rarely fail to support viewers' conviction that Tony Soprano is *not to be messed with*. And we admire the character for this. No one takes *us* seriously when we talk about "wanting to wring" someone's neck after a betrayal. Described in review after review as "lusty," the description of Tony is apt whether it is meant to suggest lasciviousness or a pronounced vitality. It is also meant to be a compliment. When it comes to what he wants, Tony has both aim and reach. And, again, we admire Tony for this. We like a man who knows what he wants and knows how to get it. Tony's having a family, a wife, and scores of other women seems an ideal arrangement to some. And just think of how Tony goes about getting money—he just takes it.

But Tony is not happy. Clearly Tony cannot attain happiness the way he acquires so much else. In the show, we look to Tony's therapist Dr. Melfi to explain what is wrong with Tony; why, despite "having it all," he feels like such a loser. In this chapter, we'll look to the diagnosis ancient philosophers would offer. That's right, what would Plato, Aristotle, the Stoics, and the Epicureans have to say about the happiness of a self-described "fat crook" from Jersey? They have plenty to say. And I would like to suggest that Tony Soprano, who has hardly changed at all from his psychotherapy, could benefit from a little philosophy.[1]

Tony on Happiness

Tony, for all of his blustering anti-intellectualism, shows signs of having thought a bit about happiness and to have discerned three different approaches to happiness: that of the "whiners," the "happy wanderers," and the "Gary Cooper"-types. Tony worries out loud that therapy is meant for the "whiners." When angry, Tony accuses Dr. Melfi of trying to get him to blame others (his parents) for his unhappiness and make him "feel like a victim" ("The Happy Wanderer"). Tony certainly does not want to become like the "fucking Americans nowadays" who he describes as "pussies—crying, complaining, confessing."

Tony disdains the "whiners," but it is animosity he feels for the "happy wanderers." These "assholes" don't need therapy and move through life cheerily oblivious to its trials and setbacks. Tony says of them, "I see some guy walkin' down the street, you know, with a clear head—you know the type. He's always fuckin' whistling like the happy fucking wanderer. And I just wanna go up to him and I just wanna rip his throat open. I wanna fuckin' grab him and pummel him right there. For no reason" ("The Happy Wanderer"). Yet, despite castigating members of this sorry fraternity for doing things like visiting zoos, Tony quite enjoyed acting the "happy wanderer" on the day he was made giddy by a trip to the zoo with his new girlfriend. Of course, this good mood was short-lived. Given the option, Tony would happily wander through life, but he seems to recognize that this is something he is not ever going to have the option to do.

---

[1] My approach is very different from that recommended by Lou Marinoff in *Plato, Not Prozac! Applying Eternal Wisdom to Everyday Problems* (New York: HarperCollins, 1999). I do not agree with Marinoff that reliance on philosophy might eliminate any need for Prozac and I disagree with Marinoff's indiscriminate use of any philosophy he thinks appropriate to a person's problems. He writes, "If you came to see me I might discuss Kierkegaard's thoughts on coping with death, Ayn Rand's ideas on the virtue of selfishness, or Aristotle's advice" (p. 6). I think such an approach fails to take ethical theory seriously, because ethical theories are not mutually compatible.

So Tony is left to aspire to the equanimity of a Gary Cooper. "Remember the first time I came here [to therapy], I said the kinda man I admire is Gary Cooper. The strong, silent type" ("The Happy Wanderer"). Of course, what it is that "Gary Cooper" has eludes Tony, who is not even clear on what he understands to be "Gary Cooper"-like. He idealizes his father by putting him in the "Gary Cooper" category: his dad ran his own crew back when the mob had "values." Yet at the same time Tony acknowledges that his mother "wore [his father] down to a little nub. He was a squeaking gerbil when he died" ("Pilot").

Does it seem far-fetched to suggest that ancient Greek philosophy can help clear up Tony's confusion about happiness? Perhaps it ought not to, not even within the context of the show. The show's writers have Tony read the following quotation in Bowdoin College's Admissions Building: "No man can wear one face to himself and another to the multitude without finally getting bewildered as to which may be true" ("College"). The author, Nathaniel Hawthorne, was undoubtedly inspired by the work of ancient thinkers in composing this line. It reflects the ideas first put forward by Plato. In *The Republic*, Plato has Socrates explain that happiness is a matter of organizing a harmony between the parts of one's self. We ought to make ourselves a "perfect unity, rather than a plurality, self-disciplined and internally attuned." But this is no static state. We must engage in activities that are consistent with this aim, so that we "preserve and promote" internal harmony.[2] Looking to ancient philosophers for an explanation of what this internal harmony consists in will show up the deficiencies in Tony's understanding of happiness. (And in doing this might explain Gary Cooper's appeal.) Because the ancient accounts are clear on both the cause and the effects of happiness, they help us to recognize that, when it comes to happiness, we have options

---

[2] "Once he has stopped his mental constituents from doing any job which is not their own or intruding on what is the other's work; once he has set his own house in order, which is what he should really be concerned with; once he is his own ruler, and is well regulated, and has internal concord; once he has treated the three aspects of the soul as if they were literally the three defining notes of an octave: low, high, and middle, and he has created a harmony out of them and however many notes are in between, only then will he have bound all the factors together and made himself a perfect unity rather than a plurality, self-disciplined and internally attuned . . . and conduct is what

beyond deciding we are a "victim" of others, and that to pursue happiness is not merely to pursue fleeting moods. And perhaps what is even more significant is that, in contrast to Dr. Melfi, who in *four years* of treating Tony has hardly breached the subject, ancient philosophy can explain what is at stake in Tony's continuing his life of crime.

The Ancients on Happiness and Tony and the Rest of Us

Despite his extraordinary talent for satisfying his more immediate desires, in the following respect Tony is not so different from the rest of us. We, like Tony, tend to think of happiness as a matter of having certain things in our lives. We expect to be happy once we get to college . . . and then once we get our degree . . . then once we have a family, and it goes on and on. Or, having got everything we could think of, and being asked if we are happy, we respond with a list of these things and ask back, "Who could ask for anything more?" According to Aristotle, people in ancient Greece were confused in the same way. In the *Rhetoric*, Aristotle summarizes what was a matter of general agreement at the time. What seems, then, to have been a matter of ancient "common sense" is the suggestion that happiness is a matter of achieving a list of things: a good family, lots of friends, wealth, reputation, honor, old age . . .[3]

But the ancient ethicists explain that happiness is not a matter of merely having things. The Stoics, in response to a list like that above, write that "not even an abundance of these goods . . . makes a difference to the happiness, desirability, or value of one's life."[4] The Epicureans believe that if we think deeply enough about happiness we will come to realize that good birth, wealth, reputation, honor and even a pleasant old age do not cause happiness and do not even directly contribute to happiness.

The difficulty of happiness, according to the ancient Greeks, has two components. First, happiness is a matter of activity—not

---

preserves and promotes this inner condition of his that he regards as moral and describes as ideal." Plato, *Republic*, 443c-d.

[3] Aristotle, *Rhetoric*, I. 5.

[4] Cicero, *De Finibus* III, 43.

acquisition. Not even a nice family, lots of friends, wealth, reputation, honor, and living long can ward off unhappiness.[5] Happiness is a matter of what we do and how we do it. As Aristotle writes, "Activities are what give life its character."[6] Second, happiness is not something we can stumble into, despite Tony's suspicions about the "happy wanderers." To live a happy life requires a conscious effort to revise and integrate the goals we have picked up from a common-sense understanding of what makes life good. This effort is required because the aims we have, before thinking philosophically about our lives, inevitably conflict. This is demonstrated in a spectacular way by Tony Soprano, who aims to be both loving father and murderer. But our aims might only be to pursue family and career. Do we have to think philosophically about our goals and revise them as well? Something as seemingly benign as trying to "juggle" family and career *can* perpetuate a misunderstanding of what it is to be happy if we think we only need to strike the right "balance" between these pursuits. Like Tony Soprano, our efforts to "juggle" different goals may keep us from following Plato's recommendation—not to strike some *external* harmony (just enough work and just enough play) but an *internal* harmony.

Happiness Requires Integrated Motivations

What is it to make ourselves internally harmonious? This can be explained rather simply. We must start by reflecting upon what it is we are *really* after when it comes to our pursuits. *Managing this* is not so simple. It usually does not occur to the power-hungry politician that she runs for office for the sake of glory, and not for the hundred other reasons she offers people in explanation. It is hard for the habitually irresponsible to realize that they are this way for the sake of pleasure, and that *this* is the problem. But if we do come to recognize what motivates us (either as a whole or in regard to particular aspects of our lives), the ancient imperative is to continue to pursue only those things whose motivation is one that can integrate *all* of our pursuits. In the case of a power-

---

[5] After studying ancient Greek philosophy, you realize that even charming adages like, "Happiness only requires good wine, good song, and a good woman," mislead us when it comes to happiness.

[6] Aristotle, *Nicomachean Ethics*, 1100b33–34.

hungry politician, glory is not what motivates her concern for her family. The habitually irresponsible are not going to find that pleasure motivates accomplishments they can be proud of. In either of these cases, the problem is going to come about because such persons harbor inconsistent reasons for their behavior (I ought to, above all, strive for political power; I want to take good care of my family; I think pleasure is most important to pursue; I want to be proud of myself for doing things that are difficult). This, then, leads to an inability to introspect.

The show illustrates this well. Tony actually tries to justify his mob activity because it allows him to financially support his family. If he were not operating with two sets of inconsistent motivations, Tony would recognize that his illegal occupation harms his family (in various ways) far more than it economically helps them. Even though this is obvious, Tony cannot see it. He is "bewildered" just as the quotation from Hawthorne suggests. There are no more memorable descriptions of such a state than Plato's. Plato describes the person operating with inconsistent motivations as being in a "civil war" with himself. He has us imagine that if we fail to reconcile our motivations to one another, different sides of ourselves "bite each other, fight and try to eat each other."[7]

In *The Republic*, Plato describes what happens if a person with unintegrated motivations gets put in a position of power over others. This exacerbates the already disorganized condition of a person, and, despite the public appearance of "having it all," the potential is for such a person to be more unhappy than any of us. Such individuals face, in addition to more common tensions, worries about enemies and usurpers, and a higher degree of self-doubt. Plato writes that such a person is like "an exhausted body" which "is compelled to compete and fight with other bodies all its life."[8] The situation renders one friendless and terrified.

So, according to Plato, it is no wonder that Tony does not feel well. Not only does he harbor inconsistent hopes. In addition, his position of power over others makes him even less secure. Like most of us, Tony needs to employ what Epicurus describes as "sober reasoning"—sober reasoning which "works out the causes of every choice and avoidance," driving out "false

---

[7] Plato, *Republic*, 589a.
[8] Plato, *Republic*, 579c–d.

beliefs" about what we ought to be pursuing.[9] Until we reflect on our pursuits and answer to our satisfaction what the point of our effort is, our happiness, in even a normal life, will consist of nothing other than good moods and perhaps our memory of these. And this is not enough to make life seem satisfying, Aristotle explains. It is necessary, for happiness, that our desires not seem "empty and pointless."[10]

To avoid this, we must find the motivation that integrates our pursuits, and we must drop any activities that cannot be integrated with the others. For most of us, this type of reflection about our lives might not mean we have to change much of what we pursue (love, career, family), though we will have to start thinking about our pursuits differently. These pursuits will have to come to mean to us what they can mean to us *consistently*. The psychological effect of this, and not some good mood, is what the ancients are willing to call happiness.

Objections to the Integrated Motivations View (and a Reply)

Some contemporary ethicists object to the ancient account of happiness in the following way: the ancients think they can recommend a happy life as if it and an ethical life are one and the same, but really, whatever the psychological benefits of working from a consistent set of motivations, they amount to neither happiness nor morality. The dispute about what constitutes happiness will be ongoing, and is capable of being settled only in the way philosophical debates typically are settled: through slow and steady attempts to incorporating the insights or to explain away the apparent advantages of opposing accounts. We can, however, begin to address the second point, on whether the ancients are recommending a moral life in recommending a life of internal harmony. In fact, the writers' portrayal of Tony Soprano will help us answer this question.

Critics of ancient philosophy contend that even a *mafioso* can work from a set of consistent motivations, so that the recommendation that we integrate our motivations has nothing to do with morality. Let us consider whether Tony could have just "one face" to himself and to the world, yet have it be that of a

---

[9] Epicurus, *Letter to Menoeceus*, 132.
[10] Aristotle, *Nicomachean Ethics*, 1094a21.

mob boss. First of all, think of all that he would have to give up. His family would be recruited to kill like he does, since all secrecy and shame about his profession would be out the window. Even if they did not become murderers themselves, if Tony became frank about his career, his family would no longer be able to pass as they do in civilized society, of course. They would be living more like outlaws in the Kentucky hills. And having embraced his criminality, would Tony be as effective as a criminal? If everyone who dealt with him knew his intentions, would they continue to deal with him? It seems that Tony sometimes needs to wear a public face of respectability. He would be out of business were he not two-faced. But the show's portrayal of Tony reveals something else as well: Tony seems to need two faces in order to live with himself. Tony needs to think of himself as not so bad a guy.

The Sopranos is tremendously helpful in making this point. If we were left to just conjure up a bad guy in our minds, we would likely overlook this feature of such a lifestyle. We tend to imagine evil villains twirling their mustaches with glee. But bad guys are more like Tony. As the show so poignantly demonstrates, they don't like themselves. They have to pretend they are not what they are. ("I'm not saying I'm perfect, but I do the right thing by my family," Tony tells Dr. Melfi at the end of Season Three.) The show makes apparent what to the ancients was evident: there is no way for a bad person to achieve internal harmony.

Gary Cooper

In *High Noon*, Gary Cooper plays a sheriff who learns a man he sent to prison for murder is returning to get vengeance for his arrest. The townspeople refuse to help the sheriff fight off the killer and his crew because they are afraid. Despite this, Cooper's character remains as Tony describes him, strong and silent.

Without the aid of a philosophical account of happiness, Tony is left unaware that the difference between "Gary Cooper" and himself is neither a matter of brute strength nor the values of an era, but *the sort of desires* each pursues. Just imagine Tony plopped into Gary Cooper's role in *High Noon*. Wouldn't he be *torturing* his old neighbors before (and then after) the noon train arrives? *You can't mess with Tony Soprano*, and the townspeople would not get away with their betrayal because Tony gets vengeance when he wants it. Gary Cooper's character doesn't want it. He does not try to get the townspeople to bend to his will either. And this is what gives Gary Cooper's character a sort of self-possession that Tony can only marvel at. We could put it this way: Gary Cooper's character "cannot be messed with" *despite* what the townspeople do or fail to do. This is an effect of one's life being happy in the ancient sense. Such a life is, as Aristotle puts it, "self-sufficient," or "what when isolated makes life desirable and lacking in nothing."[11] Gary Cooper's character does not *need* vengeance against the townspeople in the way that Tony does, Tony's life being utterly un-self-sufficient.

Tony admits as much when he describes himself as a "sad clown" ("The Strong, Silent Type"). (Hearing this shocks Dr. Melfi, as it would others who see Tony as a far more ominous figure.) A clown puts on his show for others, prancing around until he gets the reaction he wants. We mentioned that Tony has great reach and aim; he needs to reset his aims. He is not pursuing the things that will satisfy him and is instead acting under a sort of compulsion. Consider whether we can imagine Tony *not* doing the things he predictably does: Can he stop cheating on his wife? Can he forgive and forget, even once? Why is Tony's getting revenge inevitable? Perhaps it is not because Tony is stronger than we are, but because he is weaker, in this sense: he cannot *control* the desire to strike back. As much as he tries to control those around him, he has no control over himself.

When Dr. Melfi suggests that behavior therapy might help Tony to manage his "anger triggers," Tony pauses to consider the possibility. If these triggers stop working, "then how do you get people to do what you want?" ("Employee of the Month"). Tony doesn't really have the world "by the balls." That is only the illusion, perpetuated by our misunderstandings of happiness. It is the other way round; the world has that grip on Tony. Tony is, of course, aware of this, and it makes him feel like a loser. If he only also knew this: a happy man in the ancient sense attempts to control not the world but *himself*. This is no fool's errand, unlike so many of the efforts of Tony Soprano, the sad clown.

---

[11] Aristotle, *Nicomachean Ethics*, 1097b15. Later ancient ethicists use "self-sufficiency" as a euphemism for happiness.

4

"It's All a Big Nothing": The Nihilistic Vision of *The Sopranos*

KEVIN L. STOEHR

Nihilism and *Noir*

The Sopranos is anchored by an underlying moral vision, that of *nihilism*. Nihilism, first of all, is an existential attitude or orientation according to which the activities of self-creation and the search for self-knowledge either are forsaken or are undertaken against a backdrop of rejected values and decaying institutions. The term "nihilism" derives from the Latin word "nihil," meaning *nothing in particular*, a complete absence of objects or values. A genuine nihilist proclaims that "nothing matters" or that "nothing makes a difference" and *really means it* on a consistent basis.

The nihilistic current running throughout each episode derives in part from the radical perspectivism and moral relativism evidenced by the words and actions of many of the characters in the series, but most especially by those of its morally ambiguous protagonist, Tony Soprano. The bleakly realistic worldview of the show nourishes both the style and content of its episodes and also echoes the dark atmosphere and themes of those classic movies that have been labeled as "film noir" and "neo-noir." These earlier films have had a conspicuous influence on the aesthetic and thematic framework of Chase's series. Through a selective analysis of four seasons of *The Sopranos*, I hope to shed light on the overall "character" of the series, on the general underpinnings of the tradition of *film noir*, and on the nihilistic worldview that such artworks share in common.[1]

Friedrich Nietzsche (1844–1900) was one of the first thinkers of the Western tradition to point explicitly to the existential dangers, as well as to the creative opportunities, of nihilism as a cultural, moral, and historical phenomenon. He indicates that the nihilist typically recognizes the transience ("flux" or "becoming") of life and subsequently loses faith in conventional ideas and standards that had been viewed previously as fixed or permanent. The very *purpose* of one's existence is put into question. Nietzsche defined nihilism as follows: "What does nihilism mean?—*That the highest values devaluate themselves*. The aim is missing; 'Why?' finds no answer."[2]

While nihilism in general expresses a basic loss of conviction in conventional values, Nietzsche makes a clear distinction between *active* and *passive* nihilism. He tells us that passive or negative ("incomplete") nihilism is a rejection of seemingly fixed values and institutions *without* the spiritedness that allows one to become an individualistic self-creator. Passive nihilism is an existential attitude or orientation that is born of resentment and indignation toward the value of life itself. On the other hand, active or positive ("complete") nihilism is the process of becoming a creative individual while rising above mere resentment and life-negation, thereby acquiring the principle of life-affirmation in the face of existential and spiritual crisis.[3] Nietzsche associates active nihilism with "master-morality" and with his ideal personality-type of the *Übermensch* or "Superman."

---

[1] The focus of the series upon morality or the lack thereof is summarized nicely by Ellen Willis in her seminal article "'The Sopranos' Harmonizes with the Times: HBO Series Is a 'Cultural Rorschach Test'" (*The Nation*, March 16th, 2001). Willis mentions Livia's nihilistic tendencies but does not focus upon those same tendencies in Tony, though she clearly points to his basic moral ambiguity.

[2] Friedrich Nietzsche, *The Will to Power*, translated by Walter Kaufmann and R.J. Hollingdale, (New York: Vintage, 1968), p. 9.

[3] See, for example, Sections 22 and 23 of the collection of Nietzsche's unpublished writings, *The Will To Power*. In Section 28, a similar distinction is made between "complete" and "incomplete" nihilism. An allegory of the three main stages of selfhood (slave-morality, passive nihilism, and active nihilism or master-morality) is presented in the beginning chapter ("On the Three Metamorphoses") of the First Part of Nietzsche's *Thus Spoke Zarathustra*.

To comprehend the overarching moral vision of *The Sopranos* as a depiction of nihilism in its "passive" or "pathological" form, one should first grasp the ways in which the style and content of the series are rooted in *film noir*, especially the cinematic neo-*noir* of the past three decades.[4] Tony Soprano reveals his passion for *noir* classics when he is shown enjoying late-night screenings of old *noir* films such as *White Heat* (1949). His Mafia colleagues, especially Paulie Walnuts and "Big Pussy," conjure images of neo-*noir* movies by frequently comparing their experiences with scenes from the *Godfather* trilogy. Photographs of traditional *film noir* actors Humphrey Bogart and Edward G. Robinson, captured in gangster pose, flash briefly across the screen in the very first episode of the series, during a killing by Tony's nephew Christopher Moltisanti at Satriale's Meat Market. In the first episode of the second season, Christopher is shown relishing a classic *noir* scene featuring Robinson.

Film noir, I would argue, is rooted in a nihilistic moral vision that has cast its shadow upon modern Western society, especially after World War I. *Film noir* expresses the estrangement, despair, and ruthlessness that are often generated by a collapse of the conventional rules of mainstream society and by a sobering insight concerning the superficiality of traditional institutions. This condition is especially pronounced when primal, irrational instincts have eventually irrupted through the self-repressive facade of civilized life ("bourgeois culture"). *Film noir* usually revels in the shadowy alleys of *passive* nihilism, as Nietzsche defines it, typically hinting at missed opportunities for the cultivation of creative individuality.

Film noir grew out of the same war-time and post-war disillusionment with the human condition that fueled French existentialist writers like Albert Camus and Jean-Paul Sartre. This newly defined sense of cinema taught its audiences about the brute reality of life's contingencies and about our inevitable disappointment when looking ahead to a brighter future. In most

---

[4] A helpful introduction to the nature of *film noir* is Paul Schrader's essay "Notes on *Film Noir*," appearing in the collection *Perspectives on Film Noir*, edited by R. Barton Palmer (New York: G.K. Hall, 1996). See also Raymond Borde and Étienne Chaumeton, "Towards a Definition of *Film Noir*," translated by Alain Silver, from the collection *Film Noir Reader* (New York: Limelight, 1996).

classic *noir* films there is an underlying devolution or de-humanization of the main character, usually characterized by an internal descent into immorality and even amoral indifference. Such a descent is almost always occasioned by external forces (such as victimizing villains or the cold whims of fate), but the suffering or fall of the protagonist is amplified in most cases because of his or her own moral ambiguities and psychological weaknesses.[5]

The lives of the main characters in most *noir* and neo-*noir* films, much like the life of Tony Soprano, are saturated by nihilistic attitudes of alienation, disorientation, and indifference. Such characters typically reveal an underlying relativism of eth-ical values and commit themselves to one fundamental principle only: that of *sheer survival* in a world gone wrong. These anti-heroes, no matter how hard they struggle toward redemption or simple decency, are undermined in most cases by a loss or absence of clear moral values, both their own values and those of the people around them.[6] As in *film noir* and neo-*noir*, val-ues in the lives of the *Sopranos* characters are often relativized in a nihilistic manner: in terms of utilitarian *power*-relations involving materialistic and egotistic ambition. Tony is the para-

---

[5] For example, in Billy Wilder's masterpiece of *film noir*, *Double Indemnity* (1944), insurance salesman Fred MacMurray eludes his own conscience for a time when he is seduced into murder by *femme fatale* Barbara Stanwyck. In Fritz Lang's *Scarlet Street* (1945), bored bank cashier and frustrated artist Christopher Cross (Edward G. Robinson) falls victim to an unhappy marriage, then to a manipulative prostitute (Joan Bennett), and finally to his own lack of self-esteem and moral strength. In Jacques Tourneur's *noir* classic *Out of the Past* (1947), Robert Mitchum's character descends into a depressing abyss of deceit and desperation when his attempts at escaping his past ultimately fail. Abraham Polonsky's *Force of Evil* (1948) features an attorney (John Garfield) who, in working for a mobster, forsakes his moral ideals and succumbs to overwhelming greed. Nicholas Ray's *In a Lonely Place* (1950) casts Humphrey Bogart as a temperamental screenwriter whose inner volatility ruins his chances for happiness with the woman he has grown to love (Gloria Grahame).

[6] See Robert G. Porfiro, "No Way Out: Existential Motifs in The *Film Noir*," in the collection *Perspectives on Film Noir*. Porfiro discusses certain "existential-ist" categories that may be applied to a particular topic of existentialist study, that of nihilism, including the "non-heroic hero," "alienation and loneliness," "existential choice," "meaninglessness, purposelessness, the absurd," and "chaos, violence, paranoia."

mount example of an individual who struggles at times to be good but whose basic lack of conviction in his own potential goodness becomes a chief obstacle in this endeavor. Tony's character is also ambiguous because he still clings superficially to certain conventional values, despite his own frequent failures in living up to them. Nihilism results from the collapse of faith in such values, and Tony frequently sees the walls tumbling all around him.

Gary Cooper Is Dead and Gone

Tony Soprano's belief that he inhabits a world of collapsing values is a major theme of the series. In the first episode, he complains to his therapist, Dr. Jennifer Melfi, that mob members today have "no values": *"Guys today have no room for the penal experience, so everybody turns government witness"* ("Pilot"). This verdict is confirmed in a unique "prologue" to the second episode of the first season when we witness a television interview with an expert who describes the contemporary decline of the mob. The gangsters of today, according to the interviewee, "rat on" each other and engage in drug trafficking, activities that were taboo for older mobsters. Tony listens to this expert's report and simply concurs: *"The shoe fits"* ("46 Long"). The decline of traditional Mafia values is doubly nihilistic, in a sense, in that the internal values and codes of the mob are based on a complete rejection of conventional law and order.

Tony tells his therapist from the outset that he is plagued by feelings of decline and loss: "It's good to start from the ground up. I came in at the end. The best is over." Dr. Melfi responds: "Many Americans, I think, feel that way." Tony then laments the loss of the stoic hero of yesteryear: "Whatever happened to Gary Cooper—the strong silent type? That was an American. He wasn't in touch with his feelings—he just did what he had to do. See, what they didn't know is that once they got Gary Cooper in touch with his feelings, they wouldn't be able to shut him up ("Pilot"). America today is pampered, according to Tony. He tells Melfi toward the end of the second season: "[Do you] know we're the only country in the world where the pursuit of happiness is guaranteed in writing? You believe that? . . . Bunch of fuckin' spoiled brats." He mistakes, of course, the pursuit for the goal, as Melfi points out ("House Arrest").

Tony views himself (often hypocritically) as one of the final defenders and embodiments of old-style values and standards. Tony tries at times to base his life upon those virtues that are supposed to overlap between criminal and conventional life: loyalty, respect, and honor. But Tony has come to recognize that these virtues are declining in both spheres of his everyday existence. He has neither religious faith nor trust in the law to govern his feelings and actions. In addition, the usual supports of family and friendship have become increasingly fragile. Family life is more than complicated, due to Tony's own immoral choices, and he soon discovers that his professional colleagues may really be mob informants, as we discover more clearly toward the end of the first season. "Forget your enemies," Tony declares. "You can't even trust your friends" ("Big Girls Don't Cry").

Nihilism signals not only a collapse of values (both within and without) but also the loss of personal unity or wholeness. A nihilistic attitude often results from personal fragmentation in one's everyday life, a fragmentation that is reflected at the philosophical level by the principle of relativism. A relativist holds the belief that all knowledge and experience result from personal perspectives, without any over-arching pattern or structure that allows one to order these viewpoints in a definitive way. This leads to a subsequent denial of belief in objective, universal truths and of conviction in values that are intrinsic or valid-in-themselves, apart from merely subjective and utilitarian interests.

The rejection of absolute truths and intrinsic values is most conspicuous in the hilarious Episode "D-Girl" of Season Two. Here, Anthony Jr. becomes acquainted with the teachings of Existentialism through his new high school English teacher. On the eve of his confirmation as a "good Catholic," A.J. begins to infuriate his parents by spouting nihilistic paraphrases of ideas from Nietzsche ("Nitch," as A.J. says mistakenly) and Camus. (His homework assignment is Camus's *The Stranger*, a novel that deals with a nihilist who no longer cares about anything and whose utter amorality is demonstrated by a random murder that he commits.) A.J. has recently damaged his mother's car in a careless accident and is warned by Carmela that he is lucky he did not kill his fellow passengers. A.J. replies indifferently: "Death just shows the ultimate absurdity of life." When his mother then pleads in horror for God to forgive him for his callousness, A.J. replies: *"There is no God."* His parents are dumbfounded by his sudden rebelliousness against the conventional values that they had attempted to instill in him over the years. The youngster then poses the ultimate existentialist question about the very meaning and significance of his life: "Why were we born?" (Nihilism, as we have seen, is ultimately the rejection of an over-arching purpose in life.) And later in the episode, while discussing his problems with his bedridden grandmother Livia, A.J. once again ponders the overall purpose of life. Livia, the ruthless matriarch of the series, expresses her own nihilistic view of human existence, concluding with: "It's all a big nothing. What makes you think you're so special?"

While we might wonder whether A.J. is mature enough to question his own partially developed value system in a serious manner, particularly given his prior antics and responses, there are clear hints that he is merely echoing *his father's* loss of conviction in some over-arching purpose or objective moral structure. When Tony shares with Dr. Melfi his concern about A.J.'s recent expressions of doubt and disbelief, the therapist tells him: *"Anthony Jr. may have stumbled onto Existentialism."* Dr. Melfi then explains the gist of this school of philosophy, including its questioning of the possibility of life's meaning when absolute values and truths have been vanquished. Tony replies: "I think the kid's onto something" ("D Girl").

Tony's frequent sense of the meaninglessness and "nothingness" of it all most frequently occurs in association with his fear of death. This fear is apparent in the pilot episode, when Tony recounts his first collapse and, while undergoing tests, tells Carmela: "We had some good times, had some good years" ("Pilot"). His dread of death is especially evident in Episode Three ("Denial, Anger, Acceptance") of Season One when Tony obsesses about his good friend Jackie Aprile who is dying of cancer. The episode begins with a symbol of death and dying, *at least in Tony's mind*: an artwork hanging in the waiting room of Dr. Melfi, one depicting a tranquil barnyard scene. For Tony, worried about the terminal illness of his friend, death presents the specter of absolute limitation and unconditional negativity. Death becomes the concrete reminder of his own inner emptiness and meaninglessness. He is haunted by the *horror vacui* or "horror of the Void."

Death is, of course, a recurring theme in the series, and not merely in the form of murder or the threat of murder. The very title of the second episode of the second season is "Do Not Resuscitate," referring to a topic of that show. In Episode Eleven of the same season, the illness of Uncle Junior forces the elderly gangster to admit bleakly that all paths in life lead ultimately to the cemetery. Also in this episode, Tony expresses his ultimate sense of the overall meaninglessness of existence when he proclaims to Dr. Melfi (after discoursing on the indifference that he felt after watching the film *Se7en*): "What's the point? . . . You go to Italy, you lift some weights, you watch a movie. It's all a series of distractions till you die" ("House Arrest"). And Tony's later response to having learned of Uncle Junior's cancer is simple and bleak: "A lot of death" ("Another Toothpick").

Back to the Rathole

Tony is complex in the sense that his moral character appears at times to be saturated by an attitude of passive nihilism while, at other times, he struggles actively to overcome such a life-negating stance. According to Nietzsche, the passive nihilist is one who flounders in his moral ambiguities and who eventually refuses to rise above the negativity in his own life. The active nihilist or "master," on the other hand, gains clarity of purpose as he comes to view the presence of ambiguity or negativity as a creative challenge that may result in acts of self-overcoming. As Nietzsche famously puts it: "What does not destroy me makes me stronger."[7]

As the series progresses, Tony's struggle to overcome his own moral weaknesses and inner emptiness becomes more intense. And yet we begin to realize that, even though he is undergoing analysis, he is not successful in trying to overcome these defects. The "development" of Tony's character could be viewed as increasingly similar to the typical devolution of those dislocated and demoralized protagonists in *film noir* and neo-*noir*. As he finds no hope of renewed faith in traditional and conventional values, Tony clings more than ever to the past, fears the future, continues to suffer anxiety and self-alienation, and often views himself as a hapless victim of fate. These are

---

[7] Nietzsche, "Maxims and Arrows," 8, *Twilight of the Idols*.

primary characteristics of the *noir* anti-hero.[8] Tony even pronounces doom for his own son: A.J. collapses from an anxiety attack at the end of the third season and Tony remarks to Melfi that his son possesses the same old "putrid Soprano gene."

Tony remains, at the end of the day (or at least at the end of the fourth season), a merely *passive* or "pathological" nihilist. His resentment toward the value of life and toward those who possess some degree of genuine happiness grows to new heights, ironically, as he becomes more immersed in therapy. Self-reflection, as we learn from the series, does not guarantee self-improvement. In Episode Six of Season Two, for example, he tells Melfi that he wants to pick up a brick and smash the person who walks down the street with a "clear head," the individual who might be labeled as "the happy wanderer" ("The Happy Wanderer").

It is true that at one point during the third season, Tony proclaims to Melfi that his therapy sessions have been working and that he is a happier man. We see that this is a momentary lapse in self-knowledge and a pretense of serenity. He has in fact only intensified his activities as an adulterer and a murderous crime boss. When Melfi finally asks Tony if he is truly happy, Tony does not reply ("Employee of the Month"). And in Episode Ten of the third season, Tony suffers yet another panic attack and declares that he is "back to square one, back to the rathole" ("To Save Us All From Satan's Power"). In the first episode of the fourth season, Melfi pleads with Tony to give up his life of criminality and immorality, suggesting an alternative route toward happiness, one that he has never really tried. But Tony refuses ("For All Debts Public and Private"). And in Episode Eleven of the same season, Tony delivers what seems to be a definitive

---

[8] For example: "Although the storylines of *film noir* are richly varied, there are certain recurring themes. The principal character is almost always a man; he is usually isolated, either physically or mentally, from his surroundings. He is often foredoomed and, aware of his ultimate fate, he faces it with stoic resignation. The stories are usually told in the first person and a narrating voice-over is sometimes used to express bleak resignation at what is being done to the story's protagonist. Fatalism is essential, because there is often an element in the past of these men—an event or an act—from which the story and the seeds of their own ultimate destruction develop. However hard they might try, *film noir* heroes can never escape their past." (Bruce Crowther, *Film Noir: Reflections in a Dark Mirror*, New York: Continuum, 1989), pp.10–12.

self-judgment as he dramatically terminates his therapy at long last: "I'm a miserable prick. I said this since day one . . . All this fucking self-knowledge, what the fuck has it gotten me? . . . Come on. I'm a fat fucking crook from New Jersey" ("Calling All Cars"). Here, Tony clearly comes to reject the very therapy that may be one of his genuine opportunities for personal redemption. Another such opportunity is family life, but at the finale of the fourth season, he and Carmela have decided to call it quits and separate.

Tony fails in his attempts at self-mastery and self-overcoming during the first four seasons of the series. He succumbs passively to the whims of his inner and outer fate while continuing to waver between raging resentment and absolute indifference. While the *external* villains in Tony's life change from season to season, the *internal* villain in his life remains ever-present: his inability to take account of *his own* moral decline, even while obsessing about the weaknesses of others.

There are times, in fact, when Tony becomes more immoral (and even *amoral*) because he has, through his failed pursuit to attain authenticity and self-knowledge, nonetheless become more open to his ruthless and brutal instincts. His relationship with Gloria in the third season is a prominent example of this, since Tony avoids acknowledging the clear fact that she echoes the sociopathic and resentful behavior of his mother (as Melfi tries to suggest to him in subtle ways). His brutal killing of Ralphie in Season Four is another example. Tony occasionally feigns psychological well-being by *pretending* to know himself better—by accepting, that is, his *worst* instincts while learning to ignore the occasional voices of his better angels. Ultimately, Tony comes to revel in his own resentment, self-loathing, alienation, duplicity, fragmentation, and general life-negation. Like mother, like son.

The very context of the therapy session, a framing device that initiates and carries throughout the series, is crucial in that it emphasizes Tony's desire to overcome his passive nihilism and yet ultimately shows him to be even more of a passive nihilist than we had at first expected.[9] Via the therapy sessions, Tony is

---

[9] A very helpful discussion by professional analysts, especially pertaining to the question as to whether Tony's therapy has been effective or not, is

able to narrate his life to Melfi as well as to the viewer. He uses his therapy as a way of weaving together the fragments of his disjointed and seemingly purposeless existence. The therapy session serves as a matrix of emerging order because it provides Tony with occasions of active self-consciousness. So the need for balance and order and stability is articulated most clearly in these sessions that summon him to recognize and to act upon such a need. At the same time, however, the audience sees (as the series progresses) that Tony's therapy has also provided a window through which we can view his growing indifference, both to the consequences of his ruthless actions and to his own grim character.

The Sopranos eventually paints a truly stark portrait of Tony as a passive nihilist in that he cannot successfully rise above his inner negativity and ambiguity. If Tony had been consistently unaware of his moral failings due to sheer ignorance or irrationality, then we could fault him at most for being little more than an instinctual animal, wreaking havoc whenever his appetites are aroused. But with a growing recognition of his need for therapy and reflection, Tony shows himself to be worse than a merely savage animal. Tony's increasing neglect of his moral character and its required cultivation is done *self-consciously*, with an awareness of the conventional importance of values as well as the traditional difference between right and wrong. Therapy has taught him to strive for self-knowledge, but he has instead become true to the very worst aspects of himself. For Tony, being *authentic*, even if authentically *evil*, is somehow more valuable than being *good*. He substitutes psychology for ethics to suit his own selfish purposes. Subsequently he continues to feel lost amidst the moral wasteland. He can at best accept this bleak reality in a silent and stoic manner, like "the strong silent type" whom he reveres. By the end of the fourth season, Tony comes to feel a sense of accomplishment only in the fact that he has managed to survive in a broken world.[10]

presented at *Slate.com*. See also Glen Gabbard's *The Psychology of the Sopranos: Love, Death, Desire and Betrayal in America's Favorite Gangster Family* (New York: Basic Books, 2002).

[10] I would like to thank Peter Vernezze for his invaluable assistance with this chapter.

5

The Prince and I: Some Musings on Machiavelli

DAVID HAHN

TONY: "Now most of the guys that I know read that Prince Matchabelli [sic]. And I had Carmela get the Cliff [sic] Notes once, and it was okay. But this book [*The Art of War* by Sun Tzu] is much better about strategy." ("He Is Risen")

"That Prince . . ." is more correctly Niccolò Machiavelli (1469—1527), and it his classic work of political philosophy, *The Prince,* that Tony is referring to in the above quotation.

Machiavelli not only authored works of political theory but also penned history, biography, plays, and translations. In addition, as Florentine Secretary he moved in the highest circles of Italian politics. Today, however, he is known to most through the adjective "Machiavellian," which is defined as "suggestive of or characterized by expediency, deceit, and cunning."[1] The degree to which this definition accurately represents Machiavelli's own views, while a matter of some debate, is something I will not consider in this chapter. Instead, I will focus on the relevance of his masterpiece, *The Prince,* for the main character of *The Sopranos.* By examining Tony Soprano's interactions with three of his major antagonists in the show, I hope to demonstrate that Tony is at times, whether knowingly or unknowingly, a practi-

---

[1] *American Heritage Dictionary*, third edition. (Boston: Houghton Mifflin, 1992), p. 1076.

tioner of Machiaviallian wisdom and, as we will see, ignores Machiavelli at his own peril.

Florence, New Jersey

The Italy of Machiavelli was not the united country Tony knows from his recent trip to Naples. Instead, it was a fragmented peninsula, described accurately by the historian Jacques Barzun as being "divided into numerous towns and city-states, all but one subject to death-dealing factions, *coups d'état*, assassinations, aggression and defeat in war."[2] Indeed, Machiavelli saw the government of his native city overturned three times during his life, and he himself was imprisoned, tortured, and exiled. For all of its distance in time and place, Machiavelli's Italy would not be that unfamiliar to Tony Soprano. Take away the culture, the beautiful scenery, the artistic giants, and the whole Renaissance thing from sixteenth-century Florence, and you begin to get something approximating modern-day Jersey. Florence was threatened by numerous external enemies—the French, the Spanish, and Papal Rome, to name just a few—and constantly in danger of being undermined from within by political divisions; Tony confronts the FBI, the New York mob, the Russians, and has his own internal problems with traitors and malcontents. Machiavelli's advice about how a single prince can maintain a hold on power and unite divided factions has an obvious appeal to a group of men who realize that, unlike the Dave Clark Five, they require a single, strong leader. This might help explain why "most of the guys" Tony knows take time away from their *goom-ahs* to study *The Prince*. Tony, as we will see, would be well advised to do likewise.

Of New Principalities (Acquired when the Boss Dies)

Tony's first major challenge comes from his uncle, Corrado "Junior" Soprano. Junior wishes to stage a hit at Tony's friend Artie's restaurant, Vesuvio, and Tony, afraid that the possibility of being involved in crossfire might not exactly draw customers

---

[2] Jacques Barzun, *From Dawn to Decadence* (New York: HarperCollins, 2000), p. 256.

to the business, asks Junior to do the job elsewhere. When Junior refuses, Tony torches the restaurant in order to stop the killing from taking place there. Better his friend rebuild with insurance money than be driven into bankruptcy. The situation disintegrates when Junior responds to a couple of Tony's under-lings hijacking trucks under his protection by killing one of the hijackers and ordering a mock execution of the other, Tony's nephew Christopher.

With the death of boss Jackie Aprile, things threaten to dete-riorate into chaos. As Tony says, "Lack of control at the top is fuckin' up this whole family" ("Meadowlands"). It is a book on coping with elder family members, and not Machiavelli's *The Prince*, that in fact saves the day for Tony and prevents the guys from going to the mattresses. Believing she is assisting in deal-ing with his mother, Dr. Melfi recommends the book and advises Tony that he might try letting his mother think she is in charge. Almost immediately Tony begins to apply this advice—to Junior. He gets the captains to agree to make it appear as if Junior is the boss when in fact he, Tony, will be running things. The sit-uation seems ideal. Junior is content, the family has someone in control, and, as Silvio says, "We got a brand-new lightening rod on top to take the hits" ("Meadowlands").

While the advice does not derive from Machiavelli, it is cer-tainly consistent with his writing. Machiavelli asserts that the prince must know how to be wily like a fox because "those who have known best how to imitate the fox have come off the best."[3] In particular, sometimes a prince must appear to be "faithful to his word, guileless and devout," but "his disposition should be such that, should he need to be the opposite, he knows how."[4] Tony, accordingly, pretends to follow Junior's orders and heed his commands all the while holding clandestine meetings with Junior's capos at Livia's nursing home.

Tony reaches even more deeply into Machiavelli's play book when he tries to resolve growing discontent arising from Junior's tight-fisted way of running things. As one of the capos puts it, not only does Junior eat alone, "He doesn't even pass the salt." To rectify the situation, Tony tells Junior the story of

---

[3] Machiavelli, *The Prince*, translated by George Bull (New York: Penguin, 1961), sec. 18.
[4] *Ibid.*

Augustus Caesar: "Everybody loved him because he never ate alone. . . . It was the longest time of peace in Rome's history" ("Pax Soprano"). Although Tony may well be repeating something he heard on his favorite television station, *The History Channel*, Machiavelli could have helped him out here as well: "[T]he prince gives away what is his own or his subjects', or else what belongs to others. In the first case he should be frugal; in the second, he should indulge in generosity to the full. The prince who campaigns with his armies, who lives by pillaging, sacking, and extortion, disposes of what belongs to aliens; and he must be open-handed, otherwise his soldiers would refuse to follow him."[5] Machiavelli, it seems, didn't recommend eating alone either.

Machiavellian principles might have stabilized the situation had Livia been more content with her living arrangements. But her anger with Tony drives her to manipulate Junior into ordering a hit on her own son. Tony's survival of this assassination attempt is a matter of pure luck. As we'll see later, Machiavelli has a bit to say about luck. In response, Tony takes out most of Junior's crew in one swift, violent act of retribution, pulling a page from Machiavelli (although he could have received the same instruction from the end of *The Godfather*): "In seizing a state, the usurper ought to examine closely into all those injuries which it is necessary for him to inflict and to do them all at one stroke so as not to have to repeat them daily."[6]

Of Cruelty and Mercy (When Asshole Brothers of Your Dead Best Friend Get out of Jail)

Season two opens with Tony in charge and Junior behind bars. But it is not long before another nemesis appears on the scene: Jackie Aprile's brother Richie, who has just been released after ten years in prison. The relationship between Tony and Richie begins badly and quickly disintegrates. Richie is not only unappreciative at being given his loan sharking business back, but he openly disobeys Tony's request not to shake down Beansie, the owner of a pizza parlor, opting instead to use Beansie as his personal speed bump. Richie then disrespects the executive card

---

[5] *Ibid.*, Chapter 16.
[6] *Ibid.*, Chapter 8.

game that Tony runs by assaulting one of its players (a friend of Tony who owes Richie money). Ordered to build the paralyzed Beansie a ramp, Richie tears down the steps to Beansie's house but forgets to finish the project. When Richie refuses Tony's order to cease selling cocaine on the garbage routes, he is cut out of a garbage bid, and attempts to organize an overthrow of Tony.

Would a close reading of Machiavelli have resulted in Tony handling the situation differently? And might actions grounded in the principles of *The Prince* have resulted in a different outcome? I believe so. In a chapter entitled "Cruelty and Compassion," Machiavelli considers whether it is better to be loved or feared. Not surprisingly, he comes down on the side of the latter. "Men worry less about doing an injury to one who makes himself loved than to one who makes himself feared."[7] This is especially so in the case of someone who has recently assumed power. "A new prince, of all rulers, finds it impossible to avoid a reputation for cruelty because of the abundant dangers inherent in a newly won state."[8]

But from the start Tony's handling of the Richie situation runs counter to this general rule, since he seems much more interested in gaining Richie's love and approval than his respect. He sets a bad tone at their first encounter when he tells Richie that he is "like a big brother" and that he is going to be taken care of. The request to leave Beansie alone is worded, "Jesus Christ I'm asking you to do me a favor" ("Toodle-Fucking-Oo"). Tony is almost apologetic in telling Richie that the tax for breaking up the poker game will be that Tony will get paid first: "If I don't do something how's that gonna look?" ("The Happy Wanderer"). Almost nothing in Tony's encounters with Richie seems designed to generate fear. Indeed, we see Tony several times almost pleading with Richie to show him respect.

To be sure, there are a number of reasons for Tony's relatively gentle approach to Richie. For one, Richie's ten years in jail buys him a lot of leniency. There is also the fact that Richie's brother was perhaps Tony's closest friend. Finally, let's not forget Richie's unholy liaison with the Buddhist turned mob queen, Janice. Tony's desire for his sister's happiness doubtless also

---

[7] *Ibid.*, Chapter 17.
[8] *Ibid.*

affects Tony's behavior towards Richie. And though Tony ultimately cuts Richie out of a big garbage bid, not only is the action a long time coming, but it is hardly designed to generate fear. Obviously, then, Tony has his reasons for the way he handles Richie. But it is just these sorts of emotional traps that an in-depth reading of *The Prince* might have helped Tony to avoid.

If he seems oblivious to Machiavelli's advice on the relative merits of cruelty, Tony serves as a stellar example of another Machiavellian point. For Machiavelli, the personal character of the ruler—his *virtù*—was an essential component of his success. It would be a mistake to translate the term as virtuous, for there is nothing inherently moral about the characteristics that Machiavelli believes the prince should embody. Indeed, there are times when the prince will have to behave immorally in order to secure or maintain his power. Not for nothing do we have the adjective "Machiavellian." However, it is precisely by acting at the right moment in a manner deemed to be "bad" by conventional standards that the prince will demonstrate his excellence (a decidedly better translation of *virtù*) as a ruler. The excellent ruler—like the perfect storm—can be terrible, violent, and awe inspiring. More conventionally, Machiavelli declares that "a prince should . . . strive to demonstrate in his actions grandeur, courage, sobriety, strength. When settling disputes, he should ensure that his judgment is irrevocable; and he should be so regarded that no one ever dreams of trying to deceive or trick him."[9] These are also components of his excellence. The importance of exemplifying these traits cannot be overestimated, for "the prince who succeeds in having himself thus regarded is highly esteemed, and against a man who is highly esteemed, conspiracy is difficult."[10]

It is precisely because Tony is recognized as possessing Machiavellian leadership qualities by his peers that Richie's coup fails. Consider how the events unfolded. Richie enlists a disgruntled Junior to his side for another move against Tony. But when he is unable to get anyone to go along, Junior backs out and decides to side with his nephew. "He [Richie] couldn't sell it," Junior laments to Bobby Bacala. "He's not respected" ("The

---

[9] *Ibid.*, Chapter 19.
[10] *Ibid.*

Knight in White Satin Armor"). Although Junior would prefer to explain things in terms of Richie's shortcomings, it is more accurately the case that Tony's leadership qualities—his *virtù*—insulated him from this aborted overthrow.

Of Avoiding Contempt and Hatred (The Bad Endings of Psychopathic, Sadistic Capos)

Ralph Cifaretto may not have been the direct threat to Tony's power that Junior and Richie were, though he may yet prove to be his downfall. But of course Ralph was trouble from the moment that Tony passed him over for captain. Tony's "bitch slapping" of Ralph outside of the Bada Bing! after he brutally murdered his own girlfriend only increased an already existing tension. From the perspective of mob values, of course, Tony was in the wrong. Not only was Ralph a "made guy," but, as Silvio pointed out, Tracee was not related to Tony by blood, nor was she his *goomah*. Worse, Ralph now had mob-sanctioned justification for his resentment. The situation may well have spun out of control had it not been for Gigi's unseemly death on the pishtoon, which allowed Tony to utilize the face-saving measure of offering Ralph Gigi's capo position.

Rather than considering the situation resolved, however, Tony should perhaps have listened to Machiavelli: "He who believes that new benefits will cause great personages to forget old injuries is deceived."[11] Ralph may not have been great (although he was a good earner), but he certainly thought he was. Remembering this might have made Tony a little more cautious in interacting with Ralph in the future. Instead, what does he do? He slowly begins to take control of Ralph's race horse, Pie-O-My, and starts to sleep with his *goomah*—against Machiavelli's explicit advice: "The prince can always avoid hatred if he abstains from the property of his subjects and citizens and from their women . . . because men sooner forget the death of their father than the loss of their patrimony."[12] Ralph's torching of the stable, although ostensibly carried out for insurance money, is more probably intended as revenge, an act of hatred as predictable as it was cruel.

---

[11] *Ibid.*, Chapter 7.
[12] *Ibid.*, Chapter 17.

And of course it was the death of Pie-O-My in the fire that incited Tony to his most rash act. Although a backhoe and some bleach erased all evidence of Ralph's murder, it is clear that the questions about Ralph's "disappearance" will not be so easily put to rest. As Silvio cautiously stated, "If it can happen to Ralph, it can happen to any of us" ("The Strong, Silent Type"). By the end of Season Four, it is unclear what the consequences of Tony's impulsiveness will be. Indeed, he may yet be able to pin Ralph's demise on the New York mob. But sadly, the whole mess might have been avoided with some close attention to *The Prince*.

The Prince and Fortune (Double Parked Cars and Homicidal Sisters)

Machiavelli devotes an entire chapter of the notably brief *The Prince*—the penultimate chapter—to the topic of Fortune. While not ruling out a role for human activity, Machiavelli asserts, "Fortune is the arbiter of one-half of our actions."[13] Certainly, Tony has benefitted from fortune. Chris's double parked car prevents a first assassination attempt while a second one misses its mark by inches. And as much as it may have put a damper in Janice's plan to be first lady of the New Jersey underworld, her assassination of Richie is certainly a piece of good luck for her brother. Gigi's ignominious demise prevents Tony from having to deal with a sticky situation with Ralph. You can't say he hasn't had his share of luck.

Machiavelli famously compares Fortune to a river which, when flooded, destroys everything in its path. In such a dire situation, human action is powerless. However, when the river is flowing quietly there are precautions that can be taken. One can, for example, construct dykes and embankments to ensure safety should the waters rise again. Tony has certainly benefitted from fortune's unpredictability. But has he taken precautions against her inevitable unruliness?

There is some evidence that he has not. In particular, the economic downturn that constitutes the backdrop of Season Four seems to have caught Tony off guard. In Season Three, Junior had speculated that Tony's success was more a matter of

---

[13] *Ibid.*, Chapter 25.

fortune than skill, since in the booming economy "even Chinks and housewives" were betting. But economic conditions rise and fall. Even Carmela knows that everything comes to an end. Perhaps Tony should have listened to Machiavelli (or even to the Boy Scouts) and been a little more prepared. (Although, to be fair, he does seem somewhat better positioned than Johnny Sack to weather Carmine's shutting down of the Esplanade.)

Machiavelli closes with a final piece of advice on Fortune. "It is better to be impetuous than circumspect; because fortune is a woman and if she is to be submissive it is necessary to beat and coerce her. Experience shows that she is more often subdued by men who do this than by those who act coldly."[14] Leaving aside the misogyny, it is clear that Machiavelli is urging bold action at the proper time (which need not be inconsistent with the notion of planning for Fortune's inevitable reversals). The question, of course, is when is the proper time? As a young up and coming mobster, Tony scored his first success when Jackie and he robbed a protected card game. Certainly, an opportunity for bold action presents itself at the end of season four when Johnny Sack urges Tony to undertake a hit on Carmine. Tony at first accepts—and then demurs. Will Tony regret his unwillingness to follow Machiavelli's logic on this point? Only time and Season Five will tell.[15]

---

[14] *Ibid.*

[15] A special thanks to Richard Greene, Carolyn Munich, Ryan Perry, Paul Goggi, Thom Kuehls, and Dr. Stephen Kershnar for reading earlier drafts of this chapter. I would also like to thank the third-shift wait staff at a diner in Toledo for their coffee and the patience to let me type until four in the morning.

Secondo Piatto

Ethics: Soprano Family Values

6

"I Dunno about Morals, but I Do Got Rules": Tony Soprano as Ethical Manager

RONALD M. GREEN

It seems odd to bring the word "ethical" into connection with Tony Soprano. Tony commits terrible sins and crimes. He orders the death of others and kills people with his bare hands; he repeatedly betrays his wife and abandons his lovers; he runs a criminal enterprise involved in everything from theft and extortion to the corruption of public officials.

Yet in this world of criminality, Tony reveals a degree of moral integrity that makes his character appealing. Surrounded by associates whose viciousness and poor judgment threaten not just the public but the peace and stability of their own crime "family," Tony exercises managerial leadership to create order within the larger disorder.[1] If we momentarily suspend our moral evaluation of Tony's line of work, we can view him as a manager involved in pioneering a new and more ethically sensitive management style during a period of stressful change in his industry.

The Context of Evil

There are some considerations that soften our judgment of both Tony and his crew, but much of their behavior is despicable. We need to be clear about this negative dimension because Tony

---

[1] For a discussion of Tony's appeal in relation to other characters in the series see Chapter 11 of this volume.

sometimes offers a morally idealized vision of his criminal lifestyle. This occurs most notably in a conversation with his psychiatrist, Dr. Melfi. Responding to a question about whether he fears going to hell, Tony replies, "What? Hell? . . . No. . . . We're soldiers. You know, soldiers don't go to hell. It's war. Soldiers, they kill other soldiers. We're in a situation where everybody involved knows the stakes. . . . It's business. We're soldiers. We follow codes. Orders" ("From Where to Eternity").

Like all rationalizations, this self-portrait has some truth. For one thing, much of the murder and violence that takes place in the series occurs among mob members who engage in attacks on one another or reprisals for the same. Some of the more gruesome events in the series fit this description: Tony's garroting of Fabian Petrullio, the "rat" whom Tony accidentally encounters during his college tour with his daughter, Meadow ("College"); the whacking of Matt Bevilaqua following his attempt (along with buddy Sean Gismonte) to kill Christopher Moltisanti "on spec"; Tony's crew's almost "consensual" execution of close friend turned FBI informant, Salvatore "Big Pussy" Bonpensiero aboard Tony's boat, the Stugots ("Funhouse"); the back-of-the head shooting of Jackie Aprile Jr. by Vito Spatafore as punishment for young Jackie's role in leading a murderous heist of a mob-run card game ("Army of One").

Nevertheless, Tony's analogy to military ethics is far from perfect. Apart from the questionable justice of their cause, which rarely reaches beyond self-enrichment, Tony and his crew by no means confine their activities to other consenting participants in the criminal enterprise. They repeatedly and deliberately implicate innocent "civilians" in their activities. This is made clear early in the episode "Commendatori," when two thugs carjack an SUV, throw the terrified family out on the street, and almost take off with the family dog. Later, we learn that thefts like this are the first link in a new Sopranos' business, shipping stolen luxury cars to Italy. Among the innocent victims of their other schemes are the impoverished residents of Newark's ghetto who, in an operation dreamed up by Tony, State Assemblyman Zellman, and others, are left with the gutted shells of houses after federal rehab financing (and plumbing) are pilfered by Tony and his crew. We also peer into Christopher Moltisanti's brokerage operation, the heart of which is a "pump and dump" scheme that sells the "dog" stock "Webistics" to senior citizens.

When one conscience-stricken broker tries to present a client with investment alternatives, he is badly beaten by hoodlum "floor managers" Bevilaqua and Gismonte.

It's true that Tony and his associates are not the only ones involved in corruption and fraud. In *The Sopranos* the mob is often held up as a mirror to the "law-abiding" world. "Webistics" is a metaphor for much of the greed-driven technology-sector hype of the 1990s. In "A Hit Is a Hit," Carmela is astonished to learn at a barbecue with friends of their "white bread" Italian neighbors, the Cusamanos, that the wives are actively engaged in insider trading. But perhaps most telling is the brief exchange between Meadow and Tony as they drive to Colby for her college interview. Raising the question of what Tony does for a living, Meadow asks bluntly, "Are you in the Mafia?" Tony replies that some of his money comes from illegal gambling, and probes, "How does that make you feel?" Meadow replies, "Sometimes I wish you were like other dads . . . Like Mr. Scangarelo, for example . . . An advertising executive for big tobacco."

If we put Tony's crimes on one side of the balance and Mr. Scangarelo's on the other, the pointer might tilt in Tony's favor. Compared with the misdeeds perpetrated by greedy corporations and corrupt politicians, Tony's—and the mob's—crimes hardly count. In terms of business ethics, it is one of the points of *The Sopranos* that much of what we condemn in criminal behavior has its counterpart in the world of legitimate business today.[2]

But none of this excuses Tony. He knowingly plays a leadership role in an industry in which theft, fraud, extortion, and murder are routine, an industry whose best—and sometimes only—products or services are ones that feed human vices and addictions. Indeed, it is clear that much of the psychic pain tormenting Tony and causing the panic attacks that drive him to see Dr. Melfi stems from the conflict between his conscience and the way he earns a living. How, then, can Tony be regarded as an "ethical manager"?

There are two answers to this question. The first involves comparing Tony to some of the other "managers" with whom he

---

[2] David Simon, *Tony Soprano's America: The Criminal Side of the American Dream* (Boulder: Westview, 2002).

works and who characterize the mob at this moment in its history. The second looks more directly at the quality of Tony's managerial decision making. In a number of crucial episodes and scenes, we see that, although Tony often appears beleaguered and frustrated, he does remarkably well at steering himself and his team through the challenges they confront.

The Bad Examples

When we compare Tony with other managers above or below him in the Mafia echelon, it becomes clear why he has come to hold a position of responsibility. Together, these associates form a study in incompetence. Nowhere is this truer than one step above Tony in the hierarchy. Corrado Soprano (Uncle Junior) is the anti-type who highlights Tony's own leadership skills. Junior's hunger for the power and respect of office far exceed his ability to exercise power or merit respect. In decision after decision, judgment after judgment, he makes mistakes that propel the narrative. Among other things, he is ignorant of the most basic cultural facts. Following Junior's arrest, an obviously Jewish judge named Jacob Greenspan interviews him and his lawyer in quarters and asks whether Junior knows what an electronic bracelet is ("Do Not Resuscitate"). Junior thinks for a moment and replies, "It sounds like Nazi Germany to me." This elicits a sour remark from the judge about Junior's "needing a history lesson" followed by the ruling, "He's wearing a bracelet." Earlier in the series, Tony meets with the capos about who should lead the organization. He floats the idea of giving the job to Junior, who he believes has the support of the New York branch of the mob. "If anything, God bless your uncle," says Larry Barese. "But he's living in the wrong century. And New York knows it" ("Meadowlands").

Ignorance, poor judgment, and vanity underlie Junior's decision to accept the job of boss, even though it places him in the cross hairs of an impending government prosecution. Almost immediately, Junior imperils the family through a series of bad decisions ("Pax Soprana"). To assert control, he sends Mikey Palmice to beat up card players under the protection of capo Jimmy Altieri; instigated by Livia he imposes "taxes" on the previously protected operations of family counselor Hesh Rabkin; in a gesture imitative of Don Corleone in *The Godfather*, he has

Palmice throw drug dealer Rusty Irish off a bridge over the Patterson Falls as punishment for causing the drug-related suicide of the fourteen-year-old grandson of Junior's tailor. Unfortunately, Rusty Irish is one of Larry Barese's best gambling earners, and the unconsulted Barese is furious.

All these poor decisions lead to a sit-down at Satriale's, where the capos complain that Tony has created a Frankenstein. In an effort to solve the problem, Tony visits his mother, Livia, and tells her that Junior needs reining in, adding, "It's not a business that forgives bad decisions." Later, appealing to the older man's Italian sensibility, Tony attempts to teach Junior that a respected leader must share the wealth with those beneath him. As the two watch a little league game, Tony mentions Augustus Caesar. "Everybody loved him," says Tony, "because he never ate alone . . . It was the longest time of peace in Rome's history. He was a fair leader and all his people loved him for that."

Toward the end of the first season, Junior's character flaws propel him into his most unfortunate decision of all: to kill Tony. What is striking here is the role played by Livia. Furious that Tony has put her in the Green Grove retirement community and perceiving that Junior is smarting under Tony's *de facto* control of the family's business, Livia informs Junior of Tony's therapy ("The Legend of Tennessee Moltisanti"; "Boca"), and magnifies Tony's transgressions ("Nobody Knows Anything"). Of course, Livia is a monster. As Tony tells Dr. Melfi ("Pilot"), by the end of Tony's father's life, she was able to wear her tough-guy husband down "to a little nub . . . a squeaking little gerbil." The even weaker Junior is no match for Livia's passive-aggressive skills.

Junior's flaws have nothing to do with his readiness to heed feminine advice. We will see that one of the great strengths of Tony's leadership is his willingness to listen to and respect women's views. Junior's mistake is not that he listens to a woman, but that he listens to Livia. The result is a decision that is bad for Junior's biological and business families.

Several rungs down the organizational ladder, Christopher Moltisanti displays a contrasting set of flaws. If Junior suffers from poor moral judgment, vanity, and ignorance, Christopher's major vice is impulsiveness. Tony recognizes this. When Christopher accepts girlfriend Adriana's invitation to take off from the brokerage for the afternoon to go to the beach, things go badly wrong. His two office punks, Matthew Bevilaqua and Sean Gismonte, brutalize a broker and steal a Porsche Carrera from the parking lot of their own building. Later, Tony admonishes Christopher: "I been telling you to spend more time down at the brokerage. You're the fucking SEC compliance officer for Christ's sake. You gotta exercise impulse control" ("Guy Walks into a Pyschiatrist's Office").

In some respects, Christopher's problem is generational. Raised in a world of TV, video games, and widely available recreational drugs, he is accustomed to constant stimulation and expects instant gratification. It entirely fits Christopher's character that he tends to see the world through a film or video lens. ("D-Girl").

We see these flaws very clearly in "Meadowlands," a defining episode of the first season. When Christopher tries to collect his weekly payment from drug dealer Yo Yo Mendez, he learns that "it ain't my corner anymore; it's Junior's." Furious, Christopher rushes back to the Bada Bing!, interrupting Tony and the crew who have just seen a report on television about the death of mob boss Jackie Aprile. Unaware (or unconcerned?) that he is crashing a solemn moment, Christopher angrily announces that something has to be done right away. Paulie "Walnuts" Galtieri tries to put him off, urging, "Christopher, this ain't the time," but Christopher insists: "They're moving in. I say we go to Defcon four." Tony tries to slow him down. "I gotta assess this. All right?" But Christopher won't listen. "What are we, politicians? Does this look like the Senate to you, T? This is about respect of our thing." Tony's anger flares. "Why don't you shut the fuck up? It doesn't concern you." Christopher then makes his grandstand play:

> Yes it is. I represent you out there and I'm tired of putting my tail between my legs. This ain't negotiation time. This is *Scarface*, final scene, fucking bazookas under each arm. Say hello to my little friend.

Christopher's acting out of a scene from (a remake of) one of the most famous gangster movies entirely suits his personality. Raised on television and videos—at one point he tells Adriana, "I love movies. You know that. That smell at Blockbuster, that candy and carpet smell, I get high off ("The Legend of

Tennessee Moltisanti")—he often models his behavior on Hollywood formulas, leaving little time for more patient and careful deliberation. At the end of this scene Christopher says to Tony, "You don't do something; I gotta question your leadership." This provokes Tony, who pushes Christopher down on the bar and chokes him, to rage, "You ungrateful little fuck. Where'd you get the balls to question my leadership, huh?"

Leadership is the issue. Tony correctly perceives that Christopher, perhaps alone among the members of his crew, has the makings of a boss, and, possibly even, a successor ("For All Debts Public and Private").[3] Christopher is smart, tough, and culturally aware. There are even moments when he shows the ability to learn, as when he takes a pass on a second hijacking of a truck protected by Junior ("46 Long"). A contrast is drawn in this episode between Christopher and his buddy Brendan Filone, who goes after the truck and ends up, punished by Junior's man Mikey, with a bullet in his eye, "Moe Green style." Nevertheless, poor impulse-control remains Christopher's Achilles heel. In the fourth season this takes the form of a descent into heroin addiction.

Tony's Management Skills

If Junior and Christopher represent flawed management styles, Tony's exercise of managerial leadership is one of the main points of interest in the series. By means of Tony's conduct and choices, *The Sopranos* explores what it means to manage a complex human enterprise in a changing "business" environment.

Tony is by no means perfect. He has some of the flaws of the series' other, less adept managers. He shares with Christopher a problem of impulse control. It usually takes the less disruptive form of an attraction to sex or food, but it also sometimes flares in irrational anger and violence, as in his jealous beating of business collaborator, Assemblyman Zellman, for taking up with Tony's ex-*goomah*, Irina ("Watching Too Much Television"). To his credit, Tony is aware of this dimension of his personality. In

---

[3] Christopher is not really Tony's nephew. He is the son of the late Richard "Dickie" Moltisanti, a long-time street thug who was Carmela's cousin and a mentor of Tony. See Alan Rucker, *The Sopranos: A Family History* (New York: New American Library, 2001), Chapter 4.

the episode "Employee of the Month," Ralphie Cifaretto overre-
acts to an Arab businessman's failure to keep up in his debt pay-
ments by pistol-whipping the deadbeat. Later, Tony explains to
Ralphie why he has chosen to pass him over for promotion to
captain: "You got some bad tendencies, Ralphie, and I sympathize, 'cause I got 'em too."

Not only is Tony aware of his flaws: he struggles to control
them. Nowhere is this better displayed than near the end of
"Commendatori." This episode takes Tony, Christopher and
Paulie to Naples to work out the details of the car theft operation with their Neapolitan associates. In some respects the
episode is a study in how *not* to do business. Paulie spends
much of the time whoring. Christopher is so spaced out on
drugs that, on their return, he has to buy an Italian gift for his
girlfriend at the Newark Airport duty-free shop. Of the three,
only Tony keeps his eye on the ball.

It's not easy to do. Annalisa Zucca has become the effective
head of the Naples family as a result of her husband's impris-
onment and her elderly father's dementia. She is a shrewd,
beautiful woman. As she bends over to swing her golf club, the
camera—and Tony—focuses on her shapely bottom. But despite
her attractions, Tony must secure a high price for each of the
stolen vehicles shipped over by the New Jersey crew. This sexually charged negotiation culminates as the two stroll alone
through the cave of the sibylline oracles. Annalisa explains how
the sibyllines could predict future events. "Oh yeah," Tony asks,
"Got a premonition for me?" Annalisa tells Tony that he is "no
problem to read," that he is his "own worst enemy." This provokes Tony to say that Annalisa reminds him of someone back
home (presumably Jennifer Melfi[4]), but Annalisa guesses: "Not
your wife. Your girlfriend?" Tony replies, "Oh, I got one. To
answer your question. But no. Not her."

The conversation abruptly takes a sexual turn. "But she's
someone you want to fuck. I can tell," Annalisa says. Tony tries
to shrug this off, but she persists: "You don't want to fuck her?
You don't want to fuck me?"

Tony replies, "Yeah I do, but I don't shit where I eat."
Annalisa does not understand. Laughing nervously, she asks,

---

[4] This presumption is confirmed by Tony in a conversation with Jennifer in
"Bustout."

"Que cosa?" Tony translates: "No fare la merda dove mangia. It's bad business. We're in business." Annalisa's anger suddenly flares. "No, va ten. Va ten," Get away, get away, she says, and adds, "Not at those prices." She then offers a lower purchase price for each of the stolen cars.

What is remarkable about this scene is that Tony maintains his focus on business, despite what, for a macho guy, are major provocations not to do so. Not only is Annalisa's offer to have sex, fast and dirty, right there on the floor of the cave tempting, but there is the deliberate provocation to his masculinity. Antagonized by Annalisa's assertion of her allegedly superior psychological knowledge of him, Tony would see having sex with her as a natural way to regain control. Annalisa knows this. She may have set up the whole situation to distract Tony's attention from business and (literally) soften him up for the final stage of the negotiation. But for all his sexual impulsiveness, Tony does not succumb. The negotiation ends with a selling price for each vehicle that Tony later happily reports as being twice what he expected.

Tony's ability to subordinate personal desire to business necessity is one expression of his larger ability to perceive and act on what is best for his organization. Above all, Tony has good judgment where his relevant stakeholders are concerned. He is able to identify the claims of these stakeholders, and respond to them fairly and imaginatively. Unlike his more impetuous and injudicious colleagues, he does not allow his judgment to become impaired by vanity or pride. Indeed, as in the scene with Annalisa, Tony is often willing to emerge from an encounter with diminished glory, if by doing so he can preserve important relationships and achieve his larger objectives.

The series is populated with episodes where Tony's good judgment averts conflict. At the end of the fourth season, the boss of the New York family, Carmine Lupertazzi, threatens to muscle into the Riverfront Esplanade project, and war impends. Tony makes peace by offering the New Yorkers a modest share in the proceeds ("Whitecaps"). In the second season, when the vicious hood Richie Aprile uses his garbage routes to peddle drugs, Tony reacts. Pulling Richie aside at the Garden State Carting Association's annual social event, he offers a brief tutorial on the legal realities: "After five years, the cops are finally leaving garbage alone. A drug bust on one of those routes, it's a different story. You've got the FBI, the DEA, all those fuckin' pricks are gonna be breathing down our necks again." When Richie protests, "It's a little coke. What *is* the big deal?" Tony tells him bluntly "You wanna deal drugs, that's your business. You do it on Association garbage routes, it's my fuckin' business. It stops today. You got it?" ("House Arrest").

A first season episode, "Meadowlands," particularly illustrates Tony's shrewdness, breadth of vision, and attention to the complex stakeholder issues that define good management. The heart of the episode is Tony's decision to allow Uncle Junior to assume leadership of the family. We witnessed the run up to this in the tense relationships between Junior's men and Tony's during the long illness of mob boss Jackie Aprile. In a sit-down with the captains, Tony learns that the position is his for the asking. During this same period, Tony expresses to Dr. Melfi his exasperation with the old people in his life, especially his mother and uncle. She responds by urging him to read a "good book out there" that offers "strategies for coping with elder family." Tony demurs, saying, "No, I read, I go right out," so Jennifer offers advice based on the book's argument: "Would it hurt you to let your mother think that she's still in charge? You have children. You know what they're like. You know that sometimes it's important to let them have the illusion of being in control."

The scene shifts back to the Bada Bing!. We see Tony, despite his earlier protestation, sitting at the bar, hunched over a copy of a book entitled *Eldercare: Coping with Late-Life Crisis*. The television announces Jackie Aprile's death, Christopher barges in and performs his *Scarface* routine; Tony forcefully puts him in his place. The scene ends as Tony storms out of the bar. Soldier "Big Pussy" Bonpensiero announces ominously, "Here we go. 'War of '99'," and consigliere Silvio Dante adds, "Adios, Junior."

Every narrative expectation of the gangster movie genre leads us to think that Big Pussy and Silvio are right. This expectation is heightened when the scene shifts to outside the luncheonette where Uncle Junior hangs out with his pals. Tony storms up in his Suburban, gets out of the car and checks his pistol. We are reminded that Junior had last dismissed him following an angry conversation at the same luncheonette by saying, "Next time you come in, you come heavy" (that is, armed).

As Tony enters the luncheonette, we expect a shoot-out. Instead, Tony puts his hands up in the air and declares in a firm voice "I came in heavy, like you said, but I don't wanna use it." Junior's men look on nervously. Tony sits down across the table from his uncle. "Our friend Jackie has died," he says, "And we need a leader." Junior replies coldly, "We do," apparently expecting Tony to assert his claim. But Tony surprises everyone. "Sopranos have been waiting a long time to take the reins," he says, "That's why I want it to be you, Uncle Jun."

Junior is astonished. He asks Tony whether this is really his decision and whether he can speak for the captains. Tony responds affirmatively. Junior rises to hug Tony. While still in this clinch, with Tony's mouth pressed against Junior's ear so that the cronies cannot hear, Tony says, "Just one thing. You know I can't be perceived to lose face. So, Bloomfield and the paving union. It's my asking price." Junior nods assent and the scene ends as others offer congratulations.

In this and ensuing episodes, the basic wisdom of Tony's decision becomes apparent. Junior becomes nominal head of the family, avoiding war; Tony is free to control the actual direction of the family's business, while Junior becomes the main target of federal prosecutions. At Jackie Aprile's funeral, Hesh, the always-wise counselor, offers an independent assessment of Tony's maneuver: "Smart, very smart." But what neither Hesh nor the men realize is that Tony came up with this strategy as a result of his conversations with Dr. Melfi and his reading of the book *Eldercare*. Heeding Dr. Melfi's advice, he has given Uncle Junior "the illusion of being in control." As if to punctuate matters, we shortly see Tony in another session with the psychiatrist. When she asks whether he still has his doubts about therapy, he replies, with a sly grin on his face, "No. Give it another chance. Get a lotta good ideas here. You know, how to cope."

Kim Akass and Janet Macabe, in a discussion of female narrative authority in *The Sopranos*, note that Tony's relationship with Dr. Melfi introduces an important feminine perspective into the series and into Tony's thinking. "The assimilation of Jennifer's psychoanalytical vernacular by Tony," they observe, "allows a feminine voice to penetrate into a generic text that has traditionally excluded it." [5] They add that by adopting Jennifer's insights and professional manner, "Tony is being equipped with the new interpersonal skills needed for dealing with human resource problems at the beginning of the twenty-first century."[6]

We can better appreciate the magnitude of Tony's progress as a manager if we keep in mind the pervasive sexism of his world. That Tony can learn from Dr. Melfi and bring that knowledge to bear on a crucial decision reveals why he is able, in an environment marked by rapid change and emergent threats and competition, to maintain effective, and profitable control of his organization.

It might be objected, of course, that none of this has anything to do with ethics. Tony is not an "ethical manager" in the sense that he is guided by the principled and universal considerations that we associate with ethical choice and conduct. Although he is not a psychopath, because he can sympathize with others' pain and suffers guilt for some of his more injurious deeds,[7] his principal objective always is to benefit himself, his family, and his crew.

Yet within this narrowed horizon, Tony exercises moral self-restraint and a substantial degree of moral oversight. He tries to dampen the disruptive tendencies of his crew and mob associates, struggles to avoid violence, and treats his stakeholders—from a youthful Bada Bing! stripper, to a garbage route client, or an aspiring capo—with respect. He is ethical in the sense that he seems intuitively aware of St. Augustine's famous dictum that "even robbers take care to maintain peace with their comrades."[8]

In fact, Tony himself would probably not use the word "ethical" to describe himself. In an episode in the fourth season ("Mergers and Acquisitions"), Tony has a brief affair with Valentina, a girlfriend of Ralphie Cifaretto. The involvement is

---

[5] "Beyond the Bada Bing!: Negotiating Female Narrative Authority in *The Sopranos*," in David Lavery, ed., *This Thing of Ours: Investigating the Sopranos* (New York: Columbia University Press, 2002), p. 154.

[6] *Ibid.*, p. 153.

[7] Glen O. Gabbard, *The Psychology of the Sopranos* (New York: Basic Books, 2002), p. 32.

[8] *City of God*, Chapter XIX. Quoted from *The Political Writings of St. Augustine*, edited by Henry Paolucci (New York: Regnery, 1962), p. 10.

hardly underway when Tony breaks it off. Valentina tracks him down, and corners him in a restaurant to ask why. He explains that he can't be with her because she's sleeping with Ralphie. "What's the matter," she sneers, "You got morals all of a sudden." "No," Tony replies, "I dunno about morals, but I do got rules." This clarity about the conduct appropriate even to a mob boss makes Tony someone from whom other managers can learn.

7

Tony Soprano's Moral Sympathy (or Lack Thereof): *The Sopranos* and Subjectivist Ethics

SHEILA LINTOTT

In the last episode of the second season, Tony Soprano, along with Silvio Dante and Paulie Walnuts, took Pussy Bonpensiero on his very last boat ride ("Funhouse"). This unfortunate turn of events came to pass because Pussy, a longtime close friend to Tony and member in high standing of Tony's crime family, was found to be a rat—an FBI informant. The three men shot an unarmed Pussy in the chest and dumped his body into the ocean. I wish to address the moral status of Tony's actions when he orders a hit, smacks his *goomah*, or lies to his wife. Generally speaking, murder and battery are both legally and morally wrong, and lying and cheating, if not illegal, are usually morally wrong. Is Tony's behavior somehow different—excusable, understandable, perhaps not even morally wrong? Are moral standards different for Tony Soprano than they are for the rest of us?

Among philosophers there is a healthy debate over the nature of morality. Some, *Ethical Objectivists*, argue that moral judgments such as "abortion is morally permissible" are objectively true or false. For *Ethical Objectivists*, moral claims are true or false in the same way as clear matters of fact like "the earth is round." Without necessarily claiming to know which are true, or how complicated such true judgments must be, *Ethical Objectivists* claim that moral judgments, when true, are true at all times and for all persons, regardless of whether they believe or feel otherwise.[1] In other words, the *Ethical Objectivist* maintains that the truth or falsity of moral claims is independent of the agent making the claim.

On the other side of the debate about the nature of morality we find *Ethical Subjectivists*. According to *Ethical Subjectivists*, the truth or falsity of moral claims depends not on some alleged objective fact of the matter about the act, but rather on the feelings, beliefs, or attitudes of the person passing the judgment. They do not believe that moral judgments are true or false in the same mind-independent manner as statements such as "the earth is flat." In this chapter, we will consider two subjectivist theories of morality in reference to the behavior of Tony Soprano: *Simple Subjectivism* and *Humean Ethical Subjectivism*.[2] I will argue that *Simple Subjectivism* fails to give us an adequate theory of morality and to pronounce acceptable judgments regarding Tony Soprano's behavior. However, as we shall see, this failure is not sufficient to discount *Subjectivism* altogether, because *Humean Ethical Subjectivism* succeeds where *Simple Subjectivism* fails. Hume's moral theory, which is based on a common human nature, does offer us a plausible account of morality and allows us to classify much of Tony's behavior as immoral.

Simple Subjectivism

TONY: You eat steak? . . . If you were in India, you would go to hell for that.

PAULIE: I'm not in India.

TONY: What I am trying to tell you, none of this shit means a goddam thing. ("From Where to Eternity")

---

[1] The principles that Ethical Objectivists ascribe to can be rather complicated and context-dependent. That is, in some situations Ethical Objectivists might maintain that murder is morally wrong while admitting that in others, say, in cases of self-defense or defense of an innocent third party, it may be perfectly morally permissible to kill another human being.

[2] For more detailed discussion of Subjectivism and other topics in Metaethics not covered in this essay, see J.L. Mackie, *Ethics: Inventing Right and Wrong* (New York: Viking, 1991); *Theories of Ethics*, edited by Phillipa Foot (Oxford: Oxford University Press, 1967); and for a summary overview, see James

Simple Subjectivism is the most extreme version of subjectivist ethics. Like the familiar doctrine of moral relativism,
according to which moral claims are true or false relative to a
certain culture or epoch, this doctrine denies that there is any
objective or absolute truth to moral matters. But *Simple
Subjectivism* goes further than any version of relativism
because, instead of claiming that moral codes are relative to
certain cultures or epochs, this theory sees morality as radically
relative to each particular individual. Each individual defines
her own moral code, just as each individual is best qualified to
say which color is her favorite. Moral codes, according to this
view, are just matters of taste. You may think that murder is
wrong, while Tony Soprano may not. There is no problem with
this difference, just as there is no problem with your favorite
color being green and mine being blue; to each his own. There
seems to be no better evidence to support a *Simple Subjectivist*
theory of morality than the behavior of Tony Soprano. When
Tony orders a hit, smacks his *goomah*, breaks his marital vow
of fidelity, tampers with a jury, or extorts money from a small
business owner, many argue that these acts are 'right for Tony'
despite the fact that they are morally unacceptable for the rest
of us.

Simple Subjectivism is comfortable with the apparent contradictions between different people's moral codes, because on
this view the contradictions are merely that—apparent. This theory of the nature of morality tells us that "X is morally right" simply means "I think X is morally right." On this view, when Tony,
Paulie, and Silvio killed Pussy, if Tony believed that the killing
was morally right, then, for him, it was—end of story. This is
perhaps the most rampant version of subjectivism in the non-
philosophical community. It is also the most problematic.

Before examining the problems with this view, it is worth trying to understand its appeal. First, there is plenty of evidence
supporting the claim that individuals differ—sometimes drastically—in their opinions on moral matters. Different generations,
different cultures, different people all seem to espouse different
moral principles. If morality is objective, then the burden of

---

Rachels, *The Elements of Moral Philosophy*, fourth edition (New York: McGraw
Hill, 2003).

proof is on the objectivist to explain why moral systems appear to differ so much from individual to individual.[3]

Furthermore, passing moral judgments on another individual is a difficult task. When observing another person, we can see her behavior, but we are not privileged to know all of her motivations, nor do we understand completely all of the circumstances surrounding her actions. We may be attracted to *Simple Subjectivism* because we realize that if we really understood a person's motivations and fully grasped all of the nuances of the situation, what looks to be morally wrong may not be. This unwillingness to condemn another person without serious consideration and evidence, in other words, the ability to practice tolerance, is certainly a good trait. In many cases a person's moral character is best judged from the privileged position of the subject.

There are many good reasons to allow individuals to voice their opinions on moral matters and likewise to refrain from passing moral judgment on another person's character or actions. We may learn something from hearing another's opinion, or we may be mistaken about the circumstances or her intentions. However, whether the facts that lead us to such healthy open-mindedness and well-heeded caution recommend an acceptance of *Simple Subjectivism* remains to be seen.

Problems with *Simple Subjectivism*: Disagreement and Moral Outrage

DR. RICHARD LA PENNA: Call him a patient. The man's a criminal, Jennifer. And after a while, finally, you're going to get beyond psychotherapy with its cheesy moral relativism, finally you're gonna get to good and evil. And he's evil. ("The Legend of Tennessee Moltisanti")

Simple Subjectivists make ethical judgments matters of opinion. Moral judgments, on this view, are said to be abbreviated statements of personal approval. So, if an FBI agent says, "extortion

---

[3] Although I will not attempt to meet this burden of proof in this chapter, I think it can be met. For discussions of the commonalities in seemingly divergent moral codes, see Rachels, *Elements*, pp. 25–26 and Louis Pojman, "A Critique of Ethical Relativism" in *Ethical Theory: Classical and Contemporary Readings*, edited by Louis Pojman (Belmont: Wadsworth, 1998), pp. 46–49.

is morally wrong" what she really means is only "I think that extortion is morally wrong." If Tony Soprano defends his acts of extortion by claiming that "extortion is not morally wrong," he is only stating: "I don't think extortion is morally wrong." The *Simple Subjectivist* argues that although moral judgments look like statements making objective claims, they are actually only expressing personal opinions. The statements: "Agent Ciccerone thinks extortion is morally wrong" and "Tony Soprano thinks that extortion is not morally wrong" are not contradictory. They are consistent; they can be true simultaneously. However, in a genuine disagreement, there is usually a contradiction. For example, if Christopher believes that Meadow has taken drugs in the past and Carmela believes that Meadow has never taken drugs, only one of them can be right. Either Meadow has used drugs in the past or she hasn't.

Are moral disagreements really illusory, unlike this dispute over Meadow's drug use? Doesn't it seem as if there is a genuine moral disagreement between Agent Ciccerone and Tony? If so, then both Tony and agent Ciccerone are stating something about the act of extortion—not only about their beliefs about the moral status of extortion. For another illustrative example, recall Carmela and Tony's screaming match in the last episode of Season Four ("Whitecaps"). The couple argues about marital infidelity. Tony seems to be defending himself when he asks Carmela:

> Carmela, who the fuck did you think I was when you married me, huh? You knew my father. You grew up around Dickie Moltisanti and your Uncle Eddie. Where do you get off acting all surprised and miffed when there are women on the side? You knew the deal.

Despite the fact that their marriage and marital problems are admittedly complicated, Carmela is not persuaded by Tony's attempt to justify his extramarital affairs. How can we understand this apparent disagreement over the topic of adultery? If we accept *Simple Subjectivism*, we can't. It seems as if Carmela is convinced that adultery is morally wrong; Tony is at least attempting to present a case that adultery is not morally wrong. If there is a genuine disagreement here, there must be something more to their claims than mere personal approval and disapproval. If Carmela thinks X is true and Tony thinks X is false, they are in disagreement. The statement "Tony thinks adultery is not morally wrong" does not logically contradict the statement that "Carmela thinks adultery is morally wrong." But when Tony argues that adultery *is* morally permissible for him and Carmela argues that adultery *is not* morally permissible for Tony, their claims *do* contradict one another. Only one of them is right because their statements cannot both be true at the same time. This is why people bother to argue over moral matters; if matters of morality were subjective in the sense portrayed by *Simple Subjectivism*, then arguing over moral issues such as adultery, abortion, or the death penalty would be like your trying to convince me that my favorite kind of ice cream is not rum raisin (it is)![4] So, one major problem with *Simple Subjectivism* is that it does not allow us to account for moral disagreements.

Another serious problem with *Simple Subjectivism* is that it does not allow us any room to morally condemn the behavior of another person. The same problem put another way is that the theory makes each of us morally infallible. Although we should not jump to any quick conclusions about the moral status of another's actions, nonetheless, there seem to be very clear cases of actions at which we ought to be morally outraged. And sometimes our moral outrage is directed at ourselves. But, if morality is merely a matter of opinion and everyone's opinion counts equally, then we are left with counterintuitive conclusions such as that Adolf Hitler and Mother Teresa stand on equal moral ground and that any act is morally acceptable provided the agent believed it was so at the time.[5]

However, not even Tony Soprano wants to accept this sort of a conclusion. Consider the following conversation between

---

[4] Notice that you might try to convince me that butter pecan is actually the superior flavor, but this is quite different from any attempt you might make in persuading me to think at the present moment that I do not know what kind of ice cream I prefer.

[5] Serial rapist and killer Ted Bundy defended himself by appealing to a simplistic version of *Ethical Subjectivism*. He contends that since pleasure is something he values, his raping, torturing, and murdering young women is morally justified because it brings him more pleasure than other—generally deemed to be morally acceptable—activities. For more on this, see a paraphrased statement of Ted Bundy in Harry V. Jaffa, *Homosexuality and the Natural Law* (Claremont: Claremont Institute, 1990), pp. 3–4; quoted in Pojman, *Ethical Theory*, p. 41.

Tony and his therapist, Dr. Melfi, about his nephew Christopher's recent near-death experience ("Full Leather Jacket"):

> DR. MELFI: Do you think he'll go to hell?
> TONY: No. He's not the type that deserves hell.
> DR. MELFI: Who do you think does?
> TONY: The worst people. The twisted and demented psychos who kill people for pleasure. The cannibals, the degenerate bastards that molest and torture little kids and they kill babies. The Hitlers, the Pol Pots. Those are the evil fucks that deserve to die. Not my nephew.

The distinction that Tony draws between those who deserve to go to hell and his nephew (and ultimately himself) may or may not be defensible. Nonetheless, for Tony, and for most of us, it is not the case that morality is simply a matter of a variety of equal yet differing opinions. There admittedly are many differing opinions about moral matters, but that does not mean that all such opinions are equally good. At least some of the opinions of Hitler, Pol Pot, and maybe even Tony Soprano should be discredited.

We can see then that *Simple Subjectivism* fails as a moral theory. It fails because it cannot make sense of moral disagreements and it cannot explain moral defects in a satisfactory manner. We want to find a way to condemn some behavior, even in cases where a person blatantly fails to do so for himself. Is there a version of subjectivism that will allow us to make sense of moral disagreements and condemn morally reprehensible behavior, while holding fast to the intuition that there is something subjective about morality in general? For an answer to this question, let's consider *Humean Ethical Subjectivism*.

Humean Ethical Subjectivism

> DR. MELFI [to Tony]: "Do you feel like Frankenstein? A thing? Lacking humanity? Lacking human feelings?" ("Denial, Anger, Acceptance")

Hume's moral theory is subjectivist, but it is a much more promising theory than *Simple Subjectivism*. David Hume

(1711–1776) argues that rather than being based on reason, moral judgments find their grounding in the passions or emotions. According to Hume, in the claim "X is morally wrong," the predicate 'morally wrong' refers to something, namely a feeling—a moral sentiment, *in the person* passing the judgment rather than to some matter of fact about the object, 'X.' Hume explains:

> Take any action allow'd to be vicious: Wilful murder, for instance. Examine it in all lights, and see if you can find that matter of fact, or real existence, which you call *vice*. In which-ever way you take it, you find only certain passions, motives, volitions and thoughts. There is no other matter of fact in the case. The vice entirely escapes you, as long as you consider the object. You never can find it, till you turn your reflection into your own breast, and find a sentiment of disapprobation, which arises in you, towards this action. Here is a matter of fact; but 'tis the object of feeling, not of reason. It lies in yourself, not in the object. So that when you pronounce any action or character to be vicious, you mean nothing, but that from the constitution of your nature you have a feeling or sentiment of blame from the contemplation of it. Vice and virtue, therefore, must be compar'd to sounds, colours, heat and cold, which, according to modern philosophy, are not qualities in objects, but perceptions in the mind.[6]

Here Hume makes an explicit comparison between moral judgments and judgments concerning qualities that are not in objects, but that we tend to attribute to objects. Consider, for example, how we perceive color. When we see color, we are seeing light waves that are reflected by an object. If our optical system were different, grass might appear purple to us rather than green. This is because without our processing of light waves in a certain way, there is no color in the world. The claim then that "the grass is green" is true only for beings who perceive grass (and other objects of color) the same way we do. Just as colors are not, strictly speaking, properties of objects, Hume argues that virtue and vice are likewise not, strictly

---

[6] David Hume, *Treatise of Human Nature*, Book III, Part I, §1, edited by David Fate Norton and Mary J. Norton (Oxford: Oxford University Press, 2000), p. 301.

speaking, properties of actions; colors, virtues, and vices are dependent on human perception.

Perhaps the clearest example of the difference between the qualities in an object and those that we merely attribute to the object comes not from Hume, but from his fellow empiricist, George Berkeley. Berkeley explains: "When a pin pricks your finger, doth it not rend and divide the fibres of your flesh? . . . [Y]ou neither judge the sensation itself occasioned by the pin, nor anything like it to be in the pin."[7] In other words, it would be absurd to say that the pin has the quality of pain; instead, it is more accurate to say that the pin has properties that can cause the sensation of pain in us. Likewise, according to Hume, murder causes in the witness a sensation of moral repugnance—a distinct unpleasant sensation: "An action, or sentiment, or character is virtuous or vicious; why? Because its view causes a pleasure or uneasiness of a particular kind . . ."[8]

Recall the episode of *The Sopranos* in which Tony and Pussy shoot Matt Bevelaqua, the young "stock broker" who attempted to assassinate Christopher ("Full Leather Jacket"). A battered, crying, shaking, and pleading Matt calls out for his "Mommy" while Tony and Pussy pump him full of bullets. According to Hume, it is not that this murder is, in and of itself, morally wrong. Rather, the murder is morally wrong because witnessing it causes in me a feeling of moral repugnance.

So, just as color, pain, and heat perception are subjective, so too are virtue and vice. That is, we speak as if it is an absolute fact of the matter that the sky is blue, yet we realize that, independent of perception like ours, the sky isn't blue at all. Colors are perceptually dependent on the object that reflects light waves and also on the way the optical system of the perceiver processes the light waves. According to Hume, virtue and vice are also dependent on the reactions of human beings—their emotive reactions. Without human emotions, morality as we know it would cease to exist, although the acts that we call morally good or bad would still occur. Emotional reactions are

---

[7] George Berkeley, "The First Dialogue," *Three Dialogues between Hylas and Philonous, in Opposition to Sceptics and Atheists* in *The Empiricists* (New York: Anchor Press, 1974), p. 225.

[8] Hume, *Treatise*, p. 303.

indisputably subjective; but the significance of this fact needs to be considered in detail.

Evaluating Humean Ethical Subjectivism: Searching for Tony's Moral Sympathy

TONY [to Dr. Melfi]: When the laughs got old, we stopped calling him. It wasn't until years later that I found out that the poor prick was going home every night and crying himself to sleep. And when I found out, you know, I felt bad. But I never really understood what he felt—to be used, you know, for somebody else's amusement, like a fuckin' dancin' bear, till I played golf with those guys." ("A Hit Is a Hit")

Some events depicted in *The Sopranos* are especially gruesome. The scene in which Dr. Melfi was raped and the scene in which Tony and Pussy killed Matt rank toward the top of those I personally found most difficult to watch. Moreover, most viewers, I suspect, were likewise horrified by these events. Of course, the agreement here is not universal; some antisocial personalities may have actually derived satisfaction and enjoyment from viewing these scenes.[9] Given this discrepancy, one may be tempted to interpret Hume as allowing that morality is simply a matter of taste. If morality is based on subjective feelings and such feelings *can* differ from individual to individual, doesn't this make morality on Hume's theory as radically subjective as it is on *Simple Subjectivism*? If so, then this theory will be subject to the same problems that confronted *Simple Subjectivism*, the problems related to moral disagreement, human fallibility, and moral outrage.

However, Hume's theory is *not* subject to such objections, because for Hume the basis of morality is found in the natural

---

[9] I will leave aside here the issue of to what extent our emotional reactions to *The Sopranos* are rational or full-fledged due to the fictional nature of the depictions. For more on the paradox of fiction, see (among others) Gregory Currie, *The Nature of Fiction* (Cambridge: Cambridge University Press, 1990); Peter Lamarque, "How Can We Fear and Pity Fictions?" *British Journal of Aesthetics* 21 (1981), pp. 291–304; Kendall Walton, "Fearing Fictions," *Journal of Philosophy* 75 (1978), pp. 5–27.

and normal human capacity for sympathy. Since Hume bases morality on a common human nature, his version of *Ethical Subjectivism* asserts more than the *Simple Subjectivist* version which makes morality entirely idiosyncratic. He asserts: "That there is a natural difference between merit and demerit, virtue and vice, wisdom and folly, no reasonable man will deny."[10] The grounds of this "natural difference" and the "true origins of morality" are found in "the nature and force of sympathy."[11] In terms of their capacity for sympathy, according to Hume, "the minds of all men are similar in their feelings and operations." [12] In other words, Hume maintains that "X is morally wrong" is true when the sympathy of any reasonable person under normal circumstances would elicit a negative response to X. Moreover, sympathetic moral sentiments function to prescribe (or prohibit) certain behavior. For, as Hume tells us: "Nothing can be more real, or concern us more, than our own sentiments of pleasure and uneasiness; and if these be favourable to virtue, and unfavourable to vice, no more can be requisite to the regulation of our conduct and behavior."[13]

Furthermore, Hume's theory is easily supported by empirical evidence. Human beings do react in fairly predictable ways to the sight of another person's suffering. Witnessing a person in severe pain makes us cringe; seeing a child cry causes (at least) a pang of concern in us; and trying to console a person grieving a loss of a loved one stirs up our deepest sympathies. It is only the rare few—people with antisocial personality disorder—that either feel nothing or actually reap pleasure from the sight of such events. It is not difficult for us to reach agreement about such basic tenets as: whenever possible, reducing suffering is a good thing.

Tony Soprano is guilty of horrible acts of violence and indifference to human suffering. Dr. Melfi calls him on this during a particularly intense therapy session in which they discuss the death of the racehorse, Pie-O-My. She asks him straightforwardly: "You've caused much suffering yourself, haven't you?"

---

[10] Hume, "Of the Dignity or Meanness of Human Nature," in *David Hume: Selected Essays* (Oxford: Oxford University Press, 1998), p. 44.
[11] Hume, *Treatise*, Book III, Part 3, §1, p. 368.
[12] *Ibid.*, p. 368.
[13] Hume, *Treatise*, Book III, Part I, §2, p. 302.

Tony thinks, stares off in the distance, and ultimately never answers her question ("The Strong, Silent Type"). But we all know the answer is yes. When Tony acts in a vicious manner to which normal persons respond with sympathy to his victims, then we condemn him morally for those acts.

Yet, like most human beings, and contra the opinion of Dr. Melfi's ex-husband, Tony Soprano is not entirely evil. Tony is a realistically complicated character and he is not entirely incapable of feeling the flutter of normal human sympathy. He wants to care for his family, to help his friends, and to generally "do the right thing" ("The Knight in White Satin Armor"). Unfortunately, he is not always able to—sometimes his sympathy even leads him in the wrong direction. He steps out of line with Ralph Cifaretto several times because his sympathy for Ralph's victims rages out of control. He reacts violently after Ralph beats Tracee, the twenty-year-old stripper, to death outside of the *Bada Bing!* ("University"). And ultimately, Tony kills Ralph because he suspects him of having a fire set to kill Pie-O-My to get the insurance money ("Whoever Did This"). Ralph denied it, but aggravates Tony when he argues that the horse's suffering doesn't outweigh the insurance benefit: "It was a fucking animal," Ralph explains, versus "a hundred grand a piece."

To find the source of Tony's mixed up moral outlook, and frequent inability to feel sympathy when appropriate, perhaps a good place to look is to his childhood, as Dr. Melfi is constantly urging him to do. Tony discusses some early memories of his home life. As a young boy he recalls seeing his father and Uncle Junior beat up the butcher and chop off his pinky. He tells Dr. Melfi that this event was not traumatic; it was a rush. He was proud of his father's strength and power, proud that he himself didn't run away, and his father was proud of that as well ("Fortunate Son"). Perhaps Tony has been conditioned to respond in abnormal ways by being brought up in less than normal circumstances. Growing up in his family, Tony was not permitted to express sympathy, neither did he receive much. Dr. Melfi seems to think that Tony has some antisocial personality traits and suspects they are at the root of his panic attacks. She broaches this topic with him:

> DR. MELFI: There's a psychological condition known as alex-
> ithymia—common in certain personalities—the individual

craves almost ceaseless action which enables them to
avoid acknowledging the abhorrent things they do.

TONY: Abhorrent?! . . . . What certain personalities?

DR. MELFI: Antisocial personalities.

TONY: What happens when these antisocial personalities
aren't distracted from the horrible shit they do?

DR. MELFI: They have time to think about their behavior—
how what they do affects other people—about feelings of
emptiness and self-loathing—haunting them since childhood. And they crash. ("House Arrest")

Tony reacts to this suggestion with silence, but one can see his
silence as recognition of the moral contradictions in his life.
During the discussion about Pie-O-My's death, Dr. Melfi says to
him: "It is sad that you've lost something that you love. That
being said . . . It *is* a horse." An appalled Tony fires back: "What
the fuck is the matter with you!?" But clearly Dr. Melfi is on to
something. She is not chastising Tony for feeling for the horse;
rather, she is trying to coax him into seeing that the ease in
which he feels sympathy for animals is not equaled when it
comes to humans. She points out to him: "You haven't grieved
this way for people—your mother, your best friend" ("The
Strong, Silent Type"). Dr. Melfi is attempting to extend Tony's
natural ability to feel moral sympathies for animal suffering to
feel for human suffering to the same extent.

Hume's theory, which like *Simple Subjectivism* makes morality a subjective matter, succeeds where that theory fails. Humean
Ethical Subjectivism allows us to make sense of disagreements,
makes room for human fallibility, and permits us to condemn
moral atrocities.[14] We can condemn much of Tony's behavior,
despite the fact that in many cases Tony fails to acknowledge
the immorality of his actions. Unfortunately, Tony is unable to

---

[14] A Humean theory of moral subjectivity can serve to ground judgments
regarding the immorality of much of Tony Soprano's behavior. Yet, there
remains a bothersome issue that plagues this theory of moral philosophy.
Many people find this theory problematic because it entails the following: If
human beings were naturally disposed to react in an apathetic manner to
genocide, then on Hume's theory, genocide would be deemed morally
unproblematic. Worse yet, imagine that human beings were to evolve in such
a way that we actually came to enjoy watching innocent children suffer at the
hands of torturers, then torturing children would be deemed virtuous.

respond as a normal person because he is in abnormal circumstances. His childhood was such that it trained him to respond
in an abnormal way to violence and domination, and the 'occupation' that he has been indoctrinated in reinforced this abnormal way of life. Of course, this is not to claim that murder is
morally acceptable "for Tony," but rather that his circumstances
are so abnormal, and perhaps he has become so abnormal, that
he cannot respond appropriately to many situations. Dr. Melfi
was helping him work on that. Meadow is right; Tony should go
back to therapy ("Whitecaps").[15]

[15] Many thanks to the editors of this volume, Richard Greene, William Irwin,
and Peter Vernezze, for helpful comments on an earlier version of this essay;
I am also grateful to Eric Johnson for his feedback on various drafts of this
essay, as well as for his willingness to watch (again and again) and discuss *The
Sopranos* with me.

8
Staying within the Family: Tony Soprano's Ethical Obligations

SCOTT D. WILSON

Tony Soprano is a bad man. In his capacity of the head of a North Jersey crime family he is responsible for beatings, murders, extortion, and theft, he promotes prostitution and illegal gambling, and he is a racist who routinely cheats on his wife. He may not be the worst person on *The Sopranos* (no, in my opinion that distinction is Ralphie's alone), but there is no denying that Tony is a bad man. No doubt, this is part of what caused AIDA, the American-Italian Defense Association, to sue HBO for violating the Illinois state constitution.[1] According to this group, HBO has harmed all decent, hard working, and law abiding Italian-Americans by producing *The Sopranos*, a show that continues to perpetuate the negative stereotype of Italian-Americans that is so common in mass media. Not all Italian-Americans are gangsters; not all Italian-Americans are bad men like Tony Soprano.

Whatever the merits of AIDA's claim (their suit was dismissed in court), we should not conclude that Tony Soprano is a bad man and rest content with that. For anyone who has watched the show with any discernment at all will recognize another obvious truth: Tony Soprano is a good man. Often in his roles as a father, friend, and proud Italian-American, Tony does what is right. He takes care of his mother (who does not appreciate or even acknowledge his concern in the least), wants his chil-

---

[1] See their statement at http://www.italiausa.com/misc/m01e48.htm.

dren to have a better life than the one he leads, makes sure that people drive at reasonable speeds through the neighborhood, and sponsors a yearly Christmas toy give-away for the local children, complete with a rotund Santa Claus. For these reasons and more, it is hard not to like Tony Soprano. This is part of what makes *The Sopranos* the pop-culture smash that it is. While Tony Soprano is a very bad man in many respects, he is also a very good man, a man with whom most people watching the show can identify.

What may not be so obvious, however, is that the reason Tony is a bad man is the same reason that he is a good man. Tony is both a savage killer and a devoted father because he accepts a moral system that places primary importance on his relationships with people he likes and with whom he identifies. Like Tony, most of us just assume that morality begins with our duties to friends, families, and the people we can call our own, and that anything more than this is not really required. What I hope to show is that we cannot rely on this type of moral thinking, but must instead be more impartial if we are to be morally decent people. Still, a commitment to impartial morality is perfectly consistent with our giving extra weight to the interests of our friends and families. In what follows I will outline a moral theory that is at its core impartial, and thus has the resources necessary to explain why Tony is a bad man, but is also consistent with Tony's being a devoted and caring friend and father. To further demonstrate the benefits of thinking in this way, I will apply the theory to Dr. Melfi's decision to accept Tony as a patient.

Tony's Ethical Code

Tony's most explicit and elaborate statement of the ethical standards by which he lives comes to us in a speech he gives in Dr. Melfi's office in "From Where to Eternity." Melfi asks Tony whether he thinks he will go to hell when he dies. He responds:

> Hell? You been listening to me? No. . . . We're soldiers. You know, soldiers don't go to hell. It's war. Soldiers, they kill other soldiers. We're in a situation where everybody involved knows the stakes and if you're gonna accept those stakes . . . you gotta do certain things. It's business. We're soldiers. We follow codes. Orders.

Melfi then asks him whether he thinks this justifies everything he does, to which he replies:

> Excuse me, let me tell you somethin'. When America opened up the flood gates, and let us Italians in . . . what do you think they were doin' it for? Because they were tryin' to save us from poverty? No, they did it because they needed us. They needed us to build their cities and dig their subways and to make 'em richer. The Carnegies, and the Rockefellers, they needed worker bees, and there we were. But some of us didn't want to swarm around their hive and lose who we were. We wanted to stay Italian and preserve the things that meant somethin' to us. Honor, and family and loyalty. And some of us wanted a piece of the action. Now, we weren't educated like the Americans. But we had the balls to take what we wanted. And those other fucks, those other, the G.P. Morgans [sic], they were crooks and killers, too. But that was their business, right? The American Way.

There are three main elements to Tony's moral code as elaborated above that I wish to highlight.

First, Tony places a good deal of importance on the value of family. In order to do right by Tony's standards, it is imperative that you do right by your family. Tony mentions this duty in many places. In "Pine Barrens" he claims, "I'm not saying I'm perfect, but I do right by my family." He tells Meadow in "Bust Out," "Everything I do. It's all for you and your brother." This is not just idle talk for Tony either. Take his relationships with his sister Janice, and with his mother Livia, as examples. Janice is not a very good person, and Tony does not like her. I sympathize with Tony, for Janice really is no good. She is a scam artist and a leech who is on "total disability" because she claims to have gotten carpal-tunnel syndrome from working in a coffee shop. She comes home to see her sick mom, but her real reason is to take control of her mother's house and the possible riches hidden there. She is loud, rude, and opinionated. She even goes so far as to give some not-so-subtle hints to her fiancé, Richie, that he should kill Tony and take over the family business. So it should come as no surprise that Tony does not like Janice. However, she is his sister, and he must do right by his family. So when Janice kills Richie in a short but heated argument in "The Knight in White Satin Armour," Tony is there to take care of the mess. In "To Save Us All from Satan's Power,"

Tony gags and beats the Russian mobster who broke her ribs and (actually) hurt her wrist in an assault. Never mind that the Russian was only trying to get Janice to return the prosthetic leg she had stolen from Svetlana, the woman hired by Tony to take care of his mother. The fact that Janice may have partly deserved what she got is irrelevant. What matters is that Janice is his sister and those who hurt his family must be punished.

Perhaps even more telling is Tony's relationship with his mother. Livia is a black hole of depression who does not recognize any of the good things that Tony does for her. She constantly criticizes him and is thoroughly miserable to be around. Why does Tony spend so much time and effort trying to have a good relationship with her? Because she is his mother, and as he says to Melfi in "46 Long," "You're supposed to take care of your mother."

Tony cares deeply for his family, but he may care more about his "other family"—the crime family over which he presides. In "Fortunate Son," when his nephew Christopher is getting made, Tony reveals just how important this family should be:

> This family comes before everything else. . . . *Everything.* Before your wife and your children and your mother and your father. It's a thing of honor. . . . You stay within the family.

Tony repeatedly stresses the importance of "staying within the family." In "Toodle-Fucking-Oo," after Richie runs Beansie down and puts him in the hospital Tony stresses the importance of staying within the family, saying, "we wash our own dirty laundry." Tony takes this point very seriously, and behaves ruthlessly toward anyone who does not. Just ask Big Pussy Bonpensiero, who was flipped by the feds—of course it is too late now to ask him anything, since Tony made him "sleep with the fishes." You can ask his wife, Angie, for when she complains to Tony's wife, Carmela, how tough finances are since Pussy has "disappeared," Tony smashes her car to remind her of the importance of going to him if she has problems, of staying within the family.

Tony also views himself as a kind of soldier-businessman. We do not condemn soldiers for killing people in wars, and so we should not condemn Tony for killing and beating people in his role as a soldier. He also sees himself as a businessman who is not unlike other businessmen. This is a recurring theme in the show, and is expressed by many characters who are engaged in legitimate business. For example, at a dinner party at Dr. Cusamano's house in "A Hit Is a Hit," discussion turns to the mob family next door and Cusamano shrugs it off, asking: "Being a gangster—what's that mean anyway?" A business friend of his goes further: "Yeah, that's true. Some of the shit I see in the boardroom, I don't know if I'd make a distinction." Cusamano agrees, "Sometimes I think the only thing separating American business from the mob's . . . is fucking whacking somebody." So not only does Tony see what he does as just business, but his law-abiding neighbors do as well. A businessman just takes advantage where he can to earn for his family. Tony is not very different from most American businessmen—he just kills people sometimes, which is justified by his being a soldier.

Why does Tony see himself as a soldier? The answer to this brings us to the third element of Tony's moral code. Not only is Tony committed to his friends and family, but he is also committed to Italian-Americans in general. He is proud to be an Italian-American, and believes that he and his business associates are obligated to help the Italian-American community. As Tony's speech to Melfi indicates, he believes Italian-Americans were treated very poorly when they first started coming to America, and in order to fight the prejudices they encountered, they needed to stick together. So, not only must Tony do right by his friends and family, but he must also do right by the Italian-American community. He stresses the importance of this to his children, listing a number of Italian-Americans who have had great positive contributions to America. It is a duty that he believes all Italian-Americans have ("The Legend of Tennessee Moltisanti"). In the same episode, he becomes enraged when one of the feds who searches his house turns out to be an Italian-American. While the other feds are just doing their jobs, this guy is going against one of his own, an unforgivable error in Tony's eyes.

These three principles form the backbone of Tony's moral code: do right by your family, do right by your business associates, and do right by your people. If we are honest with ourselves, we will admit that we are not entirely unlike Tony. Now we may not be leaders of crime families and so may not be devoted to our mobster pals. However, the dominant moral thinking today is one of partiality—in order to do right, we must think of only a portion of the people affected by our actions. So, for example, the person who buys her family luxuries and refuses to donate money to relief organizations to provide other people with necessities is not seen as doing anything wrong in our society. Why? Well, she is doing right by her family, and that is all that morality demands of her. The ad executive who intentionally misleads people in order to sell a product is not doing anything wrong. Why? Well, business is business, and we are allowed to do things in business that we are not allowed to do otherwise. And the person who donates money to help out relatively wealthy Americans who have had their homes destroyed by a hurricane rather than helping out the absolutely poor people living in such places as Afghanistan, Africa, and South America is doing a wonderful thing. Why? Well, we have duties to people we can call our own, and not necessarily to those who are not one of us.

This, of course, is the genius of *The Sopranos*. For if the characters of the show were merely people who had no moral principles at all, or had principles with which few people could identify, then the show would be a mere curiosity. But the characters on the show are like us in many ways, and share some same basic values with the rest of us. We watch the show in part because we are able to put ourselves in Tony's shoes, because we identify with him and his concerns (to a point). But then we see this man, with whom we can identify, doing things that shock and appall us. We are entranced—how can such a good man be so bad? How can such a bad man be so good?

Impartial Morality and the Problem of Partial Relationships

We can understand better why Tony is a bad man if we look closely at how he goes about justifying his actions. Tony is the leader of an auto theft ring, among other things. He justifies this by demonstrating that in doing this he is benefiting his families (both crime and blood). That is the end of the justification for him. Once he has shown that an action benefits the people with whom he has partial relationships, he is done showing why he thinks he is permitted to do the action. For Tony, then, morality is essentially about these partial relations—they are what ultimately justify all actions.

This is Tony's major moral mistake, for morality is essentially impartial. Just what this impartiality amounts to is not an easy matter to explain—many different philosophers think of it in many different ways. However, one way of putting it is this: from the point of view of the universe (so to speak), each person's welfare is equally important, each person is equally deserving of respect.[2] The fact that Carmela is Tony's wife, for example, does not mean that Carmela is thereby more deserving of moral concern than Angie Bonpensiero. In other words, the fact that a certain action will benefit my friends or me is never the end of a moral justification for doing the act since I have not considered how the act will affect others. If the act harms others, then this speaks against doing the act because these other people matter in their own right.

Tony's mistake, then, is to assume that morality is essentially about our partial relations and the duties that arise from them. Indeed, morality is needed to combat just this way of thinking. Think about some of the moral reforms of the past that we are proud of, such as the Civil Rights movement. This movement asked us to expand the circle of people in the moral community to include everyone equally. History has taught us the dangers of failing to do so, but we sometimes need reminders. Tony Soprano is such a reminder, for he is a throwback in many ways. He cares only for his own, and will do anything to protect them.

But this leads us to a problem. Perhaps we all agree that morality should be in some sense impartial. Few of us, however, are ever completely impartial, and no one is always completely impartial. So does this mean that we are all failing to live according to what morality demands? Could it be true that morality requires us to always be impartial in everything we do?

Before we answer these questions, let's be clear on what complete impartiality would require. Suppose, for example, that Tony can either save Meadow or two total strangers from drowning, but cannot save them all (and that he is the only person in a position to save any). Wouldn't true impartiality require him to save the strangers rather than Meadow (save two rather than one)? Most people agree that he is not only permitted but

---

[2] Henry Sidgwick described the impartiality of morality in this way in his influential book, *The Methods of Ethics*, first published in 1874.

required to save his child instead of the strangers. So, it would seem, most people do not believe that morality requires us always to be completely impartial.

So here is our problem: on the one hand, we think that morality is in some important sense impartial. On the other hand, we do not think we must always be completely impartial in order to be doing the right thing. Are our views simply inconsistent, or is there some way to reconcile them? In order to answer this question, I propose that we examine Dr. Melfi's decision to accept Tony as a patient.

Should Dr. Melfi Accept Tony as a Patient?

In the very first episode of the series Tony comes to Dr. Melfi on his doctor's advice, having had panic attacks that render him unconscious. He makes it clear to her that he is part of the mob, and as such he routinely breaks the law (and possibly peoples' legs). Dr. Melfi agrees to treat Tony. Is this something she should do?

If she were to be completely impartial, then it would seem she should not. If she is able to help Tony, this would enable him to become a more effective mob boss, and thus a more dangerous person. In fact, Tony often uses her advice on personal relations to become a better mob boss. For example, in "Meadowlands," when Tony and Junior butt heads over who is to run the family, Tony remembers some advice Melfi offered in therapy. She suggests that the best way to handle his difficult relationships with his elders is to "let them have the illusion of being in control." This he does, which ends up giving him the real power in the family. In making Tony better she may end up making things worse for other people.

Dr. Melfi's ex-husband, Richard, would agree that she should not treat Tony. In "The Legend of Tennessee Moltisanti," he rails against her decision to treat Tony: "Call him a patient. The man's a criminal, Jennifer. And after a while, finally you're going to get beyond psychotherapy with its cheesy moral relativism, finally you're going to get to good and evil. And he's evil." Richard believes that Tony is evil and that she should not help an evil man. The psychiatrist who sees Carmela in "Second Opinion" agrees. After he advises her to leave Tony, he tells her he cannot accept her "blood money" and will not have anything to do with her unless she is no longer an accomplice to Tony and his evil-doing.

Before we agree with this conclusion, however, let me introduce a distinction. Let's say that when someone considers the effects of proposed courses of action on everyone concerned, and then chooses the act that will have the best consequences for everyone, considered impartially, that they have acted completely impartially. We must be careful to contrast this with an action that is justified from an impartial point of view. We can say that an action is justified from an impartial point of view when, even if it does not make things best for everyone considered, there is a good impartial reason for performing the act nonetheless.

To make this distinction clear, consider again the drowning example. To act completely impartially, Tony must save two strangers rather than Meadow, since this will make things best for everyone. However, there may be an impartial justification for Tony saving Meadow instead of the strangers. That justification would run something like this: it is a good thing, for everyone, that family members care more for each other than they do for total strangers. If parents did not care more for their children than they did for strangers, it is hard to imagine how children could live healthy, happy lives. If children do not live healthy, happy lives, they will be less likely to grow into members who contribute positively to society. So if we want to have children who grow into people who make positive contributions to society, we must show some partiality to them over strangers. So there is a good impartial reason for family members caring more for each other than they do strangers.

So if Tony saves Meadow rather than two strangers, he may have an impartial justification for doing so. He is justified in doing this because he cares so much for his child that he simply cannot save two strangers rather than Meadow, and it is a good thing that people care this much for their children.

We now have a way to justify giving priority to our partial relationships from an impartial point of view. It may seem that the moral theory we have arrived at is really no different from Tony's, but there is an important difference between them. Recall that for Tony, the end of moral justification comes once you have shown that an act has benefited a family member or friend. On the moral theory I am endorsing, that is only the beginning of the justification. In order to complete the justifying process, we must consider why these relationships are important, and this requires us to adopt the impartial point of view. Another important difference is this: using Tony's theory, we would not become alarmed if in benefiting our families we end up causing others a great deal of pain. These others do not really matter on Tony's way of thinking. But on the theory outlined above, they do matter, and as others become affected more, we should rethink the amount of partiality we are showing.

Now let's return to Dr. Melfi. Is there an impartial justification for her treating Tony, even though he is a mob boss and treatment might make things worse for everyone? Perhaps there is. The role of a psychiatrist is to treat her patients in order for them to achieve mental health. Presumably this is a good thing for society. People who suffer from neuroses and psychoses will cause problems for others, and so it is in everyone's best interest that these people get the help they need. But in order for a psychiatrist to do this job well, she cannot always think about how her actions will affect others. Her attention must be focused on her patients, on making them better.

This does not mean that Dr. Melfi should give priority to Tony whatever the consequences. To do this would be to follow Tony's moral code. Rather, Dr. Melfi should give priority to Tony's interests and be focused on treating him, and should also be aware of how doing so affects others. If the effect on others becomes too great, she should rethink her decision, and this is precisely what she does. When she is forced into hiding because Tony fears the mob might come after her, one of her patients commits suicide in part because Dr. Melfi was hard to reach at the time. She then decides she can no longer treat Tony. When he asks to be taken back, or at least referred to another psychiatrist in "Guy Walks into a Psychiatrist's Office," she replies, "I would never ask another colleague to get involved in this. How many people have to die for your personal growth?" Dr. Melfi understands that her duties to her patients have limits, and these limits are set by the welfare of others. She eventually does treat him again and with good reason. One of the goals of her treatment is for Tony to understand the origins of his self-destructive behavior so that he might eliminate it. Since the source of this behavior is his upbringing in a mob family, further treatment is capable of showing Tony that a change in his "career" is the only way to achieve good mental health.

Caring and Impartiality

It is tempting to think of Tony Soprano as a man divided—the part of him that is good causes him to be a devoted father and friend, while the part of him that is bad causes him to kill and beat people. Yet it's a mistake to think of him in these terms. Rather, he is a man who cares too much for his friends and family and not enough for the other people his actions affect. If he is to be a good man, he must temper his concern for his family with a concern for these others. I suspect that one of the main reasons the show is so popular is that people see a little bit of Tony in themselves. We are people who care for our friends and family, and would do just about anything to protect them and ensure that they do well in life. If what I have said above is correct, then we should be careful in just how devoted we are to these people. Just like Tony, we stand in need of justifying our actions from an impartial point of view if we are to live moral lives.

9

Is Carmela Soprano a Feminist? Carmela's Care Ethics

LISA CASSIDY

The short answer to the title's question is "fugheddaboutit." There are many interpretations of feminism, but all feminists believe in women's liberation from male domination. Carmela Soprano is the antifeminist. She is the salon-pampered home-maker who presides over the furniture suites and window treatments of the Soprano mini-mansion. She also happens to be married to the mob, in the person of Jersey boss Tony Soprano.

Carmela has chosen a traditional marriage that has rendered her financially and emotionally dependent on a violent and duplicitous husband. For example, Carmela needs Tony so much, as she confesses to family priest Father Phil, that she overlooks Tony's cheating and is glad it relieves her of her sexual duties. And though she has female friends, Carmela has little feeling of sisterhood for women in socially subordinate positions. Remember when Carmela patronizingly flicks her manicured nails at her caterer and friend Charmaine Bucco, as Carm flicked to her maid? Carmela has direct knowledge that her comfortable lifestyle is supported by illegal activities, which include prostitution. Carmela even helps Tony hide assault rifles before an FBI raid! And though she loves both her teenage son and daughter, her child rearing practices reinforce traditional gender roles. Indeed, many times she encourages A.J. to buck up (by taking his studies and school commitments more seriously), but urges Meadow to soften up (by sharing her emotions and private life). Finally, Carmela has denounced feminism as it would seem to challenge her position as Mobster Wife. In season four, Carmela was outraged by Father Phil's guest speaker who repudiates that stereotype of Italian-American women.

Even though Carmela is not a feminist I think she uses a kind of moral reasoning, called "care ethics," that is often associated with feminism. Care ethics is the philosophical elaboration of an idea pioneered in the 1970s and 1980s by the Harvard psychologist Carol Gilligan, whose work discusses how people solve their moral problems.[1]

Justice and Care in Moral Reasoning

Gilligan argues that men and boys often use a "masculine voice" in their moral deliberations, and for too long this voice has been the morally and psychologically authoritative one. For most men, being moral means objectively settling disputes between individuals when their rights are in conflict. This conception of morality, sometimes called the "justice tradition," has been the dominant one in psychology since Sigmund Freud's pioneering of the field, and is said to originate in moral and political philosophers such as Immanuel Kant and John Locke. People who use "justice" in their moral reasoning apply abstract moral rules and arguments to settle moral conflicts *impartially* and *universally*. For example, someone—we'll call him "Tony"— might consider murdering a business rival. Is it immoral to whack someone? According to justice thinking, Tony should realize that murdering one's rival is an immoral trespass on another's human rights and dignity. Tony should apply this argument to his own plans *impartially*, by disregarding his own personal gain in proposed murder and *universally*, by not making himself an exception to the morality that everyone else should follow.

Gilligan holds there is also a "feminine voice" in moral deliberations. Her research finds that often women feel torn between the responsibilities they have to loved ones and to themselves. When moral conflicts arise, some women hesitate to solve those conflicts by "universalizing maxims" (Kant) or preserving "inalienable human rights" (Locke). Instead, women often reason

---

[1] Carol Gilligan, *In a Different Voice* (Cambridge, Massachusetts: Harvard University Press, 1982).

that they have the responsibility to respond to their loved ones. People who use care in their moral reasoning approach morality as *particular* and *contextual*. To return to our earlier example, is it immoral for Tony to whack a rival? In contrast to the justice tradition, a care thinker would stress the *particularity* of the moral dilemma, by paying attention to how particular people are involved and the *context* of the moral dilemma, by looking at the entire situation surrounding the proposed hit. So the connections between Tony, his rival, and the surrounding "family" members matter more than abstract moral rules. While a care thinker would avoid giving a one-size-fits-all answer to Tony's moral dilemma, she might urge that Tony respond to the rival without harming him, perhaps by seeking out alternative solutions to whatever has caused their dangerous rivalry in the first place.

Gilligan writes:

> The moral imperative that emerges repeatedly in interviews with women is an injunction to care, a responsibility to discern and alleviate the 'real and recognizable trouble' of this world. For men, the moral imperative appears rather as an injunction to respect the rights of others and thus to protect from interference the rights to life and self-fulfillment.[2]

Feminist philosophers who have adapted Gilligan's psychological research into a full-fledged moral philosophy include Virginia Held,[3] Nel Noddings,[4] Sara Ruddick,[5] and Joan Tronto.[6] My descriptions of justice and care here are very broad, and some philosophers even question whether justice and care are really as separate as I have presented them here. But let's focus only on the contrast between justice and care as accounts of *how* people *reason* about moral problems. "Practical moral reasoning is intended to identify morally desirable, or at least morally permissible, actions and practices."[7] Justice and care

---

[2] *Ibid.*, p. 100.
[3] Virginia Held, *Feminist Morality* (Chicago: University of Chicago Press, 1993).
[4] Nel Noddings, *Caring* (Berkeley: University of California Press, 1984).
[5] Sara Ruddick, *Maternal Thinking* (New York: Ballantine, 1989).
[6] Joan Tronto, *Moral Boundaries* (New York: Routledge, 1993).
[7] Alison M. Jaggar, "Caring as a Feminist Practice of Moral Reason," in Virginia Held, ed., *Justice and Care: Essential Reading in Feminist Ethics* (Boulder: Westview, 1995), p. 179.

describe different modes or styles of practical moral reasoning, and I argue that Carmela's moral reasoning style is care-ethical.

Carmela on Marriage and Morality

I present Carmela Soprano as a care thinker whose moral reasoning is as layered as the lasagna at Vesuvio Restaurant. Carmela uses care ethical reasoning in her moral deliberations, even though she is no feminist role model. Specifically, Carmela's evolving attitude towards her marriage illustrates how care ethics works.

Carmela and Tony's marriage has had its rocky spots, but Carmela (in Seasons One and Two) looked to the moral authority of the Catholic Church to guide her. In Season Two's "Commendatori," Carmela counsels friend Angie Bonpensiero, who is fed up with husband Big Pussy's emotional absenteeism. Angie vows to file for divorce, but Carmela's arguments against divorce are as slick as Paulie Walnuts's hairstyle. First, Carmela mentions the Church's doctrine that marriage is a sacrament; then, she considers the welfare of Angie and Pussy's grown children; and finally, she cites the poor example divorce sets for children. Angie dismisses all of Carmela's arguments and asks, "Why you working this hard, Carmela?" At the end of the scene the two women embrace, and Carmela whispers to her, "In the end, I know you're not gonna leave him. I know you won't do that." Carmela seems to be convincing herself and might be speaking about her own marriage as well as Angie and Big Pussy's.

Carmela's moral reasoning here mixes justice reasoning with incipient care ethics. By relying on the moral pronouncement of the Church ("You know what the Church says about divorce," she says earlier in the show) Carmela draws on justice; she is impartially applying a moral rule about divorce dictated by the ultimate authority. But elements of care thinking emerge when Carm carefully weighs divorce's potential impact on Angie and Pussy's grown children. Care ethics means responding to the people about whom one cares (in this case, one's children). Here we see Carmela understands caring for others as maintaining the marriage even at the cost of one's own happiness. However, her care ethics will soon evolve beyond self-sacrifice.

Carmela versus Dr. Krakower, Care versus Justice

In Season Three, Carmela consents to couples therapy to aid Tony in his recovery from panic disorder. After meeting privately with his therapist, Dr. Melfi, she takes Melfi's suggestion to seek out separate counseling ("Second Opinion"). I think this single meeting with Dr. Krakower demonstrates how Carmela, at that time, had not yet become a mature care thinker who is able to balance her responsibilities to care for others with caring for herself.[8] Carmela first insists to Dr. Krakower that Tony is "a good man," to which the doctor responds that Tony is "a depressed criminal, prone to anger, serially unfaithful. Is that your definition of a good man?" The straight talking Dr. Krakower has Carmela's attention. Carmela expresses her anger and hurt. "[Tony] betrays me every week with these whores," but Dr. Krakower replies that that "probably is the least of his misdeeds." He further urges her to trust her initial impulse and "consider leaving him" because if she does not she will continue to suffer guilt and shame as "his accomplice." Dr. Krakower refers to Dostoyevsky's *Crime and Punishment*, musing that Tony could use the time in jail to reflect and repent on his crimes. Carmela begins to imagine what leaving Tony would entail:

CARMELA: I would have to get a lawyer, find an apartment, arrange for child support . . .

DR. KRAKOWER: You're not listening. I'm not charging you [for the therapy session] because I won't take blood money and you can't either. One thing you can never say, that you haven't been told.

CARMELA: I see. You're right. I see.

---

[8] Gilligan writes that care thinkers evolve through three phases of maturing. The first phase is survival, in which women may only look out for their own interests. Upon reflection, this moral reasoning is criticized as selfish and gives way to complete self-sacrifice of one's own needs in order to respond to others'. Finally, the "mature" phase of care ethics is being able to reason through moral problems by balancing the need to care for self with care for others. Gilligan, *In a Different Voice*, p. 74.

The next scene shows Carmela at home pathetically huddled under blankets on the couch. She demands that Tony "do something nice" for her: give Meadow's Ivy League college a fifty-thousand-dollar donation. He eventually relents and they go out for dinner.

How is it that Carmela can bitterly complain about Tony's infidelities but be apathetic about his behavior as an amoral mafioso? Is she herself incapable of coherent moral reasoning? Why aren't her thoughts as put-together as her imported, designer separates?

Notice that Carmela's moral deliberations are tortured and intricate. She moves from resenting Tony's infidelity, to defending him, to planning to escape him, to numbly and halfheartedly agreeing to leave him—finally resolving the dilemma by emotional extortion. According to care ethics, this waffling is actually indicative of careful moral reasoning. The feminine voice speaks with endless qualifications and compromises, while the masculine voice is unwavering and rigid. Carmela is trying to be responsive to her own needs while still maintaining a connection with someone who hurts her. Even as she tries to envision leaving him, she still pictures herself and her children connected to Tony. She begins to fill in the narrative of what a post-Tony life would be like before Krakower cuts her off. Carmela is trying to find a solution that would respond to the needs of all her loved ones, including herself.

In the confrontation with Dr. Krakower, Carmela demonstrates some features often attributed to care thinking. She wants Tony to respond to her needs as a person; this is plainly a desire for reciprocity of caring in her relationship, which philosopher Nel Noddings discusses as "total engrossment" with another person.[9] Carmela needs for Tony to stop hurting her. But she is oddly indifferent to the brutal nature of Tony's Mafia business. Carmela's attention to the particularity of her marital problems demonstrates a frequent criticism of care ethics: that care thinkers have no framework to address the needs of justice for those distant others who lay outside one's immediate sphere of caring.[10]

---

[9] Noddings, *Caring*, p. 100.
[10] Claudia Card, *The Unnatural Lottery* (Philadelphia: Temple University Press, 1996).

Dr. Krakower, on the other hand, does not vacillate and is coolly rational. His moral thinking draws heavily on the justice tradition. First Dr. Krakower sets up an abstract, rational moral rule or maxim: "One ought not take blood money." Then he applies this principle to himself and his patient impartially and irrespective of emotional ties. This produces a just course of action for any rational being. (The reference to Dostoyevsky, a Russian novelist associated with Existentialism, might seem out of line if we depict Dr. Krakower as a justice thinker. But Dostoyevsky's resolution to existential angst was to argue for conventional religion and morality.) By the time Carmela relents before Dr. Krakower and agrees with him, it is certain that his moral rules about blood money seem wholly abstracted from and irrelevant to Carmela's real and pressing responsibilities to care for and respond to the needs of her family and of herself. Her moral reasoning is directed towards her so-called "special" moral responsibilities, while Krakower's evokes abstract moral rules.

Her resolution to the moral dilemma is exactly what Dr. Krakower warns Carmela. It is as if Carmela's demand for the Columbia University donation will satisfy her that Tony is willing to sacrifice part of what is important to him (money) to keep her from feeling hurt, just as she is willing to sacrifice part of her needs for him. This is the kind of lopsided caring she is willing to settle for at this time in her life. Using care ethical reasoning does not automatically lead to good solutions to moral problems.[11] This is surely not the mature vision of care ethics that Gilligan describes, and Carmela will revisit this moral dilemma in Season Four.

Carmela's Mature Care Ethics

In Season Four Carmela's care reasoning becomes more sophisticated, and she finally summons the courage to balance her responsibilities to others with self-assertion. In other words, she kicks Tony out ("Whitecaps").

What has precipitated Carmela's achievement of Gilligan's mature phase of caring? We can speculate on several important changes for Carmela. Chief among them is her relationship with

---

[11] Jaggar, "Caring as a Feminist Moral Practice," p. 188.

Tony's pony-tailed Italian henchman, Furio. Over morning coffees and interior design advice, Furio and Carmela fall in love, even though that love remains unspoken. While Furio is as violent and iniquitous as Tony, Carmela falls for Furio's emotional openness and responsiveness. Furio is tender and caring, or at least that is the side of his personality presented to Carmela. Carmela's religious devotion seems to have waned; she is less inclined to rely on the Church's moral pronouncements as she did before. Carmela also seems to have been affected by the "empty nest syndrome," renewing her interest in a realtor's license as a way to find fulfillment outside her waning motherly duties. Since those to whom she has devoted herself make fewer demands on her time, Carmela is ready to turn attention towards herself. The death of Bobby Bacala's wife, Karen, also may have prompted changes in Carmela; the realization that life can be as brief as a Bada Bing! dancer's thong might have empowered her to make changes in how she reasons through moral problems.

Of course, Carmela only stands up for herself after a phone call from jealous Irina, Tony's former mistress, informs Carmela of Tony's infidelity with his mother's one-legged nurse, Svetlana. The confrontation with Tony begins when Carmela explodes: "You have made a fool of me for years with these whores and now to bring it into my home!" The last straw for Carmela is that Tony's infidelity has invaded the boundary of her home, a boundary that had shielded the family from Tony's other life. Tony slept with Svetlana, a woman Carmela knows and liked, who cared for Tony's mother. Angrier than a commuter in Lincoln Tunnel traffic, Carmela is able to finally assert herself. As she is throwing him out of the house Tony asks, "What about the kids?" "Yeah, it's horrible. God help them," she replies. Here we see that Carmela acknowledges the pain a marital separation will cause the children, but also accepts that this pain can no longer be postponed by shouldering all of the hurt herself.

It may seem strange to say that Carmela is actually caring for herself and her family by breaking up her family. After all, doesn't care ethics focus on attentiveness to loved ones in order to maintain relationships? Though it appears paradoxical, I think Carmela has actually succeeded in using mature care ethics to reason through her moral dilemma. She is finally able to balance her responsibilities to her family without sacrificing her own needs. Carmela is maintaining the integrity of the family by splitting it apart; this way the children can still enjoy a relationship with their father. When Meadow inquires into the reason for the split, Carmela spares her the details of her father's mistakes: "This is not something I want to talk about. I'm sorry. Not now, not ever." In care thinking, responsiveness to another person first involves judging what that person's needs are.[12] Despite her morbid curiosity, it's best if Meadow not know just what Dad did. Carmela sees Meadow's real needs and responds to them by shielding her from the truth.

The final, explosive confrontation comes in the garage/pool house where Tony has been sleeping. Carmela has come to terms with his sexual betrayal and can finally enunciate why she needs Tony to stay away from her: "What's done is done. We are where we are, it's for the best." Though it must sound hollow even to herself, there is surely emotional truth in this statement. Carmela reasons that she can best respond to the needs of her loved ones (even Tony himself) by severing the marriage. She then reverses her earlier position and states that she might have tolerated his infidelity if Tony's "attitude around here had been the least bit loving, cooperative, interested." The chief failure of the marriage is the failure of reciprocity in caring.[13] Tony's lack of connection and lack of effort to sustain connection now hurts Carm even more than the cheating. When Tony eventually yells that he might have been more available to her if she was a more interesting person, Carmela hollers back "I'm here! I have things to say!" When Tony later tells the children he is moving out for good, Carmela is oddly quiet. Her final words to him are "Be careful" (and not "Go to hell"). Carmela is able to wish him well in his new life, at least in so far as she recognizes her enduring connection to Tony through their children.

If Carmela were using the principles of justice in her moral reasoning, she might cite Tony's repeated violation of the marriage vows in their last showdown. She might legalistically argue that his breach of those promises to her nullifies her promise to stay married to him. Or else she might abstractly reason that if

---

[12] See Joan Tronto, "Women and Caring: What Can Feminists Lean about Morality from Caring" in Alison M. Jaggar and Susan N. Bordo, eds., *Gender/Body/Knowledge* (New Brunswick: Rutgers University Press 1989), p. 177.

[13] Noddings, *Caring*, p. 83.

everyone were to behave as Tony did, fidelity as a concept would cease to exist. Or perhaps she could say that living in a marriage that violated her spousal rights was a tyranny to which no rational person would consent. But of course, Carmela does not evoke such "theoretical-juridical" moral theories in her reasoning.[14]

Carmela and Feminism: Perfect Together?

Since Carmela uses feminist care reasoning in her moral deliberations, we can ask two questions: What does this mean for feminism? And what does this mean for Carmela?

Feminist philosophers sometimes worry that the appeal of care ethics is that it repeats and codifies existing stereotypes of women and girls as overemotional, incapable of objectivity, and subservient.[15] It might be easy to imagine that women living in psychologically oppressive conditions, such as Carmela's marriage, might be timid and self-flagellating from years of just trying to cope. (As Meadow complains: "God, Mom! How could you eat shit from him all those years?") Yet Carmela's quick retorts can be as saucy as shrimp fra diavolo, and she is shrewd and tough, even as she uses the feminine voice in her moral reasoning.[16] In this way Carmela would defy the stereotype of a yielding, self-sacrificing, deferential woman that care ethics might at first glance be said to valorize. Feminists who worry that care ethics merely reinforces harmful stereotypes of women could be assuaged by Carmela's

---

[14] Margaret Walker, *Moral Understandings*. (New York: Routledge, 1988).

[15] Marilyn Friedman, "Beyond Caring: The De-Moralization of Gender," in Marsha Hanen and Kai Nielson, eds., *Science, Morality, and Feminist Theory* (Calgary: University of Calgary Press, 1987).

[16] My favorite scene of Carmela using care reasoning while still being intimidating and tough (apart from her marital dilemma) is in Season Two's "Full Leather Jacket." Carmela wants daughter Meadow accepted to Georgetown University, and the Sopranos' neighbor coincidentally has a sister who is a Georgetown alumnus. Carmela stops at the sister's law office to deliver a ricotta pie and ask for a recommendation for Meadow. By the end of the meeting Carmela has cowed the confident lawyer into submission, though Carmela never threatens her overtly. Carmela's care for her daughter is fierce, and Carm bullies someone in order to respond to Meadow's need to be accepted to Georgetown and Carmela's own need to have her daughter attend college close to home.

simultaneous defiance of these stereotypes *and* employment of care reasoning.

A related concern is that women have developed care ethics in their moral reasoning under oppressive conditions of being forced to care for others, so care ethics may not contribute to women's liberation from that patriarchal oppression.[17] Feminist values are separable from care ethics as a form of moral reasoning. After all, Carmela uses care ethics despite the fact that she is not any more a feminist than the Five Families are a harmless civics organization. Yet perhaps her achievement of the mature phase of care ethics, in which one can respond to and balance the care for self with care for particular others, can at least coincide with a feminist awareness. We might hope that Carmela is ready to use this newly found mature caring to reevaluate her own antifeminist values. If that did come to pass, then we could argue that her eventual rejection of her patriarchal marriage began with her care thinking. While using care ethics in moral reasoning is not the same as being a feminist, perhaps for Carmela the former could lead to the latter.

If it is good (or at least interesting) for feminists that Carmela is a care thinker, is it good for Carmela? I think it might be the first step toward Carmela becoming a feminist, though I'm not holding my breath for her to attend *The Vagina Monologues* any time soon. And in the event that Carmela allowed Tony to come in from the dog house, Carmela could still retain care in her moral reasoning. Carmela could reconcile with Tony and be a care thinker, but only if she changes her current belief that being married to Tony is detrimental to herself and her children. We can only speculate on what would produce such a change. (Tony finally reforming his philandering ways and tuning in to Carm? Carmela eventually rejecting the concept of traditional, monogamous marriage?) As they say in the old country, "Attenda e veda"—wait and see.

---

[17] Card, *Unnatural Lottery*, pp. 60–65.

10

Dying in Our Own Arms: Liberalism, Communitarianism, and the Construction of Identity on *The Sopranos*

H. PETER STEEVES

Envelopes of Cash

I'm not sure how many connected men I've met in my life. At least three. Likely more. The number seems high to me as I've lived most of my life in the quiet American Midwest—not a hot-bed of *Cosa Nostra* activity by most regards. And yet, I have stories.

When I was just out of my first year of college I was in search of a summer job and thus came to tutor the only son of a rich Italian businessman in a town in Illinois. The boy was attending summer high school and it was my job to see he passed every class, especially the math and science courses, his greatest challenges. We worked for hours each day (it was a struggle; he bore more than a passing resemblance to A.J. Soprano in body as well as mind); and I would reward myself most nights by accepting the hospitality of the family, especially happy to take home a Tupperware container of the mother's manicotti or the grandmother's fresh *cassatta siciliana*—exotic foods to my Ohio-born, Hamburger Helper-acquainted, Velveeta-accustomed palate.

In my memories, twisted and interpreted as memories necessarily are, the grandmother was a lovely stereotype. Not a scheming Livia Soprano, but a Hollywood creation nonetheless: the happy Italian *nonna* committed to her family, talking about "the Old Country" with a tear in her eye, offering food as the solution to all of life's problems. She had been born in Italy and moved to the U.S. as a young girl; and after more than seventy years in this county she still seemed "Italian" to me in a way that was somehow deeper than her son's.

The father's business had something to do with construction, though it was impossible for me to imagine him ever having a speck of dirt on his clothes. The materials from which his suits were made seemed flowing and smooth, like running wine. No jogging suits and see-through socks in his closets. He seemed such a good and kind man as well. He clearly loved his family. He slapped me on the back each day with a smile, thanked me for doing a commendable job with his son, treated me with respect and good humor, and paid me every Friday. In the middle of trying to get out of a geometry lesson one particularly sunny morning, his son once spoke of the family's boat out on the lake, eventually making a passing reference to his father's work and letting the word "construction" hang in the air with an ironic tone. But it's not as if I accidentally came across $50,000 in Krugerrands and a .45 automatic while hunting for a pencil sharpener in the house. And yet. . . .

At the end of the summer, "A.J." passed all of his classes to the delight and surprise of his parents (and his tutor), and everyone insisted that I come to the house one last time that final Labor Day weekend as part of the family. Late in the day of that cool September holiday the father called me into the house, into the kitchen, and thanked me for the miracle I had worked with his son. I assured him that the boy had truly worked hard, but he wouldn't hear it. He said that he wanted to give me a bonus for having done such a fine job. I refused, sincerely needing the money but just as sincerely not wanting to take anything away from his son's accomplishment or to take a greater payment than that on which we had agreed. I had my honor as well. He definitely wouldn't hear it. With a warm smile that should have—but somehow did not—clash with his serious eyes and the determined force with which he took my hand and made the decision for me, he placed an envelope of cash against my open palm then pushed my hand up to my body toward my heart before letting go and walking away. I didn't look in the envelope but folded it and stuffed it into my pocket, playing my part. I would not see him again.

Later that evening the grandmother kissed me on the cheek and wrapped up three sausages with peppers and onions in aluminum foil for me. The creme floodlights that shone up the sides of the house were turned on, the lightning bugs scattered out of the garden, and I left for home.

Livia and René, Silvio and Thomas

Tony Soprano feels disappointed that he came in at the end of *this thing of ours.* "The best," he says with great remorse and in the grips of depression, "is over" ("Pilot"). Yet regardless of the fact that the Mafia seems to have lost the code of honor that once—at least so goes the collective myth—held it together, Tony's identity, his sense of self, his set of values, are direct creations of the community in which he finds himself today. Against the tide of modern life with its constant undertow of Liberal metaphysics and relativistic ethics, Tony treads purely communitarian waters: he *is* his roles and relationships—father, husband, lover, *don,* friend, and executioner; the point of overlap of the many narrative threads that converge in modern Jersey to constitute this man. And yet he is in a state of crisis. It is a crisis that can, in part, be traced to the tension between Liberalism and communitarianism in the Western world.

"Liberalism" and "liberalism" should not be confused. The lower-case "l" of the latter denotes a position in modern politics: the opposite of conservative, the left of the political spectrum, the Democrat as opposed to the Republican. Upper-case "Liberalism" is, rather, the political and metaphysical underpinning of our society in general: both liberals and conservatives are Liberals. Liberalism, then, finds its roots in our collective past—in, for instance, the seventeenth-century thought of René Descartes (1596–1650) and Thomas Hobbes (1588–1679).

Descartes famously argued that the only thing he could be sure of with one hundred percent certainty was his own existence. All of the rest of his experiences *could* be a dream, the external world *could* be an illusion—no matter how unlikely. But whether he was sleeping or awake or a brain floating in a vat, one thing (and only one thing) was for sure: he was having some sort of experience, he was conscious, he was thinking. And the fact that he was thinking meant that he surely existed: *cogito ergo sum* (I think, therefore I am). Descartes's project was, in part, to build subsequently all of the rest of his knowledge on this one thing he could know for sure. This set the stage for thinking of the self as radically individual and cut off from the rest of the world. Indeed, after Descartes the only thing one can ever know for sure is that one's own isolated self exists. To be is to be alone. All the rest—family, friends, society, the world—are add-ons, precarious and doubtful. Or as Livia Soprano says: "In the end you die in your own arms" ("D-Girl").

Thomas Hobbes assumes the same sort of radical individualism in his political philosophy. In Hobbes's conception of a presocietal "state of nature" we are supposedly all isolated, selfish, and equal. There are no bonds among individuals, no relationships, no community. Only violence. Every individual is in a state of war against all other individuals, competing for scarce resources and trusting no one. The only thing that can rescue us is a Sovereign who enforces a social contract that dictates how we are to lay down our individual natural rights to do whatever we wish and take up individual civil liberties of noninterference in their stead. I thus give up my natural right to steal from, harm, and indiscriminately whack you, and you give up your rights to do the same to me. We gain, in turn, civil rights such as those of private property, freedom of expression, and the general right not to be messed with as we go about "life, liberty, and the pursuit of property" (the latter according to John Locke; a line Thomas Jefferson later stole ["Hey, it fell off the truck!"] and changed to "the pursuit of happiness").[1] We ultimately leave a state of nature in which we were radically individual and enter a civil society in which we are . . . radically individual—but now

---

[1] In "House Arrest" Tony ponders the meaning of such liberties during his therapy session and hits on a major philosophical point: Liberalism guarantees we can individually try to get things (without bothering other people), but it doesn't say that we will be *provided* with them. In political philosophy this is sometimes called the difference between a negative right (a right of *noninterference*, such as the right to freedom of the press) and a positive right (a right to *have* something, such as a right to healthcare when one is ill). Negative rights are all that a Hobbesian social contract provide, but in the end they don't do much to guarantee a good life—or as Tony much more colorfully puts it:

TONY: You know we're the only country in the world where the pursuit of happiness is guaranteed in writing? Do you believe that? Hm? Bunch of fuckin' spoiled brats. Where's my happiness then?
MELFI: It's the *pursuit* that's guaranteed.
TONY: Yeah, always a fuckin' loophole. Right?

at least peacefully together, living by a common code, uniting only by agreement and with contracts and official documents to regulate it all.

Versions of this sort of thinking essentially form the foundation of our society: capitalism, contemporary democracy, the U.S. Bill of Rights, our justice system, our educational institutions, our cultural myths (the Old West, the self-made man, and so forth) all take this individualism—this view of what it is to be a self—as fundamental. Though the common person today seldom worries that he or she might be living Descartes's constant illusion (*The Matrix and Philosophy* readers aside), and though we might have rejected Hobbes's all-powerful Sovereign in favor of an elected-for-a-term official, we continue to see individualism as a good and groups or communities as somehow fundamentally oppressive and untrustworthy. To Liberal eyes, even, the Mob boss comes close to a Hobbesian Sovereign, with the *Omertà* oath which one swears upon entering the Mob akin to signing a social contract. The Mafia requires a Sovereign not a community in charge, goes the thinking—or as Jimmy Altieri remarks: "We need a supreme commander at the top, not the fuckin' Dave Clark Five" ("Meadowlands").

And yet, the Mafia is all about community, being-together, defining one's self in terms of one's relationship to the group. It is, at its very core, more communitarian than Liberal. Communitarianism rejects the assumption that all we can know, count on, or take to be fundamental in our politics, metaphysics, and ethics is the isolated individual. Instead, to be is to be a member of a group. We are born into—and throughout our life find ourselves caught up in—roles and relationships that, at a fundamental level, define who we are. The self is thus defined in terms of its relation to Others. First and foremost, one is someone's son or daughter, brother or sister, a member of this culture or that. We might then make decisions to go one direction or another, but it is always from a starting point over which we have no choice and by means of which we found our core identity. And even after we leave this initial position, we continue to be communally defined. The rejection of Liberalism is not the rejection of free will, but it is the acknowledgment that one's will is always tied to others' and thus is not radically individual. When Dr. Melfi, for instance, ushers in a discussion of free will with Tony, he rejects any radically individual formulation of it as a cause for his "chosen" line of work. "How come I'm not making pots in Peru?" he responds. "You're born to this shit" ("Down Neck").

"Commendatori, Buon Giorno. I'm from America."

Place, in fact, is an important constituent of identity: Peru, Italy, Jersey, and Ohio make different sorts of folks. Communities are always situated—always one place or another—and the particularities of place make for particularities in people. Liberals champion placelessness, and place thus begins to disappear in the Liberal world: McDonald's fool's-golden arches look the same in every city (a Liberal "landmark") and with that incessant dressing they liberally put on The Olive Garden salad, food starts to taste the same everywhere as well; one city's suburb can stand in for any other, one highway for any other; and with modern transportation (and information) technology, all places are virtually close to all other places thus making "place" a nearly meaningless place-holder. But for the communitarian, real places—with their particularities and history—are one of the defining factors of selfhood.

Living in America, one cannot help but feel the tension between the constant refrain of Liberalism's individualism and the call of one's communitarian identity. What does it mean, for instance, to be an American, an Italian, an Italian-American? Tony and his crew visit Italy with an expectation of a homecoming, of finding something familiar and inviting, only to discover that they are not really "Italian"—or at least they have to readjust what it means to be Italian ("Commendatori"). Paulie Walnuts is, perhaps, most deeply affected, though it eventually gets to all prodigal sons. The food is different over there (Paulie longs for his "macaroni and gravy"), their particular knowledge of the language fails them (Paulie's use of "Commendatori" as a greeting to each male Italian he meets doesn't go over very well), and in the end no one thinks of these visitors as "Italian" in any sense of the word (Paulie tells the prostitute he is with that his grandfather came to America from Naples and thus he, Paulie, is also "Napoletan'"; when it turns out that the prostitute is from the same part of Naples as Paulie's grandfather, he happily declares, "Our families probably knew each other!" only to be met with worse than indifference as the woman mindlessly scratches her foot and looks away).

Is this a failure of communitarianism? On the contrary. It is Liberalism that has destroyed the situated communities that inflate us to life. It is Liberalism that leaves us with the crisis. Communities do indeed define us, but communities are place and time specific. Paulie cannot be "Napoletan'" in any meaningful way if he is actually seeing Naples for the first time when he makes the claim! Others with whom we share a daily life—in face-to-face relationships, in places we actually inhabit together—are what constitute us. Paulie and Tony and all of us in one way or another look elsewhere for identity because our own communities seem to be losing coherence.

This is a dangerous claim. In the wrong hands it can become a call to tighten immigration, keep races separate, run a rival ethnic group out of town, go back to "the good old days" (which were never good for women, people of color, or other disadvantaged groups), and perpetuate the bigotry Tony professes when he condemns his daughter, Meadow, for dating a black student at school ("Proshai, Livushka"). Such racism has no place in a communitarian philosophy. The forces that institutionally destroy local communities today are those based on the radical individualism of Liberal ideology, not a group-minded communitarian ethic. But this is hard to see.

In the episode entitled "Christopher," the violence that erupts from a clash of communities—one wanting to celebrate Columbus Day and honor Italian heritage, one wanting to stop the celebration of Columbus Day in honor of American Indian heritage—seems to come from too much communitarianism, too much group identification. But in reality, every side is struggling against a false enemy, a false construction of identity. In this mad quest for purity—of body and of history—violence results.

Purity is not a communitarian notion. No real community or person is one hundred percent anything. However, when forced to live in a Liberal world where one's communal identity is hard to pinpoint let alone maintain, we struggle to be something, to be one hundred percent *anything*, and find ourselves—like Hobbes's citizens—blaming each other, blaming other fictionalized constructions of groups, rather than blaming the system that has made us so isolated, alone, and antagonistic in the first place. A Liberal society based on individual conceptions of rights is doomed to violence. True, each Italian American has a right to take part in a parade honoring Columbus. True, each American Indian has a right to freedom of speech in protesting that parade. And true, everyone involved has a right of non-interference to be left alone while using those rights of free expression. Theoretically, every individual playing piece meets on the game board, does his or her individual thing, and everybody walks away by themselves at the end a winner. But is this really what the good life is all about? Are we truly free when we have the right to complain and then be left alone? Surely it beats living in a society where one can be imprisoned or even killed for expressing an unpopular opinion, but such despotic states are not communitarian either. We have come to accept individual rights such as freedom of speech as such a cornerstone of liberty in general that we forget that responsibilities also must go along with rights; we forget that speaking is less meaningful than conversing; we forget that a speech means nothing if it is not delivered to someone, and to someone who listens rather than speaks at the same time. The game looks good, theoretically. But in practice, we end up at each others' throats. Inevitably, globalism, free-market capitalism, cosmopolitanism, and even democracy as it is practiced for the most part today are but the modern faces of imperialism and colonialism—the same forces that enslaved the Indians, sent societies out in search of new land and people to conquer, and made it such that people ever felt the need to settle away from their homes in search of better jobs and a higher standard of living.

Tony doesn't see this. His diagnosis of the Columbus Day violence is too much community identification. Gary Cooper, an American icon of individualism Tony has cited as a model citizen before, never complained about his "group" being held back. According to Tony, Silvio is a successful businessman, father, and husband because of his individual hard work and not his Italian heritage. Questioning where he and his friends get their identity and their self-esteem, Tony concludes: "That shit doesn't come from—from Columbus or *The Godfather* or Chef-fuckin'-Boyar-Dee."

Eloquently put. And yet, pretty much all wrong. First, Silvio may work hard, but he owes a good deal of his business success to his role as a Mafia *consigliere* and thus his Italian heritage. Second, Tony himself mentions Silvio's children and wife—these Others, these familial anchors of roles and relationships—as part of the origin of his friend's self-esteem. And third, *The Godfather?* *The Sopranos* is a show that constantly references *The Godfather*, constantly suggests that the Mob not only draws on its own past for its identity, but on this Hollywood account of its past as well. And Silvio, above all others in Tony's crew, is obsessed with and sees himself in terms of *The Godfather*. Plus, he does a mean Michael Corleone impression.

"Lewis Bratsi Sleeps with the Fishes"

A good deal of what it means *to be* is to be imitating, reflecting Others, playing roles. Identity—fractured as it is—is always performative; and metaphysics and aesthetics can thus be thought of as two aspects of the same inquiry. Uncovering what it is to be a self is analyzing how it is that the self plays a role: the self always lives within the context of a narrative.

It is not just that we turn our life into a story but that we turn stories into our life. Fictional Others, too, make us what we are. The most obvious occurrence of this in *The Sopranos* is the sense in which *The Godfather* and *Goodfellas* and other fictional accounts of the Mob serve to constitute the identities of these modern (fictional) Mafiosi. Of course, they are in reality postmodern gangsters, so we should not be surprised that Michael Imperioli (who plays Christopher Moltisanti on *The Sopranos*) was also in *Goodfellas*; and that Christopher had dreams of writing a Hollywood screenplay about the Mob; and that Joe Pesci's character shot Imperioli's character in the foot in *Goodfellas* for messing up his drink order; and that Christopher shot a bakery store worker in the foot for not taking his order—when he was actually mad for another reason, mad that he wasn't being recognized by his community as a gangster, mad that his role in Tony's crew seemed small and undefined and that unlike a fictional character (!) his story didn't seem "to have an arc" ("The Legend of Tennessee Moltisanti"). Add to this already self-self-self-referential mix the fact that the Soprano crew watches *The Godfather* and contemporary Mobsters watch *The Sopranos* and everyone mimics everyone else's actions, and the postmodern circle of identity becomes more like an infinite spiral.[2]

The spiral jumps easily from the fictional to the nonfictional, ultimately breaking down all such distinctions: every story becomes a part of our autobiography, every autobiography becomes collective fiction. In the second episode of *The Sopranos* ("46 Long"), for instance, Christopher sees Martin Scorsese (Imperioli's director in *Goodfellas*) at a nightclub and screams out his admiration for Scorsese's failed movie *Kundun* rather than *Goodfellas* only to be snubbed by the director. Silvio does his Michael Corleone impression three times throughout the episode as well, referencing both Michael's sense of style and the fact that the Mafia is changing, perhaps lurching into its last days, though unwilling to stop pulling these men back in. Pussy, however, is more concerned throughout about the crummy detective job to which he has been assigned by Tony, complaining: "I'm fucking Rockford over here!" The reference to *The Rockford Files* not only speaks to how we see our lives in terms of narrative, but how it all necessarily has a postmodern twist: series creator David Chase wrote these lines for Pussy, and Chase got his big break as a television writer when he was hired on *The Rockford Files*.

We all do this—we all live our lives as narrative. But the startling claim is that this is all that we do, even when we are not aware of it. As with communitarianism in general, Tony does not want to accept this. When told that the meat-inspired memory of the first time he had a panic attack ("All this from a slice of gabagool?!") is just like Marcel Proust's *Remembrance of Things Past* in which a dainty tea cookie sets off a memory from childhood that spans hundreds of pages, Tony's dismissive response is, "This sounds very gay. I hope you're not saying that" ("Fortunate Son"). Even when Tony finds himself caught up in contemporary fictional narratives, he dismisses them as meaningless. After telling Dr. Melfi that he was enjoying the movie *Se7en*, for instance, Tony admits that "halfway through it, I'm thinking, this is bullshit. A waste of my fuckin' time. Why do I give a shit who the killer is?" ("House Arrest"). Dr. Melfi agrees;

---

[2]See, for instance, *The E! True Hollywood Story: "The Sopranos,"* Emily Puk, producer, E! Entertainment Television Productions, 2003.

but she shouldn't. She should realize that the narratives with which we surround ourselves make us what we are, and Tony has made an interesting choice of rentals. Moreover, she—above all others—should have heard the true meaning of Tony's question to her. Of course Tony does care and should care who the killer is. *He* is the killer. He *is* a killer. He is trying to come to terms with his own fractured identity in these psychoanalysis sessions, and it is, for him, something like a murder mystery. Indeed, Tony's dismissal of *Se7en* as irrelevant to his life is particularly telling in that he clearly learned something (about himself) from the movie. Two years later in "Whoever Did This," he will be playing Kevin Spacey's role, murdering someone out of anger (along with a mix of pride, lust, and greed; four of the seven deadly sins), covering his tracks even as everyone is silently figuring out who did it, chopping off Ralphie's head in place of Gwyneth Paltrow's.

This is our common fate, though hopefully we will be cast in less violent roles. Yet, against all of our wishes, how often our obsessions become Ahab-like, our lusts Lolita-ish, our weariness Sisyphusean, our fears Ichabod Crane-ic, and our furies as furious as Furio Giunta.

In the end, perhaps the *agita* of identity is a sign, the trace of violence inherent in all becoming and all being. Perhaps it is an indication that we are never fully realized, never truly made, never free from the responsibility of choosing right over wrong even when the choice is less than free, the story less than fully ours. This, then, is what it means to be a wise guy: to know just how little we know as we simultaneously refuse to accept our short cut. It is to know that even envelopes of cash stuffed into youthful pockets on quiet Midwestern nights make us who we are, and we will echo these moments the rest of our lives in a world that was never truly innocent.

Contorno

Aesthetics:
The Beauty of
Crime

11
Sympathy for the Devil

NOËL CARROLL

The marriage of *The Untouchables* with the sit-com, of violent action with the soap-opera, and pornography with domesticity, *The Sopranos* seems to be a strange brew, appealing to high-end critics and popular audiences alike. But much of this apparent paradox disappears when one realizes that the hair-pin mood shifting—from mirth to mayhem and from parody to rage—admired by the highbrow clientele is a matter of shuffling rapidly between genres—such as the gangster film and crime show, the sitcom, the soap-opera, the family drama, and soft-core pornography—already familiar to the general audience and beloved by them. *The Sopranos* has taken the family theme of *The Godfather* and split it in two, augmenting the literal kinship side of the analogy and adapting it to enshrined TV formats: TV does the natural family so well, because it is the family that is its coveted audience, one to whose narcissistic inclinations it congenially caters with the sit-com and the soap-opera. Juxtaposing mundane family life with life in the "crime family," while enabling the two terms of the comparison to inform each other in insightful (sometimes comic, and sometimes unsettling) ways, also relieves the banality of everyday family life with a dash of excitement, much in the manner that an evening of crime shows leavens the routine of actual family existence either after or even during dinner.

However, even if *The Sopranos* is not as altogether bizarre as it may appear at first blush, it possesses some stubbornly anomalous features that invite philosophical reflection. Perhaps the strangest of these is what we might call "sympathy for Soprano"—that is, the pro-attitude that most viewers, including the most law-abiding, bear toward the central figure of the show, the mobster-boss, Tony Soprano. What is, of course, strange about this response is that most viewers would feel anything but care and concern for Tony Soprano's real-life counterpart; indeed, many would feel moral revulsion. Nevertheless, many—perhaps most—of us do appear to care for the fictional Tony Soprano, whereas we would loathe an actual person just like him. Does this make any sense? How is it possible?

Maybe needless to say, the preceding paradox is not unique to *The Sopranos*. It's an instance of a broader paradox that is sometimes called "Sympathy for the Devil." The problem is basically how a viewer can be sympathetic (care for, or have a pro-attitude) toward a fictional character whose real-world counterpart she would abhor totally? Using Tony Soprano as our particular specimen of the devil, let us consider why, maybe to our own surprise, we may find ourselves on his side.

Perhaps the best way to begin to appreciate this mystery is to remind ourselves of Tony Soprano's many crimes. He is the head of a New Jersey crime family that traffics in drugs, prostitution, extortion, usury, money laundering, murder, bribery, theft, suborning witnesses, pornography, and crimes of which I don't even know the names; he contributes to the corruption of policemen, assemblymen, clergymen, unions, and various businesses, large and small. Nor is it the case that Tony Soprano is merely a distant CEO, presiding over all this criminality from afar. He is a hands-on gangster, relishing, as he acknowledges more than once to his psychiatrist, the adrenaline rush of violence, the "thrill" of beating a man to death with his bare hands, or running down a welcher with a car. Tony, at one point, is on the verge of suffocating his mother with a pillow, and he is prepared to kill his own uncle.

Nor are his transgressions only legal in nature. He is a tireless philanderer and adulterer. He is an inveterate liar, dishonest to his family, doctor, friends, and lovers, not to mention to enemies and the law. He is a man of large appetites; he is closely acquainted with virtually every vice and, at one time or another, seems to indulge each one excessively, sometimes in turn and sometimes in tandem. He is a man that most of us would give a wide berth if ever he came anywhere near our neighborhood. Few of us would hesitate for a moment to condemn the real-life Tony Soprano. If we read of his death in a gang war, we would not shed a tear; if we learnt that he was imprisoned and that they threw away the key, we would cheer.

But that is how we would react, if Tony Soprano were an inhabitant of the actual world. As a denizen of the fictional world, called *The Sopranos*, however, he somehow engenders our sympathy (understood as "care"), or, if that is too strong a word here, he at least elicits from us a pro-attitude. Yet how can this be?

It Was Fascination

An initial response to this apparent paradox is to say that it is just that—merely "apparent." In fact, it might be said, we do not really have a pro-attitude toward Tony Soprano. Admittedly we do feel something toward Tony—indeed, we feel something rather strongly—but it is not sympathy. Instead it is fascination. Tony is this bizarre amalgam of the ordinary and the exotic. He is a family man beleaguered by everyday trials of the sort that one might encounter in a sit-com, or a soap-opera, or, to a certain extent, in one's daily life. There are disciplinary problems with the kids, arguments with aging relatives, household squabbles of every sort, bickering over the family finances, sicknesses, troublesome in-laws, issues concerning the children's education, and so on. But Tony Soprano is no ordinary family man; his business is in an underworld of violence and forbidden desires which he rules, often with great brutality. He has a Good Housekeeping suburban dream house, but his office is in a dingy strip joint, the Bada-Bing!

The disconnect between his unexceptional family life and his exceptional professional life is nothing short of staggering. Among other things, his family life seems absolutely contemporary and conventional, whereas his professional life appears to be both a throwback to a bygone era and extraordinary in its transgressiveness. These two opposed life-worlds clash audibly.

Tony and his cronies sit around planning murders, robberies, and scams, but they also gossip about ailments like the hypochondriacs with whom we are all familiar, use the current psychobabble, and speak about stolen property like consumers parroting advertising copy. They obviously read the same magazines and catalogues that everyone else does, but when they talk to each other about it in their New Jersey cadences, it seems so strange coming from their mouths. Undoubtedly, this is realistic. Actual gangsters are probably not as aphoristic as Don Corleone. But it is nevertheless jarring to hear every day consumer-speak issuing from the lips of these thugs. And in almost every way, Tony Soprano himself is an oxymoron: a ruthless Mafia chieftain with a soft spot in his heart for ducks.

In addition, there is Tony's psychiatric treatment. The sessions with his doctor, Jennifer Melfi, are dazzling. The layers of intentional dissembling, unconscious self-deception, understatement, knots, hypocrisy, and misdescription that Tony puts in motion are consistently engrossing; one is constantly comparing what he says and what he is aware of with his actual situation (as we know it). Both in terms of his strikingly bifurcated and oxymoronic life and his labyrinthian mental gymnastics—often the result of depression but also sometimes of simple guile— Tony Soprano is an undeniably fascinating character—one whose doings frequently strike us with their unprecedented juxtapositions of elements and their continuing potential to take us by surprise.

For these sorts of reasons, we are interested in Tony Soprano; we keep coming back for more. But it would be a mistake, it may be argued, to regard this kind of interest as a matter of caring for Tony Soprano. It is more like being bewitched by him. We can't take our eyes off him, because he so amazes us. But amazement and fascination do not add up to a pro-attitude, since we can be transfixed by what we find despicable.

However, even though it is true that we are fascinated by Tony Soprano—often for the reasons just given—it does not seem quite so easy to dispel the paradox that concerns us. For there are a number of oxymoronic characters in *The Sopranos* who also wear symptoms of denial on their sleeves but who, however fascinating for those reasons, do not mobilize in us the kind of pro-attitudes that Tony does.

Consider Richie Aprile. A devotee of yoga, this self-consciously short gunsel with a Napoleon-complex is at the same time sociopathic in his brutality, repeatedly running over his former associate Beansie with his SUV to the point where Beansie is paralyzed for life. Richie can show as much barely explicable rage as Tony, and his occasionally New Age lingo sits uneasily with his sado-masochistic sex games with Tony's sister Janice. Given his curious alchemy of attributes, Richie is as riveting as Tony. But surely no one has a pro-attitude toward Richie Aprile. The series mandates quite the opposite stance toward him and, for probably everyone, it is an assignment we discharge effortlessly.

Fascination and caring are distinct. Even if we are fascinated by Tony Soprano, that does not preclude that we also have a pro-attitude toward him. Acknowledging how very arresting for us he is does not make the fact that we also care for him disappear, since there are equally "thought-provoking" anomalies populating the world of *The Sopranos* for whom we have no sympathy.

Wish Fulfillment

One way of trying to explain the pro-attitude we bear toward Tony might be to argue that he fulfills our darkest wishes. Tony is Rabelaisian in his self-control: he eats, fucks, drinks, and smokes whatever he pleases. He permits his rage to flow in torrents. He beats the Jersey assemblyman, Zellman, who is on his payroll with his belt because the politician is having an affair with Irina Peltsin, one of Tony's former *goomahs*. Vengeance is his and he metes out his own version of justice unconstrained by anyone. In her dream, Melfi associates Tony with a huge panting dog—a rottweiler. Often Tony seems to be nothing short of a personification, in the lineage of King Ubu, of the unbridled id. Moreover, he seems to be able to get away with the worst crimes and misdemeanors—at least with regard to civil society.

Given all this, one might speculate that Tony represents the symbolic realization of deep repressed fantasies, especially for the males in the audience. They wish to be as unrestrained as Tony. Insofar as he enacts their dreams, they give him a pass. That is the basis of our pro-attitude toward Tony. Our sympathy for Soprano is nothing but our egoistical love of our own egoism. We have a pro-attitude toward Tony because he actualizes, albeit fictionally, the sort of abandon we want for ourselves— the capacity to pursue our desires unshackled and, in large measure, unpunished.

However, this is an unpromising strategy for explaining our pro-attitudes to Tony Soprano. The reason for this is of a piece with our preceding objection to the fascination-hypothesis: there are many characters in the world of *The Sopranos* who behave as wantonly as Tony does, if not more so, but we do not regard them positively in any way, whereas we do Tony. Ralph Cifereto, the psychopath who inherits the mantel of Richie Aprile, is at least as incontinent at Tony. Yet we never feel inclined in his behalf. He is always menacing. His humor is generally more mean-spirited than funny. Like Tony, he denies himself nothing. But when he beats his pregnant girlfriend Tracee to death, the audience hates him. Sinning, at least when Ralph does it, is not a way to our hearts. We are consistently supposed to regard him with disdain, distrust, and disapproval and we readily do so. Ralph is as clear-cut an image as Tony of the dark forces of the psyche. Nevertheless, no normal viewer has an inkling of sympathy for Ralph. Therefore, our pro-attitude toward Tony cannot be explained simply on the grounds of his transgressiveness.

Identification

Undoubtedly, the notion that Tony might function as a wish-fulfillment fantasy may call to mind the different but related idea that we have a pro-attitude toward him because we *identify* with him. Insofar as Tony is a figure of what one wishes to become, one is, by definition, not *yet* identical to him. Tony must be different from us in order to satisfy our wishes. But, it might be suggested, our link with Tony is not based on the grounds of what we wish to become, but on the grounds of what we already are.

Especially in terms of the quotidian side of Tony's existence, many of us can recognize our own lives in Tony's—broken water heaters, rebellious or otherwise misbehaving children, querulous elderly relatives, marital tensions, annoying extended family members and overbearing in-laws, and so forth. Like many of us, Tony finds himself—to his chagrin—in a world where the rules he grew up with are rapidly changing. Many of his complaints—for example, about his children's schools or about the self-indulgence of the me-generation—may be our complaints. On the basis of these and other points of tangency between ourselves and Tony, it might be argued that we identify with him—regard ourselves, in some sense, as identical to him. And if we identify with him, then, it could be observed, our pro-attitude toward Tony would follow fairly straightforwardly from our own partiality to ourselves.

Understood one way, the suggestion that we identify with Tony Soprano is patently absurd. For however many similarities there are between any audience member and Tony, no one of them is literally *identical* with him, nor, and this is perhaps more important, do any of them take themselves to be strictly identical with him—often, for example, we are *appalled* at those of Tony's very actions that *thrill* him.

Moreover, to suppose oneself to be identical with Tony would be to court paradox: if I thought myself Tony Soprano, then that would imply that I could meet myself (Noël Carroll); but I know it is logically impossible to meet oneself. So identification cannot explain the pro-attitude we bring to Tony because strict identification seems an inadmissible state of mind.[1]

But maybe when people claim that they identify with Tony Soprano and other fictional beings they are thinking of something less than strict identification. They do not take themselves to be identical with such characters in every way, but only in some ways. They do not imagine themselves being Tony Soprano but only as sometimes feeling or desiring as he does. This imaginative state is aspectual.[2] When Tony desires revenge, we imagine ourselves into his situation and likewise desire revenge; when he wishes to kill his mother, we take on his murderous rage; when he is exasperated by Gloria Trillo's temper tantrums, we are too. As well, we find Jackie Junior's incredible stupidity as frustrating as Tony does; we merge our frustration and his. And insofar as we imagine our feelings and Tony's to be the same, we are as disposed to regard his feelings as posi-

---

[1] For objections to the notion of strict identification, see: Richard Wollheim, *The Thread of Life* (Cambridge, Massachusetts: Harvard University Press, 1984); and Noël Carroll, *The Philosophy of Horror* (New York: Routledge, 1990).

[2] The idea of aspectual identification is developed by Berys Gaut in his "Identification and Emotion in Narrative Film," in *Passionate Views: Film, Cognition, and Emotion*, edited by Carl Plantinga and Gregg M. Smith (Baltimore: Johns Hopkins University Press, 1999), pp. 200–216.

tively as we regard our own. And this, of course, adds up finally to a pro-attitude toward Tony.

Though this version of the notion of identification appears less problematic than its predecessor, I am not convinced that it is plausible. It too has unhappy consequences. If I imagine feeling what Tony feels, then if Tony imagines becoming infatuated with someone, say Valentina La Paz, then I should imagine becoming infatuated with her. But then wouldn't I be jealous of Tony and wish his affair ill? Yet I don't. So it cannot be the case that I am imagining having the same feelings as Tony Soprano. In point of fact, I would argue that what I feel is quite different than what Tony feels. The object of his emotional state is Valentina, whereas the objects of my state, I conjecture, are Tony and Valentina, neither of whom I am infatuated with and both of whom I wish well.

Nor is infatuation the only feeling state where the aspectual conception of identification goes haywire. If Tony desires a certain "business" account then I should want it too. But that would make us competitors and I should desire that my rival's efforts come a-cropper. However, I don't. Furthermore, if I possessed Tony's particular desire for revenge, then shouldn't I resent it when he, rather than I, gets to wreak violence on its object? But that is not how most of the fans of *The Sopranos* feel; indeed, we might suspect anyone who reacted to Tony in these ways to be someone with a screw loose. So this model of our responses to Tony is not adequate.

Audiences cannot be identifying with Tony where identification is understood as aspectually imagining themselves to have the same feelings and motivations as Tony does. And if they cannot be identifying with Tony, since the very process would appear to have dubious implications, identification cannot explain our pro-attitude toward Soprano.

Of course, it may be charged that we are taking the notion of identification too literally. But if it is not intended to model our relations to the emotions and desires of characters, what identities are at issue here? Surely if the process is called identification, there must be some dimension of congruence. And one would think that the likeliest vein of correlation would be in terms of shared desires, feelings, motivations, and emotions. But, as we've seen, in a number of significant cases, postulating identification along these lines has unacceptable results.

Perhaps it will be said that, however strange it sounds, identification has nothing to do with identity. Maybe all people mean by saying that they identify with a character is that they care for him. Though I doubt that people actually have so weak a notion in mind, if this is really all identification means, then it will not help us account for why we bring a pro-attitude toward Tony, since, on this interpretation, saying people identify with him alleges no more than that they have a pro-attitude toward him. That is, under such a watered down construal, identification would have no explanatory power for our purposes; it would merely be a way of redescribing what already mystifies us.

Paradox Solved

Though I have argued that we do not identify with Tony Soprano (or, for that matter, any other fictional character), it is evident that we do have some kind of affinity for him. In order to avoid the untoward implications of the concept of identification, let us say we are *allied* to Tony Soprano. This, of course, does not explain why we have a pro-attitude toward him. However, it may suggest a way of working out such an explanation. Let us ask why we would find Tony Soprano to be an appropriate ally? Why might we form an alliance with him? If we can answer these questions, then maybe we will be in a position to explain our pro-attitude toward him.

Talking about forming an alliance with Tony may sound weird. What lawful citizen in their right mind would contemplate being in league with Tony? Well probably no one, if we are speaking of the real world counterpart of Tony. But the alliance we strike is not with an actual gang lord, but with the fictional Tony Soprano, an inhabitant of a very unique fictional world. Moreover, when we look at the moral structure of that fictional world, it seems to me that Tony is the most likely candidate or, at least, one of the likeliest candidates for an alliance, given the entire available array of characters as they are portrayed in the series. Nor is he the most suitable ally because he is putatively just the strongest or the smartest character. He also has a fair claim to being the most moral or, at least, no less moral than the other significant figures in the series.

This is not to say that Tony is moral, but only that within the relational structure of the fictional world of *The Sopranos,* he has an equally strong or stronger claim to morality than any of the other major players to whom we are extensively exposed.[3] Compared to the other mobsters, especially to the more maniacal ones (like Ralph, Richie, Paulie, Furio), Tony seems *relatively* less volatile and sadistic, and more judicious and prosocial. Within the bounds of the Mafia code, he appears to be the fairest gangster (not absolutely fair, but relatively fair) and he has a capacity for compassion (albeit obviously not fully developed).

Furthermore, the law is not represented as a positive moral counterweight. Virtually all the Jersey policemen (save one) whom we encounter are corrupt—on the take—as is the state assemblyman. The FBI are not outright venal, but the side of them that we observe is not morally unambiguous. We do not see them protecting the weak and the innocent. We see them trying to blackmail felons like Adriana La Cerva and Big Pussy Bonpensiero into spying on their friends and loved ones; and we watch them planting a listening device in Tony's home. Rather than witnessing the FBI engaged in heroic activities, we find them involved in these more unseemly or shady subterfuges which are apt to strike many as possibly questionable intrusions into the private sphere, if not illegal then intuitively immoral and perhaps verging on abuses of power. They are, in other words, cast in a light that makes them seem at least somewhat compromised and unscrupulous, and which, in any event, is not offset by showing them to be forthright representatives of justice.

Other representatives of moral authority also appear tarnished. Black civil rights leaders are revealed to be in cahoots with the mob, betraying their own people (something Tony would never do). The Catholic priests whom we encounter are hypocrites, willingly feeding at the Mafia trough. Indeed, hypocrisy of one sort or another is the characteristic that marks most of the "civilians" who receive appreciable air time in *The*

---

[3] The importance of the relative moral standing of characters in eliciting audience affiliation was introduced in my "Toward a Theory of Film Suspense" which is anthologized in Noël Carroll, *Theorizing the Moving Image* (New York: Cambridge University Press, 1996). The approach is also developed in Murray Smith, "Gangsters, Cannibals, Aesthetes, or Apparently Perverse Allegiances," in *Passionate Views*, pp. 217–238.

Sopranos. Furthermore, many of those who bear the brunt of Tony's ire have brought it upon themselves—Davey Scatino by gambling beyond his means, despite Tony's warnings, and Shlomo Teittleman by trying to renege on his deal with Tony.

In important instances, Tony is more sinned against than sinning: no one deserves a mother as manipulative and as poisonous as Livia, whose namesake is a scheming character from *I, Claudius*.[4] Tony's sister Janice has inherited all of her mother's malefic low cunning and, if she does not cause as much damage as Tony, that is only because her theater of operations is much smaller. One senses that in Tony's position, she would be far more dangerous. Nor is Tony his uncle Junior's moral inferior; it is Junior who initiates plots against Tony's life, not vice-versa. In some respects, though Tony would be the last to cop this plea, Tony is a victim and, although this hardly exculpates him, it does shift a modicum of weight onto his side of the moral scales. Of course, Tony should know better and the fact that he inherited his criminal role does not exonerate him, but it does garner him some slight measure of mitigation.

In addition, Tony does possess some positive moral characteristics. He is loyal to friends and family, including his nephew whom he forcibly enrolls into a detox program. Tony makes a serious effort at being a good parent and he plans for a better life for his children, one free of any taint of the mob. He does play by certain rules; even if those rules are those of a criminal society, Tony is nevertheless undeniably conscientious. He has a sense of justice, not in the legal sense, but in the sense of trying to give people their due within the bounds of the peculiar code to which he is sworn. And Tony agonizes over the various conflicting loyalties that pull him in opposite directions. In short, Tony has some virtues that we may unblushingly refer to as moral in addition to a number of nonmoral virtues such as brute power, raw tactical intelligence, and a quick wit.

In the world of *The Sopranos*, Tony is far from the worst character.[5] Of course, there are characters of whom we know

---

[4] "Appendix B," in David Lavery, ed., *This Thing of Ours: Investigating the Sopranos*, (New York: Columbia University Press, 2002), p. 245.
[5] Our moral estimation of Tony Soprano also benefits from what we might call the "out of sight, out of mind" phenomenon. That is, we are not shown many of the long-term repercussions of Tony's criminal activities and, as a

too little to compare to Tony morally and others who do not elicit comparison because they are too secondary to the plot, like Tony's sister Barbara. But, for the most part, when we situate Tony Soprano on the field of the pertinent cast of characters in the series, he turns out to be one of the most savory, morally speaking. This is not to deny that Tony Soprano is morally defective, but only to suggest that among an array of ethically challenged characters, he is one of the least deplorable.

There is a joke, a shortened variation of which Hesh tells at the party after Livia's funeral, which illustrates Tony's moral standing in the world of *The Sopranos*. The full version goes like this:

> Because the town has no rabbi of its own, its citizens hire one from another village to officiate at Moshe's last rites. At the end of the service, the rabbi says, "Since I am not from this village, I can say little about this man's life. So I would like someone from this shettl to tell us something now about Moshe's good works." This is followed by a resounding silence. The rabbi repeats his request with no results. Finally he says: "I don't think you understand; we are not leaving here until someone says something good about Moshe." Eventually an old man stands up and offers the following: "I knew his brother; he was worse."

This, I submit, is how Tony figures in the moral economy of *The Sopranos*. Of most of the relevant characters in this fictional universe, they are worse or no better than Tony Soprano.

Furthermore, this provides us with our grounds for our willingness to ally ourselves with Tony. In most situations, it is pragmatically urgent for us to ally ourselves with the people whom we assess to be the most moral. This is a simple matter of prudence. The people we estimate to be the most moral are the ones who are the safest to interact with, the most trustworthy, and the most reliable. Alliance with the most moral agents avail-

---

result, do not figure them into our moral calculus. We do not see how his calling-card scam might have effectively taken food off the table of an immigrant family with undernourished children. This phenomenon, of course, is related to the fact that much of the program is narrated from Tony's point-of-view in the sense that he too is oblivious to a great deal of the destruction that his actions ultimately engender.

able, in effect, is an insurance policy of sorts. They are our best bet for securing reciprocal relations of exchange[6] and fair treatment. Tony is not a moral man in any absolute sense, but inasmuch as most of the other characters in *The Sopranos* are worse, Tony is a natural candidate for solidarity.[7] Thus the pro-attitude that we extend to Tony Soprano is a result of the fact that we are allied to him. And we are allied to him because in the fictional world of *The Sopranos* alternative alliances would either be worse morally or irrelevant. This is not to say that we are not appalled by features of Tony, like his racism, or by many of his actions, including the murders he perpetrates. But in a world of moral midgets, insofar as he is the closest approximation of probity we find, we ally ourselves with him.

It might appear contradictory that we can muster a pro-attitude for the fictional character Tony Soprano, whereas we would not be similarly disposed toward his real world counterpart. That is, we seem to be staring at the following inconsistency:

1. Audiences have a pro-attitude toward the fictional Tony Soprano.
2. In terms of every pertinent moral property, the fictional Tony Soprano is identical to a real-life Tony Soprano.
3. Audiences would morally abhor a real-life counterpart of Tony Soprano (that is, by definition, they would not bear a pro-attitude toward him).

Nevertheless, the contradiction that looms in this triad of propositions is avoided once we realize that the second proposition above is false. It is not the case that Tony Soprano and his real-life counterpart are morally the same in every respect because relative to the fictional world of *The Sopranos* Tony is more morally palatable than his real-world counterpart would be,

---

[6] On the importance of reciprocal exchange for relations with non-kin, see Robert A. Hinde, *Why Good Is Good: The Sources of Morality* (New York: Routledge, 2002), pp. 72–94.

[7] Of course, it might be said that there are other major characters who are not so compromised morally as Tony, such as his wife Carmela and Melfi. Carmela is a tricky case, since she is also evidently an accomplice of Tony's and somewhat of a hypocrite, but, in any event, both Carmela and Melfi are themselves allies of Tony's and, consequently, our putative alliance with them would not conflict with our alliance with Tony.

since the real-world has much more morality in it than what we find in *The Sopranos*.

For example, the actual police, FBI, civil rights leadership, and so on are more ethically upright than what is pictured in *The Sopranos*. A Tony Soprano would not occupy the same relative position morally in the real world that he stakes out in the fiction. In the fiction, a fallen world if there ever was one, Tony is the best of the worst, and, thus, a natural ally for the viewer who has scant other options to negotiate. That is the basis of our pro-attitude toward him. However, an actual Tony Soprano would not present us with the same bargain, given the difference between the actual world and *The Sopranos*. The divergence of contexts entails that it is not the case that our two Tonys are identical in every respect morally. Thus, there is no inconsistency in bearing a pro-attitude to the fictional Soprano, while finding an actual Soprano to be morally despicable. That is, sympathy for the Soprano in the fiction is compatible with antipathy for an actual gangster with all the same intrinsic properties.

A Remaining Problem

Though we have answered the question of how it is possible for us to have a pro-attitude toward the fictional Tony Soprano, our answer may have provoked another question: is it morally permissible for the creators of *The Sopranos* to produce a fiction that elicits our alliance with a creature like Tony? Isn't it simply immoral to do this? Perhaps one might suspect this on the grounds that eliciting a pro-attitude toward Tony is likely to have some carry-over effect upon our judgments of real-life miscreants.

I don't think this anxiety is serious. First of all, even with respect to *The Sopranos*, our pro-attitude toward Tony is highly circumscribed. Though allied with him on various fronts, our allegiance is not unconditional. We are still repelled by a great many of the things he says and does. Our capacity for sympathy for Tony is limited. Our appreciation of his relative merits in his fallen world does not impair our capability to be morally outraged by many of his criminal behaviors and ethically deficient attitudes, such as his racism and sexism. Thus, there is little cause to fear some slippage from our assessment of the fictional Soprano to our judgments of real-world criminals. As indicated by our disapproving reactions to the fictional Tony,

The Sopranos leaves our capacity for moral indignation generally intact.

Nor do I think that it is problematic that *The Sopranos* exercises our talent for calculating the most morally optimal alliances possible in ethically murky situations. Certainly it is not a moral deficit that we have such a mechanism at our disposal; it enables us to navigate all those situations in life that compel us to make the best morally of a bad set of choices. That *The Sopranos* engages this ethically beneficial capacity in a way that may sharpen it cannot count as morally reprehensible.

In all likelihood, there are some who are prepared to charge that by encouraging audience-alliances with Tony Soprano the television program invites viewers to emulate his actions—the bad ones as well as whatever good ones there might be. *The Sopranos* should be condemned morally, then, because it will have immoral consequences in the form of nefarious copy-cat behavior. But, of course, no one is really in a position to substantiate this hypothesis. My own suspicion is that people will only be likely to replicate onscreen behaviors that they already regard to be morally permissible. Normal viewers will not reproduce what they believe is immoral behavior just because they see it on television. That which audiences are disposed to imitate from fictions, I conjecture, is only what they already judge to be acceptable ethically. Therefore, *if* anyone ever imitates Tony's immoral behavior, I reckon that they were already morally corrupt before the show and not that *The Sopranos* corrupted them.

And finally, on the positive side of the ledger, it may be argued that the sympathy we have for Soprano contributes to the very salutary moral message that the series promotes. In an interview with Peter Bogdanovich, David Chase, the creator of *The Sopranos*, suggests, alluding to something that the character Octave says in Renoir's *Rules of the Game*, that a major theme of the program is that "the problem is that everyone has his reasons."[8] That is, everyone has justifications and/or explanations

---

[8] Peter Bogdanovich, "Interview with David Chase," *The Sopranos: The First Season* (HBO Home Video, 2001), DVD Disc 4. For an exact quotation of what is said in *Rules of the Game*, see Octave's remarks on p. 53 of the Classic Film Scripts edition of *Rules of the Game: A Film by Jean Renoir*, translated by John McGrath and Maureen Teitelbaum (New York: Simon and Schuster, 1970).

for their actions which legitimatize them—at least in the minds of the agents in question. But it is precisely our proclivity to see ourselves as always in the right that makes human life so full of strife and resistant to conflict resolution.

Through the ingenious psychoanalytic sessions with Melfi and by narrating the world of *The Sopranos* primarily in terms of a point-of-view convergent with Tony's, Chase shows us that Tony has *his* reasons, reasons made especially pressing to us in the process of our allying ourselves with him. But, of course, it is just because Tony can have what he takes to be self-justifying reasons that enables him to persist in his evil ways. That is the very problem that *The Sopranos* discloses. By eliciting our sympathy for Tony, Chase reminds us how obdurate a problem this really is. Chase casts this issue in relief by strategically punctuating the show with outrageous behaviors and views on Tony's part that shake us from our sympathy for him and from our inclination toward his point-of-view, thus alerting us to the danger that sympathetic understanding may risk moral misunderstanding.

In a manner of speaking, David Chase is committed to questioning the commonplace coined by Alexander Chase that "to understand is to forgive, even oneself." *The Sopranos*, most notably with respect to Tony, presents us with situations that we understand, but ultimately should not forgive nor allow Tony to forgive, nor do we forgive with regard to many of Tony's crimes and attitudes. But inasmuch as we frequently find ourselves allied with Tony, often preferring Tony's reasons and assessments relative to other characters, we see how slippery the moral slope can become and how easy it may be to lose one's footing. Or, to change metaphors, by taking note of the pro-attitudes Tony elicits from us we may come to appreciate how subtly our moral compass can be demagnetized. Thus, by inciting us to care for Soprano, David Chase makes vivid our realization of the moral threat of rationalization.

12

A Moral Never-Never Land: Identifying with Tony Soprano

JAMES HAROLD

I like Tony Soprano; I can't help it. I like him despite the fact that I recognize that he's a vicious and dangerous criminal. I don't particularly *want* to like him, and I certainly don't think I would like him if he were a real person who lived down the street from me. If he were really my neighbor, I think I'd feel for him what the Cusamanos do: a mixture of fear, fascination, and disgust. Nonetheless, recognizing that he is fictional, I like him. I find myself sympathizing with him: when he is depressed, I pity him; when he is wronged, I feel anger towards those who have betrayed him; and when he is successful, I share in his happiness. I want him to do well. I root for him to defeat his opponents, and, at the end of Season Four, for him to win back his wife Carmela.

Is there anything *morally* wrong with caring about Tony Soprano in this way? If Tony Soprano were a real person, then most people would agree that liking him is a least a little bit morally unsavory. This is Charmaine Bucco's opinion, for example, especially with regard to her husband Artie's friendship with Tony, and it's also the view of most of the other non-Mafia related characters on the show, such as Dr. Melfi's friends and family, the Cusamanos, and so on. But Tony Soprano isn't real—he's fictional, and I know that even if the Cusamanos don't. So what could be wrong with my liking Tony Soprano, given that I know that *The Sopranos* is a work of fiction?

From time to time, as political winds change, politicians, including, for example, Tipper Gore, Joseph Lieberman, and Bob Dole, have weighed in against various artworks in popular culture on the grounds that these artworks are morally dangerous. *The Sopranos* has attracted its fair share of this kind of criticism. Usually these criticisms are answered by proponents of freedom of expression, and the discussion turns to censorship and the necessity of toleration and diversity of viewpoints. What often gets left behind in these debates is the crucial issue of whether or not there really is any reason to think that a series like *The Sopranos* can be morally corrupting. It is often unclear exactly how artworks like *The Sopranos* are supposed to be bad for us. One of the things that worries some of us is that television shows like *The Sopranos* make very bad people seem, well, likeable.

When Is Art Dangerous?

The first Western philosopher to worry seriously about the moral effects of fiction on its audience was Plato. Plato worried about the way that the dramatic poets like Homer played on the emotions of audience members in ways that could be dangerous and manipulative. Poetry, Plato believed, evokes strong emotion in ways that could undermine social stability. In Plato's time, a dramatic poem like *The Odyssey* would be read aloud or sung in a public performance, and so poetry, for Plato, is more like theater for us. An ideal society, Plato thought, would be governed by principles of reason, and our willingness to follow through on these rational principles could be weakened by desires arising from strong emotion—the province of poetry. Poetry was supposed to be dangerous because it can lead us to sympathize with fictional characters, and thus the feelings of the fictional characters come to infect the audience. Plato wrote:

> When even the best of us hear Homer or one of the other tragedians imitating one of the heroes sorrowing and making a long lamenting speech or singing and beating his breast, you know that we enjoy it, give ourselves up to following it, sympathize with the hero, take his sufferings seriously, and praise as a good poet the one who affects us most in this way.[1]

---

[1] Plato, *Republic* (605c–d), translated by G.M.A. Grube and C.D.C. Reeve. (Indianapolis: Hackett, 1992).

In the end, the feelings of the audience and the feelings of the character are the same, and the audience may feel pity, or grief, even when it's not appropriate to do so. Further, we may carry these inappropriate emotions home with us, and they can become part of our character, and affect the way we act. Plato recognized how strongly we can feel about poetry, and the power that this passion can have: sympathetic attention to art, he said, "nurtures and waters them and establishes them as rulers in us."[2] These passions can become so strong that we can no longer control them in our everyday lives. Plato's example is of a man who enjoys comic plays and who then comes to act like a buffoon at home; but someone who enjoyed a show like *The Sopranos* could well be possessed by more dangerous emotions, like rage, revenge, or contempt for ordinary people.[3] If you are inclined to think that Plato's arguments don't apply to modern audiences, consider the following quote, taken from a fan website discussion of "University," which speaks to just this kind of worry.

> When my boyfriend and I watch *The Sopranos*, he gets so caught up, you would think it was happening to him. This gentle man, who wouldn't harm a fly. It's strange phenomena [*sic*], and not unlike soap addicts who confuse TV with reality.[4]

In the nineteenth century, Leo Tolstoy expressed similar concerns about art (including much of his own writing) in his book *What Is Art?* Tolstoy had undergone a deep religious experience late in his life, and he came to believe that most art was morally corrupt. Like Plato, he held that art evoked strong emotions in its audience, and he believed that many such emotions are, in his view, morally corrupting. Only art motivated by true Christian feeling, according to Tolstoy, could be morally acceptable. Tolstoy therefore rejected virtually all art, except popular Christian peasant art, which, he believed, conveyed only simple Christian love. Other artworks transmitted corrupt feelings to their audiences—feelings of unjust pride or lust, for example.[5]

---

[2] Plato, 606d.

[3] See Chapter 11 in this volume for a critical discussion of this issue.

[4] <http://www.the-sopranos.com/db/ep32_review.htm>. The post was anonymous.

[5] One important difference between Plato and Tolstoy is that Tolstoy thought that the feelings transmitted were the feelings of the artist or author, whereas Plato thought that they were the feelings of the character.

These feelings make people worse morally, because the feelings are selfish, and they alienate people from one another.

Plato and Tolstoy are separated by thousands of years, but their views share certain features in common: they both hold that art corrupts its audience by playing on emotion; they both hold that some art is worse than others in doing so; they believe that the emotional impact of art is great enough to influence how we act and what kind of people we become, so that art can make us bad people; they were both particularly critical of the most popular artists of their day. There is little doubt that both of them would have disapproved of *The Sopranos*. Should we, like Plato and Tolstoy, be worried that we might be infected by watching *The Sopranos*, and caring about the immoral protagonists?

Plato and Tolstoy have their present-day counterparts, too. Some cognitive scientists believe that when we watch a television show like *The Sopranos*, we simulate the feelings of the characters portrayed on screen. That is, we use our own minds to imitate what we imagine is going on in the minds of characters, and we feel an emotion that is in some ways like the emotion that the character feels. This emotion can then affect us in a number of ways. We sometimes call this "sympathizing" or "identifying" with a character onscreen. Though in many cases we are able to separate the character's emotion from our own feelings, sometimes our imaginings of the fictional character's emotions infect and affect our own.[6]

Tony Soprano does this himself in "Proshai, Livushka." After the death of his mother, Tony watches his favorite film, *Public Enemy*. In this movie, Jimmy Cagney's character is a gangster with a gentle, loving mother. As Tony watches, he sympathizes with the Cagney character, and imagines having a loving, trusting relationship with his mother. This makes him smile, at first, and then cry, as he compares this imagined mother-son relationship with his own experience. We understand why Tony is so deeply affected by this film, because we can also be affected by works of fiction. Tony is moved by identifying with the Cagney character, and we are moved by identifying with Tony.

---

[6] This phenomenon is discussed by Robert Gordon in his "Sympathy, Simulation, and the Impartial Spectator," in *Mind and Morals: Essays on Ethics and Cognitive Science*, edited by Larry May, Marilyn Friedman, and Andy Clark (Boston: MIT Press, 1996), pp. 165–180.

A key feature of this view is that we pick out a character to identity with, and we focus on that person's feelings and emotions. It is this character that we identify with; he or she is the one that we know the best, and often, he or she is the one that we like the most. In the case of *The Sopranos*, despite a large, strong ensemble cast, the primary character with whom audiences identify is Tony himself. This is how I come to care about Tony, and why I feel relief when he is successful, even when his "success" consists in murder, as when he strangles the mob informant Febby Petrulio in "College."

The problem with this sympathetic identification is that sometimes the character with whom we identify has thoughts and feelings which are morally reprehensible, and by identifying with that character, we risk being infected by these vicious sentiments. We might start to think that Tony's views about violence and vengeance are reasonable, or we might come to share his propensity for anger, jealousy, rage, and suspicion. If imagining these feelings leads us to share them (even to a small extent), then liking Tony could make a person morally worse.

Why *The Sopranos*?

There are so many works of popular art that feature gangsters—not to mention other kinds of vicious people—as protagonists that it hardly seems fair to pick on *The Sopranos*. *Godfather Parts I, II, and III, Goodfellas, Carlito's Way, Scarface, Casino,* and *Public Enemy* are just a few examples of films that feature gangsters as main characters. (Most of these movies are referenced and discussed by the characters in *The Sopranos*, especially by Silvio Dante, who loves to imitate Al Pacino's character from *The Godfather*). But *The Sopranos* distinguishes itself from these other works in three ways. First, *The Sopranos* is an ongoing television series, not a two-hour movie. As of this writing, four seasons comprising fifty-two episodes have been shown, and at least two more seasons are planned. That will make more than three *days* worth of material if one were to sit down and watch them all back-to-back. By contrast, all the films of the *Godfather* series, taken together, would take fewer than ten hours to watch. So loyal viewers of *The Sopranos* spend a long time with these characters, getting to know much more about them, and potentially, to care much more about them than viewers ever could with a film character. Not surprisingly, we are more deeply affected by characters we spend more time with and get to know better, and we get to spend a lot of time with Tony and friends.

Second, the gangsters in *The Sopranos*, especially Tony, are portrayed in deeply psychological and often quite intimate ways. We often get to see Tony's dreams (occasionally we see other character's dreams, such as Christopher's and Dr. Melfi's, but not often). Through Tony's sessions with Dr. Melfi, we get to know Tony's feelings much better than we could otherwise. In those sessions, we get to understand his childhood (through flashbacks), his hopes and concerns, and his fears. We get a very strong picture of Tony as a complete human being. The character himself is a rich and complex one. In addition to being a gangster (with all that implies) we also learn that Tony tries, in his own way, to be a good father and husband, that he cares deeply about his children and wants them to do well. We learn that he loves his friends deeply, even those (like Big Pussy) that he ends up killing. He has a strong sense of responsibility, and when he says he will do something, he feels bound to do it. Despite (perhaps because of) his evil, vicious qualities, Tony has some good features, as well. Tony Soprano is a more fully-developed character than any other fictional gangster ever created, and we get to know him intimately.

Third, *The Sopranos* strives for verisimilitude. It does not have the ironic stylishness of *Goodfellas*, nor is it an idealized period piece like *The Godfather*. With one major exception—the number of gang killings[7]—the show is strikingly realistic. Virtually every element, including the psychoanalysis, the New Jersey settings, the language used by the characters, Tony and Carmela's family dynamics, the FBI surveillance techniques, and the mob structure and organization is very close to what is found in the real world. The show is set in our own time and many of the phenomena that the characters deal with—for example, Prozac, 9/11, Attention Deficit Disorder, coaches sexually assaulting student athletes, the competitiveness of college acceptance, teen drug use—are phenomena that we deal with

---

[7] One fan website counts thirty-nine deaths over the first four seasons (http://www.the-sopranos.com/db/bodycount.htm). The number of killings on the show far exceeds the number in real life for similar mobs.

as well. The characters on *The Sopranos* are aware of the fictional portrayals of gangsters and they discuss these. In "Christopher," Carmela and her friends attend a lecture about the portrayal of Italian-American women as mob wives; Dr. Melfi's ex-husband Richard complains over and over again about the stereotyped portrayal of Italian-Americans in gangster films. The psychiatrist who Tony consults when Dr. Melfi won't see him makes a reference to the Robert DeNiro comedy *Analyze This*. *The Sopranos* thus continues the tradition of gangster fictions, but in a deeper, more reflective way than most do: like us, the characters on *The Sopranos* know that these other stories are fictional.

All of these features conspire to make Tony Soprano a very sympathetic character. When Plato says, "We enjoy it, give ourselves up to following it, sympathize with the hero, take his sufferings seriously," the hero he describes could be Tony. But sympathizing with Tony is not like sympathizing with Artie Bucco; Tony is a terribly vicious and violent man. Tony personally commits five murders that we see on screen: he strangles Febby Petrulio in "College"; he shoots one of Junior's hired killers in "I Dream of Jeanie Cusamano" (this one, at least, is self-defense); in "From Where to Eternity," he kills Matt Bevilaqua with Big Pussy; and then he, Paulie, and Silvio turn around and shoot Big Pussy in "Funhouse"; finally, he kills Ralph Cifaretto in "Whoever Did This." On top of these five, he orders many, many other killings which are carried out by other members of his gang (some shown onscreen and some off). He loses his temper continually, administering beatings to girlfriends (Irina, Gloria) and business associates (Mikey Palmice, Georgie the bartender, Ralphie Cifaretto, Assemblyman Zellman). He doesn't ever hit Dr. Melfi, but he comes quite close. On top of his propensity for personal violence, we have his virulent racism and homophobia, his profiting from corruption, gambling, drugs, and other enterprises that presumably ruin the lives of people we never see on screen. There is no doubt that Tony Soprano is evil, vicious, and morally bankrupt. Yet we like him.

Is It Morally Wrong to Watch *The Sopranos*?

The Sopranos leads its audience to identify with a terrible person. Is it then wrong to watch the show? Could identifying with

Tony make us worse people too? In the end, I doubt it. There are a number of reasons why *The Sopranos* as a whole does more than just make bad people look good. First, although Tony Soprano is the main character on the show, some of the main characters of *The Sopranos* who are quite sympathetic are not gangsters and are pretty good people, particularly Dr. Melfi and Meadow Soprano. Many other characters, if not good, at least suffer pangs of conscience for the evil they do (or the evil men they love), and they try to do good from time to time: Carmela, Artie Bucco,[8] and Adriana, for example. These characters struggle continually with their moral positions, and their complicity in the crimes being committed all around them. Even some thoroughly bad characters like Christopher and Paulie are forced from time to time to reflect on the moral consequences of what they do ("From Where to Eternity").

But the primary moral center of the show, which serves to balance out the immoral facets of these attractive characters, is Jennifer Melfi's psychiatrist's office. It is here that the viewer is most often led to identify not just with Tony, but with his victims, and to see Tony's life in a richer, more morally sophisticated way. In a long-running series like *The Sopranos*, we see things from more than just one point of view. Tony's psychoanalysis sessions with Dr. Melfi afford us an opportunity to see Tony from the outside as well as from the inside, and to remind us of the self-deception and flimsy justifications that Tony uses in order to continue his life of crime and violence. Tony likes to compare himself to a soldier at war, or a "captain of industry," but he doesn't convince anyone with these analogies (perhaps not even himself). Dr. Melfi's facial expressions make clear her contempt for these facile attempts at justification.

Consider the episode entitled "House Arrest." In this episode, on the advice of his lawyer, Tony has decided to distance himself from criminal activity and spend his time with his legitimate businesses. He grows increasingly restless and agitated; he develops a serious rash; he becomes irritable and frustrated, and

---

[8] Artie is a very interesting character, morally speaking. For the most part, he is not involved in Tony's activities. Artie did have a brief fling with loan sharking in season four, but it didn't work out, and he wasn't really up to the nasty side of it. But he does indirectly profit from Tony's business, and he keeps silent about some of his wrongdoings.

he complains of this to Dr. Melfi. Dr. Melfi asks him: "Do you know why a shark keeps moving? . . . There's a psychological condition known as alexithymia[9], common in certain personalities. The individual craves almost ceaseless action, which enables them to avoid acknowledging the abhorrent things they do." When Tony asks what happens when such people are forced to stop and reflect, she answers, "They have time to think about their behavior. How what they do affects other people. About feelings of emptiness and self-loathing, haunting them since childhood. And they crash." Tony gets her point, but he chooses to respond to this lesson not by reflecting, but by returning to Satriale's with the other mobsters and getting back into action—thus, the shark gets back in motion rather than think about the ethical consequences of how he lives.

Jennifer Melfi continually reminds us as an audience of the dangers of seeing things exclusively from Tony's point of view, and her character provides an alternative point of view on Tony's life and actions. When she complains to her psychiatrist, Elliot Kupferberg, that she is in a "moral never-never land" with Tony Soprano, "Not wanting to judge but to treat," we know exactly how she feels ("From Where to Eternity"). Dr. Melfi, and sometimes other characters such as the Buccos, Meadow, or even Carmela, provide us with an alternative moral center that allows us to see Tony and his actions from the outside, and they remind us of the moral consequences of what Tony does. After Dr. Melfi's rapist goes free, she realizes that she could tell Tony about her rapist, and be revenged on him, but she does not do so ("Employee of the Month"). During this sequence, we sympathize with Melfi, and her moral choice, not with Tony. The finale of the second season ("Funhouse") concludes with one of the few montage sequences ever used in the series.[10] We see

---

[9] Alexithymia, strictly speaking, is somewhat different than Jennifer Melfi's account of it here. Ordinarily, alexithymia refers to a condition wherein the patient has difficulty in recognizing her or his own emotions. Melfi is describing how alexithymia manifests itself in sociopathic personalities like Tony's.

[10] The second season has more of these moments of moral reflection and serious moral examination than any other season: from the very beginning of the season, when Dr. Melfi has to decide whether she has a moral responsibility to take Tony back as a patient, to this final sequence, the characters and the creators grapple with right and wrong in a very direct way. None of the other seasons has as much sustained, direct attention to morality.

alternating shots of the Soprano family celebrating Meadow's graduation, and various shots of the criminal activities that will be paying Meadow's tuition. By juxtaposing these two scenes, the producers of *The Sopranos* remind us that what we like about Tony cannot be separated from the evil he does.

The problem with Plato's and Tolstoy's moral criticism of art is that their emotional theories of artistic identification are simplistic. We do not just take on one character or one point of view, and we do not respond emotionally in only one way. *The Sopranos* provides us with many different ways of seeing the life of a gangster, and it also invites us to feel in a variety of ways about it. Sometimes the show does make Tony and his crew look quite sympathetic; but it also provides us with other perspectives, and permits us, if we try, to formulate a complex and sophisticated personal moral response to gangster life, and not merely to imitate Tony.

This does not mean that Plato's and Tolstoy's concerns about art should be dismissed lightly. They are right that artworks can affect us deeply, and sometimes cause audiences to identify with immoral characters. But whether or not these artworks are morally corrupting depends on other factors as well. Television shows like *The Sopranos* which provide multiple moral perspectives on evil characters, and which offer room for moral reflection, might even be good for us, rather than evil.

13
Know Thyself, Asshole: Tony Soprano as an Aristotelian Tragic Hero

MIKE LIPPMAN

Although there are many reasons for the immense success of *The Sopranos*, one part of its appeal surely comes from its use of tragic elements established long ago in ancient Greek drama. Had the term "pop culture" existed in antiquity, it would certainly have been applied to tragedy of the fifth century B.C. Twice yearly, playwrights including Aeschylus, Sophocles, and Euripides submitted plays at dramatic competitions dedicated to the god Dionysos. Besides being immensely popular with the masses of the world's first democracy, Athenian tragedy became one of the most influential literary contributions to Western Civilization. The philosopher Aristotle, realizing that this pop phenomenon was worthy of serious consideration, wrote an analysis of tragedy, *The Poetics*. Aristotle's work was not a mere how-to book for aspiring poets, like a sort of "Writing Tragedy for Dummies." Instead, he sought to understand why and how successful tragic drama works its magic upon an audience.

In this chapter I want to show that Aristotle was a pretty bright guy who knew what he was talking about. An analysis of *The Sopranos*, particularly Season One, will show that the elements Aristotle identified as "tragic" remain effective. Aristotle's take on ancient tragedy can help explain why audiences today have such a powerful response to a flawed character like Tony Soprano.

Pity, Fear, and the Man In-Between

Aristotle's definition of tragedy reads in part: "An imitation of an action, complete and of a certain magnitude . . . which through pity and fear achieves a *catharsis* of these emotions."[1] For the moment let us leave aside discussion of the complicated term *catharsis* (which most simply means "a purging") and focus on pity and fear, the primary emotions for tragedy. The violent backdrop of the Mafia world makes fear a constant component of *The Sopranos*. We feel fear at Tony's violent temper at the same time as we fear for Tony's safety and well-being. Viewers remain in a constant state of suspense and dread. We constantly anticipate the next violent act, who will perpetrate it and who will suffer from it. But fear and violence alone do not constitute tragedy. Horror films contain fearful elements, but are not tragic. Nor, according to Aristotle, is tragedy when bad things happen to good people, despite the way we use the word "tragedy" today (as in: "What a tragedy! I heard dear old Livia Soprano accidentally ran over her neighbor with her car"). In fact, the simple translation of the term means no more than "goat song"—whatever that may have meant to ancient Athenians. Aristotle believes tragedy can only occur when characters occupy a particular moral space. He says:

> One must not show good people changing from good fortune into bad. This is neither fearful nor pitiable, but brutal. Nor should one show evil people changing from misfortune to fortune. This is the most untragic thing of all, since it does not contain the crucial components for tragedy, having neither compassion nor pity nor fear. By the same token, it is also not tragic to have a bad man fall from good fortune to bad. Although we may feel such a thing is acceptable, it contains neither pity nor fear. We experience pity for a man who does not deserve his misfortune and we feel fear for a man similar to ourselves . . . Our remaining option is the man in-between. This man, being of high station and fortune but not outstanding in regards to virtue or justice, falls into misfortune; not through his own evil and depravity, but through some sort of flaw within him.[2]

---

[1] Aristotle, *Poetics* (1449b). All translations are my own.
[2] *Poetics* (1452b–1453a).

Tony Soprano fits Aristotle's description of this man in-between. An upper echelon mob boss with a suburban palace in northern New Jersey, a luxurious yacht down the shore, and wads of cash to buy expensive trinkets for his various women, Tony clearly qualifies as a "man of high station and fortune." Due to the way he earns this fortune, Tony is hardly "outstanding in regards to virtue or justice." For Tony to be a tragic hero he also needs qualities that make him worthy of pity and, paradoxical as it may seem, be a somewhat moral mobster. Despite being a cold-blooded killer, Tony does have a set of values that distinguishes him from your typical Mafia psychopath and that permit the audience to look upon him with compassion. Tony's relationships may be flawed (and let's be fair, whose aren't?) but they do serve to humanize him. He genuinely attempts to do the right thing by the people he loves. We identify with his attempt to be good, even though his solutions may sometimes have some morally dubious aspects (like burning down Artie Bucco's restaurant so his Uncle Junior wouldn't stage a hit there). He respects and one could even say loves his business associates and friends. The hint of Pussy's betrayal causes Tony immense pain, and he genuinely mourns at the death of former boss Jackie Aprile. But we identify most with Tony's moral side in his relationships at home. He may not be a perfect father or husband, but Tony supports, provides for, and loves his family. There is certainly something positive about any working dad, acting mob boss or not, who is a constant presence at Sunday night family dinner and shows up regularly at his daughter's soccer games. Tony tries hard to live up to what he perceives as his family responsibilities. Despite the fact that his mother, Livia, is impossible to please and fills his life with misery, Tony tries again and again to fulfill his duty to be a good son to her.

Unfortunately, Tony's concepts of honor and responsibility contain an inherent strain of violence. In order to continue functioning as a good boss, son, provider, or whatever, Tony is often put into morally compromising situations. So, although we may admire Tony's desire to take care of friends and family, at the same time *The Sopranos* constantly reminds us that he is also a violent, murderous, selfish, racist, philandering, hypocritical bully. We identify with him only just so much before some action of his prevents us from getting too sympathetic. Every episode plays off the juxtaposition between the two aspects of

Tony's life, but they are brought out with particular clarity in the episode "College." During his tour of New England colleges with Meadow, Tony is at the same time both ideal father and brutal thug. While on the trip, Meadow and Tony undergo significant father-daughter bonding. They have a mature discussion about each other's secrets—the sort of conversation that few children have so openly with their parents. Meadow admits to having taken speed, while Tony admits, albeit reluctantly, that he is involved in the Mafia. Tony's reaction both to Meadow's questioning of his lifestyle and her admissions about her own, if a bit overprotective, is nevertheless very paternal and loving. Although a little disappointed in Meadow when he finds her drunk later that evening, Tony helps his daughter into her room to kiss her goodnight. The only punishment she receives is his good-natured teasing about her hangover the next morning. Still, Tony's model fatherhood is undercut by his "business" actions. At a gas station, Tony spots a former associate who had gone into the witness protection program after turning state's evidence, and he begins begins lying to Meadow right on the heels of their mutual, honest confessions. From that point forward, all of Tony's good paternal actions are compromised. His seemingly open-minded offer to let Meadow spend time with college girls she meets at the restaurant is only a pretext to give him the time he needs to investigate the rat. Tony's decision to handle the hit personally instead of delegating it to Christopher puts Meadow in direct danger. She is almost shot when the rat follows Tony back to their hotel. After missing one of Meadow's college interviews, Tony invents a shallow series of lies to cover up the fact that he was really off brutally strangling a man to death. The viewer, left with a powerful sense of brutality and hypocrisy with lingering paternal identification, remains unable to categorize Tony as either good or evil. Clearly, Tony fits Aristotle's model of the tragic hero as a "man in-between."

Tony's Tragic Flaw

Tony's fall, such as it is in season one (we'll discuss his ultimate downfall at the end of the chapter), is consistent with Aristotle's definition of a man "who falls, not through evil or depravity, but through some sort of flaw within him." Aristotle's concept of a tragic flaw is much debated and it gets far more attention than it actually should. A tragic flaw is not a sin, nor should it be simply summed up in one word (the most commonly cited is *hubris*, meaning foolish pride). A tragic flaw is not necessarily a "bad" or condemnable aspect of a character's personality. What Aristotle means by a tragic flaw is that aspect of a character's personality that makes him vulnerable enough so that he himself ultimately contributes to his own downfall. Tony certainly is a flawed character in many ways. But his tragic flaw is not the moral failing that makes him kill people, cheat on his wife, or draw his income from extortion and illegal gambling. Bad things happen to Tony, but only those that are not due to his own evil and depravity are tragic. If, for example, we saw the FBI haul Tony in for being a mob boss, it would not be the "undeserved misfortune" Aristotle pegs as necessary for inspiring tragic pity. In this case, he'd be getting what he deserved. We identify with his mental anguish as a tragic hero insofar as he is a guy struggling under difficult family relationships and a hard job. His flaw, manifested physically by his panic attacks, is his inability to successfully live up to his conflicting moral roles and responsibilities. In season one, much of Tony's stress comes from his conflict with his mother and Uncle Junior. Both play significant roles in Tony's two worlds, home and business. The frustration he feels from dealing with his mother's reluctance to enter a nursing home combines with his *agita* at his uncle's stubbornness about business. The departure of the ducks, later recognized as Tony's fear of losing his family, taps into Tony's sense of helplessness and dread. The combined weight placed on his shoulders from all his various family related anxieties causes his panic attacks. To help himself move beyond this flaw, Tony begins therapy with Dr. Melfi, setting in motion the tragic plot.

In the background to Aristotle's favorite model tragedy, *Oedipus Rex*, Oedipus had fled from his hometown of Corinth because he had heard a prophecy that he was to kill his father and marry his mother (he had not yet realized that he was adopted). Oedipus's decision to fight fate and leave home brought about the very circumstances that put him in the position to kill his father (who he met on the road to Delphi) and marry his mother (since he traveled to Thebes rather than return to Corinth). Just so, Tony's decision to seek professional therapy for his panic attacks further aggravates his dealings with his mother and uncle. The cure for Tony's flaw may be to go to therapy, but ironically, at the same time therapy adds to his overall misery. Therapy undermines Tony's sense of self-control, masculinity, and independence. Because of the value system his Mafia life forces upon him, Tony also lives in perpetual fear that he'll be caught by one of his crew, which adds to his already considerable stress. But in the end, his mother is the one who makes his therapy public. Already furious about being placed in a nursing home (O.K., a retirement community), Livia discovers through A.J. that Tony is seeing a psychiatrist. Feeling as if Tony's need for counseling somehow calls into question her fitness as a mother, she at first limits herself to snide comments about Tony's mental weakness. But in the end, she reveals her knowledge to Junior at a crucial moment, fueling his suspicions of her son. After mutual taunting of each other's weakness on the golf course, when Tony mocked Junior's oral sex skills and Junior retorted that at least he can deal with his own problems, the tension between them gets out of control, and Junior tells Mikey about Tony's therapy. In Junior's mind, Tony's going to a shrink opens up the possibility that he is openly blabbing family secrets at a time when everyone is terrified of indictments. Spurred on by Mikey, Junior accordingly decides to set up the hit on Tony in front of the place where he goes for therapy. Tony sums up the tragic plot line well: "Cunnilingus and psychiatry brought us to this" ("I Dream of Jeannie Cusamano"). Had Tony not had panic attacks and had he never gone to a psychiatrist, the final tragic conflict with his mother and uncle could have been avoided. Unfortunately, as Carmela notes, with a mother like Livia, there was no way Tony could avoid ending up in therapy. Tony, like Oedipus, although he had little choice but to follow his fate, still remains partially responsible for having brought it about.

All in the Families

According to Aristotle, the best tragic plots come from those few noble families of the past who underwent such high drama. He says:

> Dreadful and pitiable events must either be the actions of friends against each other, enemies, or strangers. If enemy harms enemy, there is nothing pitiable in either action or intention, except inso-

far as the actual misfortune itself. The same applies if characters are strangers to each other. But whenever misfortunes occur between close relations, such as when brother kills brother or a son kills his father or a mother her son or a son his mother, *or even if they intend to do so*, these sorts of plots should be sought after for tragedy.[3]

The Sopranos, like Greek tragedy, is filled with stories of family members trying to kill each other in horrible ways. Between Tony's Mafia family and dysfunctional blood family, almost every action occurs within a family dynamic. It's difficult to see where one family ends and the other begins. Tony's buddies in his crime family are like brothers to him. But also, the crime family is largely made up of people from Tony's blood family. Christopher is Tony's nephew and sometimes even seems like a son. Junior, Tony's blood uncle, is almost like a surrogate father to him. In addition to the crime family, Tony has the very real pressures involved with a marriage and raising teenage children. Looming large over Tony's life is his mother. Livia is the dominant figure and the real boss over both families. Her war with Tony is the tragic focus of the first season.

As Aristotle points out, pity and fear are heightened when violence takes place, or is even planned, between close family members. Simply put, a story where a mother tries to kill off her son has far more tragic potential than a war between rival mob factions. The family-driven plot of *The Sopranos* echoes the family conflicts that lie at the heart of the most influential Greek tragedies. Livia, just like Medea, tries to kill her son. She had been threatening to do so for years. In a flashback from Tony's childhood, we see a utensil wielding Livia scream at him, "I'll stick this fork in your eye!" ("Down Neck"). In another flashback, she shrieks at Tony's father that she would rather smother her children with a pillow than take them to Nevada. When her plan for manipulating Uncle Junior to whack her son fails, Tony parallels Orestes, the man who avenged his father Agamemnon by killing his mother Clytemnestra in Aeschylus's *Orestia*. Although Tony's attempted hit on his mother doesn't succeed either, in a way, he does kill off his mother. "She's dead to me," he'll protest throughout Season Two. Even before

---

[3] *Poetics* (1453b).

their final showdown, Livia portrays Tony as hurting and trying to kill her. When he tells Livia he is going to put her in a home whether she likes it or not, she cries out: "Then kill me now! Go on, go into the ham and take the carving knife and stab me . . . here . . . it would hurt me less than what you just said" ("46 Long"). Orestes, after killing his mother, is pursued by the Furies, avenging monsters who represent the guilt he has for being a matricide. Likewise, Tony has to fight off his own version of the Furies while confronting his guilt over his actions in therapy.

Of course, anyone's relationship with his mother must naturally brings to mind Oedipus. Tony may protest that no matter what Dr. Melfi says, he cannot believe that anyone would want to fuck his mother. But we know from his dreams that he cannot fight the insights of Sophocles and Freud. Or, as Oedipus's mother Jocasta once ominously said, many men sleep with their mothers in their dreams. Tony may never literally step into Oedipus's shoes, but we learn how his desire to please his mother bleeds into his relationships with other women in his life. Tony's love for Dr. Melfi is revealed to be his need for a caring sensitive woman (read: mother figure) who will listen to him. The connections between Melfi and Livia are emphasized in Tony's sex dream when Melfi's face suddenly transforms into Livia's at crucial (dare I imply climactic?) moments. Tony's lithium-ridden fantasy about Isabella the Italian dental student, whom he perceived as a mother nursing a child, was ultimately revealed to be his subconscious screaming warnings at him about his mother's tragic action. Even after Livia dies, her specter will continue to haunt Tony both in therapy and in the form of the screeching, roast-throwing Gloria Trillo.

Recognitions and Reversals

Aristotle mentions two devices, *reversals* and *recognitions*, as the most important methods in a well-written plot to elicit the emotional response of fear and pity. A *reversal* is a sudden change in a character's fortune. A *recognition* is when a character comes into a particular piece of knowledge that brings on a radical alteration in his or her understanding of a situation. A *recognition* scene crucially linked to the plot that also brings with it a *reversal* is the most effective way of stirring up emotions of fear and pity.[4] For example, Aristotle notes how Oedipus suddenly undergoes recognition at the play's climax that he killed his father and married his mother. He then undergoes a *reversal*, falling from the king of Thebes to end up as a blind about-to-be exile. *Recognition* scenes occur many times in *The Sopranos*, often at crucial moments in the plot. Sometimes Tony has *recognitions* in therapy that give him sudden flashes of self-awareness and knowledge, as when he learned what the ducks signified, or realized the significance of why he kept thinking of his father taking Janice to the amusement park. The most important *recognition* scene in season one is when Agent Harris plays for Tony the tapes of his mother speaking to Junior at Green Grove. Tony suddenly recognizes what his subconscious had been telling him all along. No longer can he fool himself that his mother is harmless, or that he ought to continue trying to please her as a good son should. Once he sees the full extent of his mother's hatred for him, his change of heart is so great that he rushes to smother her with a pillow.

Tragic Endings and Catharsis

You may be protesting that in the end, Tony had no real fall at the end of Season One. On the surface, this is true. In fact, he seems to end up unscathed and stronger than ever, free and in control of New Jersey while Junior, the figurehead boss, is carted off to prison. But remember that for Aristotle, a tragedy does not need to end badly. The mere intention of family members to do violence against each other is enough to make a tragic plot. Although it didn't turn out this way, Tony came very close to being either dead from his mother's machinations or his mother's killer. But more importantly, Tony is only a successful mobster at the expense of his relationships to his mother and uncle. In a way, then, he does undergo a *reversal* and a tragic fall; but not in terms of his Mafia life. He falls insofar as the dreadful *recognition* brought about by the departing ducks has begun to come to pass; through his feud with Junior and Livia he has lost part of his family. Likewise, despite the fact that Tony's career continues to rise, the climax of each subsequent season (the deaths of Pussy and Jackie Jr. and the separation

---

[4] *Poetics* (1452a–b).

from Carmela) all emphasize Tony's failures to succeed in his non-business life. He fails as a friend, father-figure, and husband. His Mafia lifestyle will not allow him any way to avoid disaster. Tony will likely end up dead or in jail, but he will certainly become more and more isolated from the people he loves along the way. He will change from a man surrounded by family to a man who will ultimately suffer alone. Therapy may allow us to pretend that Tony is redeemable, but even from season one we learn that Tony's personality and lifestyle will make it impossible for him to escape his destiny. In the end, Tony is bound to fall.

So, what benefits, if any, do we get by watching a depressed and doomed mobster vacillate between being a decent human being and a violent thug? If we identify at all with Tony as a flawed tragic hero, we follow along on his emotional journey. Like Oedipus, Tony follows the advice of the Delphic Oracle, "Know Thyself." Tony begins his quest psychologically damaged, or in tragic terms, cursed. Searching for the cure in therapy brought him more pain and suffering. Of course, the search for self-knowledge is often painful. Somewhere along the line, Western Civilization decided this quest was also emasculating and turns us into wimpy "sopranos." But Greek tragedy and *The Sopranos* invite us to do just that. For Aristotle, the beneficial effect to experiencing all this pity and fear is to achieve a *catharsis* of these emotions. Although some have interpreted *catharsis* as a method of ridding oneself of these emotions in order to achieve a beatific detachment, I believe the opposite effect happens both to Tony and to any viewer who gets involved in the show. Instead, emotions that were bottled up are now purged outward and brought to the surface. If we believe in the efficacy of *catharsis* in therapy or in its counterpart tragic theater, we are mentally healthier by bringing our emotions forward. Compared with lethargy and depression, self-awareness and the improved ability to express our humanity that results from viewing tragedy can hardly be a bad thing.[5]

---

[5] The author would like to thank his brother Jeff Lippman for starting him down the road that led to this paper, Gil Renberg for taping every episode off HBO so they'd be accessible to poverty-stricken graduate students, Peter Vernezze and Richard Greene for their helpful comments on earlier versions of this paper, his girlfriend Laura Gross for emotional support, editorial advice, and not wearing him down to a nub so he'd be a squeaking gerbil when he died, and most of all his spiritual guru, Ace the philosopher dog.

Dolce

Language and Knowledge: Metaphysics and Made Guys

14

This Thing of Ours: Language Use in *The Sopranos*

MICHAEL E. GETTINGS

In "Meadowlands," we find Tony and Uncle Junior clashing over who is to become boss of the family after Jackie Aprile's death. Tony visits Junior at the Sit Tite diner, and they have the following conversation:

> JUNIOR: That nephew of yours we gave a high colonic, he earns good?
> TONY: He's comin' up.
> JUNIOR: Okay, he works for me now.
> TONY: Excuse me?
> JUNIOR: Maybe he gives you some *agita* for a change.
> TONY: You got some set of balls, you know that? Absolutely not.
> JUNIOR: I show you my hand, and you slap it away.
> TONY: What's the matter with you? Why can't we talk like adults anymore?
> JUNIOR: Out. And next time you come in, you come heavy or not at all.

As with so much of *The Sopranos*, the language here is not only colorful, but of utmost importance to understanding the characters and the plot. The *Sopranos* characters use slang, metaphor, indirect speech, and other devices to communicate with one another. In addition, the things they say do much more than describe their world; in saying what they say they perform a variety of actions, such as ordering, agreeing, acknowledging, granting, and threatening. Such uses of speech were dubbed by Oxford philosopher J.L. Austin "performatives," since in speaking we often perform actions.[1] Austin first developed what has come to be known as "speech act theory," a theory which distinguishes types of actions that are performed when we speak and explains how those actions are performed. Austin's main idea was that what we do with words is far richer than simply conveying information. This richness of language use is well illustrated in *The Sopranos*. Following the storylines requires the viewer to understand not only what is said, but what the characters mean by what they say, and most importantly, what they do in speaking. Understanding language use in the series involves the viewer, and this contributes to the show's great appeal. In this chapter we will look at merely a few of the many examples of speech acts in *The Sopranos*, focusing on the use of mob slang, the relevance of power relationships between speakers and listeners, the use of language in mob business transactions, and, finally, the particularly interesting case of Tony's mother.

We begin with one of several distinctions Austin introduced—a distinction among three kinds of act involved in an utterance: the locution (the sentences, phrases, or words one utters); the illocution (what is done in uttering those words); and the perlocution (the resultant effect on the listener). Junior's initial question above, "That nephew of yours we gave a high colonic, he earns good?" is his locution. The illocution performed is a question; that is, by his words he is performing the act of asking a question. The perlocution is the act of eliciting a response from Tony. Notice that Junior avoids using the name "Christopher," instead employing the phrase "that nephew of yours we gave a high colonic." Given that Tony only has one nephew who earns for the family, the additional reference to Junior's crew having scared Christopher so much that he lost bowel control is likely intended to remind Tony of Junior's power. This reminder is yet another illocutionary act, in addition to the act of posing a question, that Junior performs on this

---

[1] See J.L. Austin, *How to Do Things With Words*, second edition, edited by J.O. Urmson and Marina Sbisà. (Cambridge, Massachusetts: Harvard University Press, 1975).

occasion. One often performs several actions at once with a single utterance. Minimally, Junior performs the acts of saying something (the locution), asking a question and reminding (both illocutions), and eliciting a response (perlocution).

The rest of their conversation can be similarly analyzed. Had this exchange been straightforward and direct, it might have gone something like this:

JUNIOR: Does Christopher earn well for you? I remind you that I wield power.

TONY: Christopher has been improving.

JUNIOR: I decree that now he will start working for me.

TONY: I am surprised and I do not recognize your authority to make that decision.

JUNIOR: In the future Christopher may give you troubles when he is working for me.

TONY: Your suggestion is bold, it offends me, and I do not accept it.

JUNIOR: I offered this to you as a means for you to make peace with me, and you have rejected me.

TONY: Your suggestion was inappropriate and your belief that it is your decision to make is condescending.

JUNIOR: I order you to leave, and if you return, come armed.

This lacks the punch that we get from the characters, but this is roughly what is going on when Tony and Junior speak. The illocutions performed include responding, decreeing, predicting, offering, rejecting, and ordering. The perlocutions include surprising and offending. Some of the illocutions, particularly ordering, deciding, and offering play crucial roles in the business of these mobsters.

Slang

The actions performed by the speakers also have a lot to do with their choice of words. In the example above Junior uses phrases such as "gave a high colonic" and "come heavy" as slang terms for "literally scared the shit out of" and "come armed." Some of these, such as the latter, are more or less firmly ingrained in mob talk. Others, such as the former, are invented on the spot by the speaker. Among the examples of established mob slang are terms such as "hit," "clip," "pop," "put a contract out," "whack," "burn," and "take care of," all of which refer to murder, at least on many occasions. There are occasions in which characters (even the mobsters) use these terms with their ordinary meanings, but the circumstances and the speaker's intent dictate whether the term is used in its slang sense.

Other established slang terms in common use on the show are "this thing of ours," which refers to the mob family and its operations, "pinched," meaning arrested, "rat," a traitor who informs for the feds, and "a friend of ours," used to refer to another mob family member. Much of the established slang has its origins in Italian: *"capo"* (a captain—one who leads a crew); *"mulignan"* (an African-American person); *"goomah"* (a mobster's mistress); *"cugine"* (a foot-soldier or low-level member of the mob family) and the like.

Many of these terms are born of necessity—since the mob's business is almost entirely illegal, the words the mobsters use should not betray their illocutions to any outsiders who might be listening, such as the FBI. One philosopher interested in Austin's work with speech acts, P.F. Strawson, claimed that for a speaker's illocution to be successfully communicated to the listener, the listener must recognize the speaker's intention.[2] This means that if I ask you a question (illocution), that question can only be successfully communicated to you if you recognize that I intended to ask you a question. So if Tony orders a hit, he needs to ensure that his subordinate recognizes his intention to issue the order, but the FBI does not, in case they are listening. Terms such as "whack," however, are so well-known that they are of little use in avoiding getting pinched. So Tony usually uses less direct means to order a hit. In "Another Toothpick," the renegade Mustang Sally has "done a Lee Trevino" off the head of one of Tony's friends (an inventive slang way of saying that Mustang Sally beat the guy in the head with a golf club). Tony says to Gigi Cestone, one of the capos who works for him, "Gig, you get him under control?," and Gigi replies, "With extreme fuckin' prejudice." Tony's locution takes the form of a question, but the illocution he performs is an order. Asking whether Gigi

---

[2] See P.F. Strawson, "Intention and Convention in Speech Acts," *The Philosophical Review* 73:4 (1964), pp. 439–460.

will get someone under control is merely an indirect way of telling Gigi to have Mustang Sally killed. Gigi's reply is a reference to Capt. Willard's order to "terminate" Col. Kurtz "with extreme prejudice" in *Apocalypse Now.* Gigi says this to let Tony know that he understands and will obey Tony's order. Tony's illocution is an order, Gigi's illocution is acceptance of the order, and finally, Tony recognizes Gigi's intention to carry out the order.

Power

In this same example, we see how the relative positions of power between speaker and listener have a lot to do with the content of what is said. The same locutions uttered by different characters would not be performances of the same illocutions. If Gigi were to ask Tony, "You get him under control?" it most likely would be a request, not an order, and if Tony were to say, "With extreme fuckin' prejudice," it would be a promise or an offer, not an acceptance. This is because Gigi is one of Tony's subordinates, not the other way around.

On some occasions the characters use language to establish power relationships, as when Tony says to Ralphie, "I'm making you a captain" after Gigi Cestone's untimely death in "He Is Risen." Ralphie gets his own crew and moves to a point in the hierarchy directly under Tony. In uttering those words, Tony promotes Ralph to his new position (illocution) and pleases Ralph (perlocution).

A more complex change of power relationships occurs after Tony's first confrontation with Junior at the Sit Tite in "Meadowlands." Tony returns, and this time he comes "heavy." But now their exchange is much less heated:

TONY: Sopranos have been waiting a long time to take the reins. That's why I want it to be you, Uncle Jun.
JUNIOR: This is your decision?
TONY: It is.
JUNIOR: You speak for the captains?
TONY: I can.

This is the point at which Junior becomes the boss of the family, at least in name. The action performed here is one of conferring a title. Of course, Junior thinks that Tony is conceding to him, and Tony wants Junior to think that. Tony also presumably believes that Junior will not wield power, since Tony knows that the captains stand behind him. Unfortunately for Tony, Junior does wield some power as the new boss, and this creates problems for Tony, which are eventually resolved when Junior is indicted and put under house arrest. Still, in this instance, Tony's locution, "I want it to be you, Uncle Jun," is a way of performing the illocutionary act of conferring a title, while at the same time performing the perlocution of leading Junior to think he wields ultimate power in the family. Junior takes Tony's illocution to be a concession of power, not a conferral of title. After all, one's equal or subordinate does not have the power to confer a title or promote. But that is what makes Tony's utterance clever—Uncle Junior doesn't know what power Tony already has, and he sees Tony as a subordinate in at least one way— Uncle Junior is Tony's elder, making Tony an upstart kid in Junior's eyes. Thus, Junior thinks Tony intends to concede power, not confer a title.

What follows in their exchange only highlights this. When Junior asks "You speak for the captains?" he intends to ask whether Tony is the spokesperson for all the captains, but the locution "speak for" can imply that one who speaks for another does so with authority as a decision-maker, not merely as a spokesperson. The contrast is the same as that between the way the White House Press Secretary speaks for the President and the way the President speaks for the White House. In the former case, the spokesperson is a mouthpiece; in the latter case, the speaker is the authority whom others follow. Junior takes Tony to mean that he is the mouthpiece for the captains, but of course Tony is a spokesperson in the second sense—what he says the other captains will follow. Tony even suggests this in his response to Junior's question; rather than saying, "I do speak for the captains," he says he *can* speak for them, implying that he speaks for them not only in this matter, but also in others. This subtlety escapes Junior's notice, as he continues to believe that he wields full power as boss.

Richie Aprile uses language to subordinate himself to Junior in "Toodle-Fucking-Oo." Junior is under house arrest, and Tony has been distancing himself from day-to-day business to protect himself as acting boss. Richie and Junior take this distance as aloofness or self-importance, which meets with their mutual disapproval. At one point Junior says, "What are you gonna do?," performing the illocution of accepting the hopelessness of the situation, that there is nothing to do about Tony's acquisition of power. An appropriate response to such an acceptance is typically an acknowledgement or commiseration. Richie could say "Yeah" or "Nothing, I guess." Instead, Richie's response is an offer—he steps forward to Junior and says, "Whatever you tell me." By doing so he treats Junior's acceptance as a direct question, rather than as an indirect commiseration. It's not that Richie doesn't recognize Junior's illocution; it's that he intentionally responds to it as if it were a different illocution to make his point. Richie's utterance surprises and pleases (both perlocutions) Junior, who can't help but think of it as an offer to kill Tony, since the offer comes on the heels of Junior and Livia's failed attempt to have Tony killed. To clarify his illocution, Richie adds, "You tell me this is the way it is, then so be it. You tell me otherwise, I'm yours, Junior. Whatever, whoever. You just say it." The offer to do Junior's bidding is clear, and it establishes the relationship of authority and subordinate between Junior and Richie, at least for the time being.

The Waste Management Business

More than just power relationships are affected by the characters' use of language. Again, because of their illegal nature, business transactions must be carried out without documentation. This makes the speech of these mobsters particularly important, since agreements and decisions are conveyed by spoken word. Such emphasis on speech requires a proportionately heavy emphasis on honor and loyalty, since there is no evidence of such agreements and decisions beyond what is said. For the utterances to carry weight, all involved parties must abide by what is said. In a typical case, Tony meets with Bobby Bacala, Uncle Junior's henchman, in "Do Not Resuscitate." Tony has become boss, and explains to Bobby what part of the business Junior may keep. He adds, "As far as the rest of everything Junior owns? It's now mine." His illocution here expresses his decision, and with his utterance, he takes control of most of Junior's business. As boss of the family, he has the power to do this. Notice that it is when Tony speaks that Junior's business is transferred to him, not when papers are signed or property is conveyed to Tony. Again, the illegal nature of mob activity requires that as little evidence as possible remains of their business dealings. The evidence of business deals remains in the memories of the involved parties, and those parties are sworn to remain loyal to the family.

In "Fortunate Son," we see the ritual that is meant to ensure that loyalty—Christopher becomes a made man. Tony explains the importance of loyalty by saying, "Once you enter this family, there's no getting out. This family comes before everything else. *Everything.* Before your wife and your children and your mother and your father. It's a thing of honor." The deal is sealed by Christopher reciting these words: "May I burn in hell if I betray my friends." This locution, in these circumstances, suffices to confirm (induct into the family of made men) Christopher. The locution is similar whether Christopher utters these words or Jackie Jr. does, but Jackie Jr. was never in the right circumstance with the right people to be able to perform the illocution of becoming a made man.

Once the ceremony finishes, a party is thrown in honor of the newly made guys, and Paulie sits down to talk with Christopher:

> PAULIE: You've been doing really good this year with the sports book.
> CHRIS: Yeah, it's been good.
> PAULIE: I'm gonna give it to you my boy, it's yours.
> CHRIS: I was wondering what it was gonna be.
> PAULIE: You're a made guy now. It's your turn to make some real money and I get to relax a little. Your only problem in life now is you give me ten points of your take every settle-up day. Other than that you got no problem. My only problem in life, I gotta kick my points to that man over there (points to Tony). On it goes, this thing of ours.

It is the speech act itself, "I'm gonna give it to you my boy, it's yours," which constitutes the transfer of the sports book from Paulie to Christopher. Of course, he owes Paulie a cut of the earnings, and Paulie owes Tony a cut of what he gets as well. The agreement is made under the conditions Paulie sets. This is typical for such business transactions.

Madre

It's not only within the mob family that language is used in such ways. One of the shrewdest and most indirect speakers is Tony's mother, Livia. Although she doesn't officially wield power in the family business, she pulls the strings behind the scenes by manipulating people, especially her brother-in-law, Junior. In "Pax Soprana," Junior has become boss of the family, and visits Livia at her retirement home, Green Grove:

LIVIA: How's your Jewish friend?
JUNIOR: Hesh? What about him?
LIVIA: Who ever heard of a Jew riding horses?
JUNIOR: He owns a horse farm.
LIVIA: Ehhh (swats at air dismissively).
JUNIOR: He's Tony's friend, not mine. What do you got against him anyway?
LIVIA: Who, me? Nothing. Johnny liked him. And my son thinks every word that comes out of his mouth is pure gold.
JUNIOR: Are you telling me that since I'm the new boss I should tax Hesh? Boy, Anthony must've really gotten under your collar. Admit it. You're looking to crack his caglioni for putting you in here.
LIVIA: I don't know what you're talking about.

In this scene, we find Livia manipulating Junior by performing certain speech acts. The locutionary acts are relatively straight-forward. It is the illocutions and perlocutions that are difficult to identify, which leads Junior to conclude that Livia is advising him to tax Hesh. There may be more direct ways for Livia to bring about what she desires, but that is not her character, and had she said simply, "You ought to tax Hesh" to Junior it probably wouldn't have had the intended effect anyway. As it is, her veiled way of conveying the message to Junior is effective enough; Junior demands two percent of Hesh's income and $500,000 in back taxes. Livia's illocutionary act is advising, though the locution itself doesn't make the illocution clear at all. A naïve observer would identify Livia's illocutionary act as one of informing, namely informing Junior of her late husband's and son's opinions of Hesh. Junior recognizes her intention, how-ever, and acts accordingly. Once Junior reveals that he has recognized Livia's intention, she denies that she intends to advise him so as to protect herself.

This is only the prelude to Livia's more insidious way of getting Junior to put a contract out on her son. In "I Dream of Jeannie Cusamano," Tony hears an FBI tape of his mother's conversations with Junior. Livia says, "A psychiatrist. He's been seeing one for a while now. God only knows what he says. He must've really taken me for an idiot." Here Livia plants the seed that will result in Junior ordering the hit on Tony. The mention of a psychiatrist in this context raises the question in Junior's mind of whether Tony is revealing family secrets to outsiders. If he is, he is a rat, a transgression punishable by death. Livia's illocution here is a warning, and although she talks as if she is worried about what Tony will tell the psychiatrist about her, she must know that that is not what will worry Junior. The tape continues with Livia saying, "My cousin Kiki after he had his lobotomy, looked exactly like my son, empty, a shell. Better Kiki had died than go on living like that, that's what his own mother always used to say." Here Livia's illocution may appear to be to inform or remind Junior of her cousin, but her real illocution is either to permit Junior to kill Tony or express her desire that Tony be killed. Her direct comparison between Kiki and Tony, and her acknowledgement that Kiki's mother believed he would be better off dead lead Junior to conclude that Livia is at the very least comfortable with, and possibly desires, her son dead. So her utterance is at least an act of permission, and maybe even an expression of her desire, to kill her own son.

The last excerpt Tony hears on the tape is this:

JUNIOR: What are you talking about, meetings? Who for Christsake, Livia?

LIVIA: All of them! Raymond, Larry . . .

JUNIOR: Three of my capos have their mothers in this place? If this is true, Livia, you know what I . . . I mean I'm the boss for Christsake, if I don't act, blood or no (stops) . . . I have to.

Again, Livia's locution seems to be straightforward enough, but given the effect it has on Junior, and the fact that Livia knows well enough what effect it will have on him, she must intend the illocution to be other than the simple imparting of information.

In fact, by saying what she says she also persuades Junior to order the hit. The act of persuasion is a perlocution of Livia's, one that is quite successful. When Tony hears the tape, he knows what his mother did in saying what she did. Even though he doesn't want to believe that his own mother wants him dead, he recognizes her intention. This recognition of Livia's intention on both Tony's and Junior's parts is what ensures the successful communication of her illocutions, and in general those who know a speaker best are the most successful at recognizing such intentions. Livia conspired with Junior, not in any clear, explicit manner, but it was a conspiracy nonetheless.

Livia occupies a position of power, but not like her male relatives. Her power does not allow her to issue orders or make decisions for the family. Those illocutions are beyond her power. Instead, the illocutions she performs are those of informing, warning, advising, and the like. But those illocutions are often combined with perlocutions such as convincing, persuading, and motivating. Because she cannot order or decide, she must exercise her power through more indirect means than even her mob counterparts, who themselves keep their speech indirect to stay out of trouble with the law. Livia needs to stay out of trouble with her family members, which means that she has to manipulate them to get what she wants.

This Show of Ours

We have briefly analyzed a few of the speech acts found in *The Sopranos*. The show is full of such exchanges between characters, from hits ordered (on Jimmy Altieri, Richie Aprile, Carmine, and others) to business deals (such as the many negotiations about the Waterfront Esplanade project) to the countless times Tony issues orders to his biological family which are subsequently ignored (he often speaks to Meadow, A.J., Carmela, Janice, and his mother as he would to his mob subordinates, to humorously little effect). And at times, when things get difficult in Tony's life and we viewers get drawn into his world, we find ourselves trying to comprehend the characters' intentions so as to better understand their speech acts. After Ralphie's son is injured ("Whoever Did This") he apologizes to Rosalie Aprile for not being there for her after Jackie Jr.'s death. Is Ralphie sincere? Are his locutions to be read as illocutions such as apologies for his past and promises to be a better man? Or is he putting on an act, the way he did with Tracee, the Bada-Bing! stripper, just before he killed her in "University?" These and similar questions entice us to keep watching. And though it's hard enough for the characters to recognize each others' intentions, trying to do it ourselves keeps us coming back to *The Sopranos*.

15

Is Tony Soprano Self-Blind?

RICHARD GREENE

An important storyline that runs throughout *The Sopranos* focuses on Tony Soprano's arduous quest for self-knowledge. Through his therapy sessions with Dr. Jennifer Melfi, Tony attempts to gain knowledge of his character, motivations, and attitudes or intentional states in order to stop having panic attacks and improve his overall mental health. Intentional states are mental states that are *about* something. For example, my worry that *my dog Scout will jump over the fence* is a state that is *about* my dog (in other words, my worry takes Scout as its object). Similarly, my belief that *the Giants will win the World Series someday* is a belief *about* the Giants.

Two claims stand at the forefront of philosophical writings on self-knowledge: Socrates's injunction that one should "know thyself," and Descartes's claim that humans have an infallible and direct access to the contents of their own minds. If Descartes is correct, meeting Socrates's injunction (at least with respect to certain forms of self-knowledge, such as knowledge of what one thinks, feels, desires, or believes) should not be very difficult. But most present-day philosophers working on issues in self-knowledge deny Descartes's claim. They don't dispute that people have direct access to what's in their own minds, but they do dispute that knowledge gained in this way is infallible.

I come to know the contents of my own mind in a way that is different from the way I might come to know the contents of someone else's mind. For example, I come to know that *I'm sad about the death of Pie-O-My* by going through some process of introspection—I consult my feelings, as it were. On the other hand, I might come to find out that *you are sad about the death of Pie-O-My* by observing what you say or what you do after you hear about it. So it appears that at least part of what Descartes is claiming must be correct: we do have direct access to the contents of our own minds. The part of Descartes's theory that contemporary philosophers object to is the claim that access to our own mental states is infallible. That is, they say that we can possibly be mistaken about one's own mental states.

Assuming that Descartes's critics are correct—that we might be mistaken about one's own mental states and processes—two issues are raised: the issue of precisely how one might be mistaken about one's mental states and processes and the issue of how self-knowledge should be understood.

Just how could a person be mistaken about his or her own mental states and processes? Well, he or she (1) might simply be in a state of denial, or (2) might fail to have knowledge of the sources or motivations of his or her behavior (and by extension of his or her overall character), or (3) might fail to have knowledge of intentional mental states.

Regarding our second issue, how we should understand self-knowledge, recent discussion of this question by philosophers shows that there are two rival views or theories of what self-knowledge is, which we can call the *perceptual model* and the *constitutive model.*

In the perceptual model, we know ourselves, or become aware of our own mental states and processes, by some sort of inner sense, by looking inwardly at what is going on in our minds. In the constitutive model, no "observation" is necessary. For instance, if I am in fact fearful of being whacked by Tony, then (so says the constitutive model) I'm aware than I'm fearful of being whacked by Tony. I don't have to do any "observing." It's just part of being fearful that I know I'm fearful, and the same applies to being elated, being vaguely anxious, being in love, or being puzzled by the plot line of a TV show. In short, if I'm in a mental state then I'm aware of it, and if I'm aware of being in a mental state, then I'm in that mental state.

In this chapter I'm going to take a close look at a handful of episodes in the lives of Tony Soprano, Dr. Jennifer Melfi , and

Christopher Moltisanti (Tony's nephew). This will illustrate the various ways in which one can fail to have self-knowledge. It will bring out some of the differences between the perceptual and constitutive models, and it will help me to explain why I think the perceptual model is better than the constitutive model.

The Perceptual and Constitutive Models of Self-Knowledge

Before turning to the cases in *The Sopranos*, let me say a bit more about the two models of self-knowledge. According to the perceptual model, self-knowledge is the result of "cognitively viewing" one's mental states. On this view one has a privileged access to one's mental states by means of some form of inner sense. This model is thought to parallel our perception of everyday external objects like plates of ravioli or automatic pistols. Just as I might use vision to view objects in the room that I'm presently in, I might also use my "inner sense" to "view" the contents of my mind (such as my beliefs, desires, fears). In simple terms, I can look into my mind and see what it contains.

Constitutive theories of self-knowledge, on the other hand, hold that self-knowledge is constitutive of mental states. Being aware that one is in a mental state is a necessary condition for being in a particular mental state. According to the constitutive theory, to have a second-order belief (a belief about a belief) is just to have a first-order belief about something and be rational (that is, to believe that thing while meeting certain background conditions). Thus, constitutive theories are so called because the second-order belief is literally constituted by the first-order state (again, provided that certain background conditions of rationality are met). On this view there is no "inner sense" or "cognitive viewing."[1] So, for example, according to the constitutive view if Tony Soprano believes that Jimmy Altieri is a rat and Tony is being rational in forming this belief, then Tony also believes that he believes that Jimmy is a rat.

---

[1] Akeel Bilgrami puts the matter as follows: "There is *a* clear sense in which, unlike the case of ordinary perception, there can be no exceptions to the claim that if someone believes that he believes that p, then he believes that p, and vice versa." Akeel Bilgrami, "Self-Knowledge and Resentment," in *Knowing Our Own Minds*, edited by Crispin Wright, Barry C. Smith, and Cynthia Macdonald. (Oxford: Oxford University Press, 1999), p. 211.

One worry that defenders of the constitutive view have about the perceptual model is that it allows for brute error (errors in judgment that "do not result from any sort of carelessness, malfunction or irrationality on our part"[2]). Beliefs about intentional states (second-order beliefs) are considered, by defenders of the perceptual model, to be the result of reliable, but not infallible, causal processes. So, according to the perceptual model, just as one may be mistaken when one forms a belief about the external world that is based on perception, one may be mistaken when one forms a belief about one's own intentional states. For example, when Tony looks inward to see how he feels about Jimmy being a rat, it is entirely possible that he may be mistaken about how he really feels about it. Defenders of the constitutive model, while in some cases denying infallibility (the view that one cannot be mistaken when one forms beliefs about one's own mental states), reject the possibility of brute error.

By way of summary, since our primary concern is the ways in which one can fail to have self-knowledge, we can take the perceptual model as holding that failures of intentional state knowledge occur as a result of brute error. The constitutive model holds that failures of intentional state knowledge occur as a result of carelessness, malfunction, or irrationality, but there can be no brute error because there are no causal processes (such as inner perceptual processes) to break down.

Fallibilism and Denial

We can now turn our attention to the three ways in which one can fail to have self-knowledge. As mentioned above, one way in which one might fail to have self-knowledge or be mistaken about one's mental states and processes is by being in a state of denial. Denial is a state in which one's unconscious mental processes cause one to fail to recognize some unpleasant aspect of external reality. Typically denial occurs as a means of eliminating some anxiety-producing emotional conflict.

As Season Two of *The Sopranos* begins, Tony's close friend and fellow Mafia family member Big Pussy Bonpensiero has been arrested for selling heroin and has agreed to become a

---

[2] Tyler Burge, "Individualism and Self-Knowledge." *The Journal of Philosophy* LXXXV, 11, 1988, p. 657.

police informant. That Pussy is "wearing a wire" should have been readily apparent to Tony by the end of Season Two. All the signs were there: Pussy disappeared for a long time right after Tony had asked Paulie Walnuts (a third member of the Soprano crime family) to check him for a wire; Pussy offered an extremely implausible explanation for his prolonged disappearance; Pussy had been asking Tony questions about the details of mob activities in which he otherwise would not have been interested; Pussy wasn't asked to provide the police with a statement about a crime in which Tony and "his husky friend" had been identified (Pussy, being quite husky, would have been the obvious choice for questioning); and Pussy's being labeled as an informant by corrupt police detective Vin Makazian had never been disconfirmed.

On some level Tony *knew* that Pussy had turned police evidence, but Tony failed to know that he knew. Tony's conscious knowledge of his subconscious awareness of Pussy's betrayal emerged during a strange dream sequence (induced by bad Indian food) in which Pussy's voice, emanating from a dead fish (undoubtedly a reference to Luca Brasi's swimming with the fishes in *The Godfather*), tells him, "You passed me over for promotion, Ton. You knew" ("Funhouse"). So Tony had all the relevant information and his behavior certainly indicated that he had knowledge, but he was in a state of denial.

Fallibilism and Knowledge of Motivation

When Socrates adjures us to know ourselves he is commanding us to have self-knowledge of our own characters—to have knowledge of the things that motivate us. Knowledge of motivation is fundamentally different from knowledge of intentional states in that it is not something to which one is thought to have a direct or privileged access. In the simplest cases, one examines what one was thinking at the time one performed an action and then reasons from there to an underlying motivation. In more complex cases one must examine both thoughts and behaviors, perhaps over an extended period of time, to draw a conclusion about what motivated a particular action. It is generally with the latter that failures of self-knowledge occur. A couple of incidents from the season two nicely exemplify this phenomenon.

In "The Happy Wanderer," Tony receives an SUV from a friend of the family, Davey Scatino, who owes Tony money that he borrowed and subsequently lost in a poker game that Tony hosted. Tony, in turn, gives the SUV to his daughter, Meadow. The truck originally belonged to Davey's son, Eric, who happens to be one of Meadow's closest friends. Meadow, of course, is offended by Tony's gesture and doesn't want the truck. Meadow's rejection of Tony's kind gesture drives him into a rant: "Everything this family has comes from the work I do . . . A grown man made a wager. He lost. He made another one. He lost again. End of story. So take that high moral ground and sleep in the fucking bus station if you want." At this point it would appear that Tony was motivated by kindness to give Meadow the truck and became irate upon her rejecting his generosity.

In "Full Leather Jacket," Tony discusses this incident with Dr. Melfi. He states that he must have known that Meadow would realize how Tony got the truck and "freak out." Dr. Melfi asks him why he gave it to her, to which Tony replies, "I don't know. For all these years I've been shielding her and protecting her from certain truths. So now what? I want to rub her nose in it?" Dr. Melfi offers an alternative explanation. "Meadow's going to be going away to college next year—leaving the nest . . . maybe you were preparing her for reality." The question of Tony's motivation in this case is never quite resolved. Tony and the audience are left wondering whether he ultimately wanted to perform an important fatherly act or lash out at his daughter's indignation about the way he makes a living.

In "From Where to Eternity," Tony and Dr. Melfi are discussing Christopher's near death experience (Christopher spent several hours in a coma after having been shot by two young gangsters wanting to build a reputation for themselves). Christopher claims to have visited Hell. Tony tells Melfi that he (Tony) will not end up in Hell, as he is a soldier, and that Hell is for degenerate types (such as people who kill for no good reason). Tony considers himself a good hardworking person who is just getting his piece of the action—a piece of the action out of which Italian American immigrants were screwed. Melfi, for the first time in her professional relationship with Tony, lashes out him in a judgmental way. "What do poor Italian immigrants have to do with you and what happens every morning you step out of bed?" Melfi, on discussing this incident with *her* psychiatrist, Dr. Elliot Kupferberg, asks, "Was I insensitive? And, perhaps, did I do it deliberately? Do I hate him?" Melfi is clearly angry with herself, but she has no clear idea what motivated her action.

Fallibilism and Knowledge of Intentional Mental States

The question of how self-knowledge with respect to intentional states is to be understood is a controversial one. The two views we're looking at—the perceptual model and the constitutive model—each embrace fallibilism, but they differ in their treatment of it. In this section I want to look at four incidents from *The Sopranos* in which a failure of self-knowledge occurs. The way these incidents are treated by each of the models of self-knowledge will provide some reason for favoring the perceptual model. I'll begin with two cases that both theories are able to handle with relative ease.

In "The Legend of Tennessee Moltisanti," Christopher, after failing to be named in a television report which identified Soprano crime family members who soon may be indicted, performs two reckless and unwise actions: he shoots a shopkeeper in the foot, and he digs up a person that he shot and killed some months before (Christopher is worried that he left some damning evidence behind). Christopher is informed by Tony that his behavior indicates a desire to get caught. So Christopher is in an intentional state of which he has no knowledge (prior to Tony informing him of his being in the state).

Throughout season two, Dr. Melfi becomes increasingly afraid of Tony. She doesn't recognize the fear right away, but still exhibits fear behavior: her overall consumption of alcohol increases; she begins drinking before her sessions with Tony; her body language is frequently that of a frightened person while Tony is speaking to her. In the second season finale ("Funhouse"), she says to Tony, "I became frightened of you; maybe I should have seen that clearer in the beginning." Like Christopher, Dr. Melfi was in an intentional state of which she was not aware.

Both of these cases can be handled with relative ease by our two theories of self-knowledge. Proponents of the perceptual model will argue that in both cases self-knowledge failed to occur because the "inner sense" simply was not employed. Christopher simply didn't engage in the kind of introspection necessary to make him aware of his *desiring* to get caught, and Dr. Melfi didn't engage in the kind of introspection necessary to make her aware of her *fearing* Tony. Eventually their behavior made them aware of their intentional states (although in the case of Christopher, it was Tony's observing Christopher that lead to his being aware). Proponents of the constitutive view will tell a very similar story about these cases, albeit one that doesn't make reference to an "inner sense." Recall that on the constitutive view, failures of self-knowledge occur as a result of carelessness, malfunction, or irrationality. If we take careless-ness to include simply not attending to or reflecting on one's mental states, then both Christopher and Dr. Melfi exhibited carelessness. According to the constitutive view, if either Christopher or Dr. Melfi thought about the way they were feel-ing, they would have recognized their respective desire and fear.

To illustrate the essential difference between the perceptual model and the constitutive model, we need to look at cases in which the person who fails to have self-knowledge of inten-tional mental states is attending to his or her mental states in the appropriate way. The constitutive model is committed to the view that if one attends to his or her mental states in a careful and rational fashion and no malfunction occurs, then there can be no failure of self-knowledge. In other words, the constitutive theorist is committed to the view that there can be no brute error when it comes to self-knowledge of intentional states. According to Sydney Shoemaker, in order for the perceptual model to be correct, what he calls "self-blindness" must be a conceptual possibility.[3] A self-blind person is one who has intentional states (such as beliefs and desires), has all the con-cepts associated with those intentional states (such as the con-cept of a belief and the concept of a desire), but only gains knowledge of his or her own mental states via observing his or her own behavior. The sort of brute error that the perceptual model postulates involves self-blindness. A person's being self-blind doesn't mean that he or she is never directly aware of his

---

[3] Sydney Shoemaker, "On Knowing One's Mind," in his *The First-Person Perspective and Other Essays*. (Cambridge: Cambridge University Press, 1996), p. 31.

or her intentional states; rather, if a person ever has an intentional state that he or she is not aware of (and is not careless,
irrational, or malfunctioning in the ways discussed by constitutive theorists), then he or she counts as self-blind.[4]

To see how self-blindness might occur consider an ordinary
case of perception in which someone fails to perceive something upon which he or she is focused. Suppose that in my present visual field each of the following things is occurring: a
waitress is serving me gnocchi; my friend, Vinny, gets whacked;
Vinny's *goomah* spills her drink. Were you to quiz me on everything that happened at precisely the moment that Vinny got
whacked, I may well neglect to report that Vinny's *goomah*
spilled her drink. I clearly saw her spill the drink, but failed to
take notice of it in virtue of my attention turning to Vinny's getting whacked. I wouldn't describe my perceptual faculties as
malfunctioning; in fact, they were doing precisely what they
were supposed to be doing—focusing on the more significant
events. Nor would I characterize myself as being careless in any
sense. So why didn't I notice the *goomah*? I was simply distracted by something more perceptually compelling.

I contend that the same kind of thing can occur when one
examines the contents of one's mind (one's intentional states).
If while attending to one's intentional states one comes across
something that is so "perceptually compelling" that it serves to
mask or hide one's other intentional states, then self-blindness
may result. For example, suppose that I'm in a very precarious
situation (perhaps I'm being fitted with a pair of cement boots).
It's not implausible to suppose that I both desire to be out of the
situation and fear that I might be harmed. I may equally be
aware of both states. On the other hand, my fear may become
so overwhelming that I don't notice that I have a desire to exit
the situation. My fear, in this case, serves to mask my desire or
any other thing I might be thinking or feeling. To the extent that
self-blindness is a possibility, the perceptual model must be
favored over the constitutive model, as the constitutive model
attributes all failures of self-knowledge with respect to intentional states to carelessness, malfunction, or irrationality.

---

[4] Shoemaker provides an argument against the possibility of self-blindness, see
Ibid. pp. 32–42. Discussion of Shoemaker's argument is beyond the scope of
this chapter.

Two cases from *The Sopranos* will serve to support my position that self-blindness, via a masking of one state by another, is a conceptual possibility. In "Everybody Hurts" Tony, upon hearing about the suicide of a former girlfriend, Gloria Trillo, begins to wonder about his role in Gloria's death and whether he is a good friend, in general. When his longtime friend, Artie Bucco, needs a short-term loan, Tony insists on giving him the money. He even gives Artie a rate that is below what he normally charges. Artie's business deal eventually falls through and in virtue of his owing fifty thousand dollars to the mob (combined with his having feelings of failure) Artie attempts suicide. Tony gets Artie to the hospital, and tells Artie not to worry about the loan. He'll recover the money provided that Artie erases Tony's tab (six large) at Artie's restaurant. Tony, at this point, is feeling pretty good about himself as a friend to Artie. In the hospital, however, Artie tells Tony, "You saw this whole thing. You knew exactly what was going to happen. Somebody mentions 50K . . ." Tony later tells Dr. Melfi, "I don't know [whether I saw it]. Is that the kind of person I am?" It is unclear whether Tony knew that he was going to take advantage of Artie, but it is clear that he is not able to "perceive" whether he had such knowledge. Tony's stronger desire to know what kind of friend he is served to mask whether he had knowledge of his own intentions. The perceptual view handles this case correctly. The constitutive view is committed to the position that some sort of carelessness, malfunction, or irrationality occurred. The problem is that there doesn't appear to be any of these things occurring. Tony is attempting, in a direct and rational fashion, to determine what he knew in this instance, and he is unable to do so.

Perhaps the best example of Tony's self-blindness lies in his attitudes toward his mother, particularly during Season One. In "46 Long," Tony clearly exhibits feelings of rage and anger toward his mother, which Dr. Melfi, at one point, asks him to acknowledge. Tony, however, doesn't see that he has these feelings. When Dr. Melfi points out to Tony that his mother "has a difficult time maintaining a relationship with anyone," and that she's "not an ideal candidate for parenthood." Tony responds that "she's a little old lady," and that "she's an old sweetie pie," and most importantly for our purposes, "She's a good woman; she put food on that table every night. I'm the ungrateful fuck because I come here and I complain about her." During another

Season One exchange, Dr. Melfi states, "Your mother has, at the very least, what we call 'borderline personality disorder'." To which Tony replies, "You fucking bitch, that's my mother we're talking about" ("I Dream of Jeannie Cusamano"). While Tony feels anger and rage toward his mother, he is not able to perceive that he has these feelings because they are masked by other feelings that he has—feelings that are stronger or more compelling. Specifically, Tony has been raised to feel that "good boys" don't hate or have negative feelings toward their mothers. Whenever he carefully and rationally attends to his feelings toward his mother, he only perceives the positive feelings, even though his actions and the things he says would indicate that he also has very negative feelings toward his mother. Thus, the constitutive view doesn't appear to correctly handle this case. Tony Soprano is self-blind.[5]

[5] I would like to thank John Collins and William Larkin for helpful comments on this paper.

Vino

Philosophy of Religion: The God of *The Sopranos*

16

Tony Soprano in Hell: Chase's Mob in Dante's *Inferno*

PETER J. VERNEZZE

Midway along the journey of our life
I woke to find myself in a dark wood.
—DANTE ALIGHIERI, *The Divine Comedy*[1]

Tony: Lately, I'm getting the feeling that I came in at the
end. The best is over. ("Pilot")

Dante—not Silvio, but Alighieri, the author of *The Divine Comedy*—will be the focus of this essay. To be more precise, the epic journey through Hell described in the first part of the work, *Inferno*, will serve as the backdrop for a moral and religious exploration of David Chase's masterpiece, *The Sopranos*. Chase has said his show is "all about people who have made a deal with the Devil" (DVD Commentary to "Amor Fou"). Who better than the author of *Inferno* to help us discover the implications of that bargain for its signatories? In this chapter, we will follow Dante through the respective levels of Hell he so richly describes in order to speculate on where various cast members might be interred.[2]

---

[1] *The Divine Comedy. Volume I: Inferno,* translated by Mark Musa (New York: Penguin, 1984), p. 67.
[2] Technically, in Dante's world no one's place in Hell can be assigned before that person is actually dead, since the possibility of eleventh-hour repentance

Preparations for the Journey

A classic of world literature, *The Divine Comedy* tells the story of Dante's travels through Hell, Purgatory, and Paradise. It begins, famously, with a lost Dante encountering the Roman poet Virgil, who offers to guide him "through an eternal place where you will hear desperate cries, and see the tormented shades, some old as Hell itself, and know what second death is, from their screams."[3] Not surprisingly, Dante is a bit reluctant to join in. But informed by Virgil of the Divine origin of their mission, Dante regains his courage and consents.

Before we begin our descent into the underworld, let's review the moral geography of the terrain. Dante divides Hell into three main regions: the Incontinent, the Violent, and the Fraudulent. Although in Dante's eyes each of these groups has "lost the good of the intellect,"[4] they have done so in varying degrees and are punished with corresponding severity. Incontinence, which consists of knowing the better but doing the worse, "offends God least, and merits the least blame."[5] The sinners in this group are consigned to Circles Two through Five. The next level contains those who are guilty of one form or another of violence, including (but not limited to) murder. These sinners are confined to Circle Seven. Finally, the most controversial element of Dante's moral scheme places those guilty of fraud and deception in the lowest levels, Circles Eight and Nine, below even the murderers. Why is Dante so hard on fraud and deception? "While both [violence and fraud] are sins that earn the hate of Heaven, since fraud belongs exclusively to man, God hates it more, and, therefore, far below, the fraudulent are placed and suffer the most."[6] Animals commit violence; only man deceives. Just as Aristotle defined reason as the distinctly human function that constitutes our greatest good, so Dante

---

or deathbed conversion must always remain open in a universe pervaded by God's grace and mercy. Hence we can only install with certainty in the afterlife those who have already met an untimely demise in the series (no small number to be sure). Any of the other characters could undergo a change of heart and be saved; personally, however, I wouldn't count on it.

[3] Musa, p. 71.
[4] *Ibid.*, p. 90.
[5] *Ibid.*, p. 170.
[6] *Ibid.*, p. 169.

views fraud and deception as the greatest corruption of this faculty and hence as our greatest evil.[7]

Level One: The Sins of Incontinence

Dante's first encounter with sin occurs in the Second Circle of Hell, which contains the souls of the lustful. In one of the most powerful episodes of the entire *Comedy*, Dante confronts Franscesca de Rimini, who relates in emotional detail her affair with her brother-in-law Paolo, which came to a violent end when her husband discovered the two *in flagrante delicto* and slaughtered them both. Just as they were once swept up by their love, so now the two condemned souls (like all of those in the Second Circle) are blown about for eternity by gusty winds. Will anyone in *The Sopranos* suffer a similar fate?

Clearly *The Sopranos* contains more than its share of illicit relationships, primarily between the various mob members and their *goomahs* (mob mistresses). But it is doubtful that any of these affairs will land the perpetrators in the realm of the lustful. Keeping in mind what the sin entails, we recall that those condemned to the Second Circle are first and foremost guilty of the sin of incontinence: they know what they are doing is wrong yet do it anyway. But this hardly fits the description of the relationships with the *goomahs*, since neither the husbands nor the wives perceive anything amiss about the whole situation. To the husbands, these mob mistresses are a part of the lifestyle, a tradition passed down through generations. Although it is not as formalized as in the old days when you used to take your wife out on Friday and your *goomah* on Saturday—or was it the other way around? ("Mergers and Acquisitions"), the banal acceptability of this relationship becomes especially clear, for example, when we witness the men openly discuss the gifts they bought their *goomahs* for Christmas in the same way they

---

[7] To fill in the gaps, the first level contains what are generally referred to as the virtuous pagans, those who were unfortunate enough to live before the time of Christ or outside the reign of Christendom. Despite the merit of these individuals, they must reside in eternal limbo, not enduring any positive suffering but deprived forever of the presence of God. The sixth level contains the heretics, whose sin does not really fit into Dante's schema but who must be accounted for anyway.

might talk about what they got their kids ("To Save Us All from Satan's Power"). There is no sense among the men that anyone is sinning. But the wives take essentially the same attitude. Carmela declares to confirmed schnorer and family priest Father Phil Intintola that she long ago accepted the affairs as a form of masturbation to lighten her workload ("Pax Soprano") and resignedly informs the soon to be married Janice that it won't be long before she'll have to accept a *goomah* ("The Knight In White Satin Armor"). Nor is Carmela the exception. Whether it is sympathizing with the plight of Hillary Clinton ("Amor Fou") or commenting knowingly that the recently widowed Bobby Bacala was the only one who didn't have a *goomah* ("Christopher"), it is clear the wives have accepted infidelity as part of the bargain. Since the men neither perceive themselves as wrongdoers nor are perceived by their wives as engaged in indiscretion, we will be unable to deposit anyone among the lustful (except, perhaps, Father Phil).

Next, Dante ventures into the Third Circle of Hell where the souls of the gluttonous lie in mud and are besieged by the elements. Here we seem to be on more congenial territory. For the boys certainly like their gabagool, no one more than Junior's personal assistant Bobby Bacala. But it is Johnny Sack's wife, Ginny, who takes the cake (and eats it too) when it comes to gluttony. Her weight is the butt of a joke that causes a rift between Johnny and Tony and almost leads to Johnny's assassination, an event that is short-circuited when Johnny returns home and discovers Ginny slumped over a stash of candy bars, a sight which causes him to delay what would have been a fateful trip ("The Weight"). Unless she mends her ways, Ginny will almost certainly wind up among the gluttonous.

The realm of the incontinent is rounded out with the greedy and spendthrifts in the Fourth Circle, and with the angry and the sullen in the Fifth. Although various characters would qualify for placement in one or the other of these territories, Dante generally (though not always) deposits individuals at their greatest level of culpability, so that one who hoards money or has a particularly large appetite but whacks someone will find himself in the realm of the violent rather than the incontinent. Before leaving, however, we need to consider a final, difficult case: that of Carmela.

The level of Carmela's culpability can certainly be debated, but it is abundantly clear that she is no innocent. Early on in the series she confesses to her priest that she believes Tony has committed "horrible acts," but that she has turned a blind eye to his iniquities because she wanted material comforts for herself and her children: "I have forsaken what is right for what is easy," she confesses to Father Phil ("College"). She admits to an even greater level of cognizance of the situation after Chris is shot, prefacing a prayer on his behalf with the admission that "we have chosen this life in full awareness of the consequences of our sin" ("From Where To Eternity"). Her own suspicions about the level of moral danger involved in remaining in her marriage are confirmed when a psychiatrist directs Carmela to, "Go home and pack. Leave the state . . . take only your children and go." When she tries to defend Tony, he merely tells Carmela that "you can never say . . . you haven't been told" ("Second Opinion").

Clearly, Carmela is aware that staying married to Tony is not without moral consequences. As she tells another priest, she is certain that if she dies she will never be with God in eternity ("Amor Fou"). But it is just this practice of knowing something is wrong but doing it anyway that is the defining concept of the sin of incontinence. Because, then, she is willing to remain in a marriage that she realizes endangers her soul—and even though Dante has no particular region designated for this transgression—we must, I fear, assign Carmela to the realm of the incontinent. True, by the end of Season Four she has separated from Tony. But this seems driven more by Tony's shortcomings as a husband than by his activities as a mob boss.[8] As she tells him: "I might actually have gone on, with your cheating and your bullshit, if your attitude around here had been the least bit loving, cooperative, interested" ("Whitecaps"). Moreover, she is still living off Tony's blood money, even having stolen some of it from a secret stash he had hidden in bird seed. The situation is, to say the least, complicated. But it is clear that at the end of season four Carmela's moral fate hangs in the balance.

---

[8] For a different view of Carmela's separation see Chapter 9 of this volume.

Level Two: The Sins of the Violent

Circle Seven is the next major level of Hell. Here, three transgressions are punished: violence to others, violence to oneself, and violence to God. Dante describes the first of these sins as follows: "By violent means a man can kill his neighbor or wound him grievously; his goods may suffer violence by arson, theft, or devastation."[9] Although this is probably where he will wind up, this is not exactly Christopher Moltisanti's vision of Hell as an Irish bar that never closes. Instead, these perpetrators are set in a river of boiling blood, their depth to be determined by the amount of violence, with those who have killed and plundered more placed deeper in the hot liquid. No one who watches the show needs to be reminded that it contains more than its share of killing, wounding, arson, theft, devastation, as well as a few other forms of mayhem Dante could not have even imagined. According to one web site, the official body count through season four stands at thirty-nine.[10] It's a fair bet you can find Paulie, Ralphie, Richie, and most of your favorites lodged here.

The second tier of the violent contains "suicides, self-robbers of your world, or those who gamble all their wealth away."[11] In one of the more innovative punishments of *Inferno*, the members of this sorry circle are transformed into trees, retribution for their decision to abandon human form. The show offers two notable suicides. Lt. Vin Makazian, a "degenerate fucking gambler with a badge" who served as Tony's sometimes informant before being busted in a prostitution raid and "doing a header" off a bridge, and Gloria Trillo, the Mercedes saleswoman who kills herself after a brief stint as one of Tony's unstable mistresses (does he have any other kind?).

Before leaving the Seventh Circle, let's pause briefly at its Third Level, which houses the souls of those who have committed violence against nature, the most prominent sin here being sodomy. Most relevant to this topic is the show's attitude towards homosexuality, which can best be described as hovering somewhere between silence and hostility. Indeed, these

---

[9] Musa, p. 169.
[10] http://www.the-sopranos.com.
[11] Dante, *Divine Comedy*, p. 169.

guys who spend a lot of time together certainly have a thing about, well, guys who spend a lot of time together. From Tony's comment to Meadow about all the Ph.D.'s in Berkeley who have a "Nobel Prize in fudge packing" ("Full Leather Jacket") to Richie Aprile's hitting Janice for saying it is no big deal if his son is gay—a punch he certainly wished he hadn't thrown ("The Knight in White Satin Armor")—one searches in vain for any suggestion that this lifestyle would be acceptable. Even Carmela gets into the act, responding to Meadow's homosexual interpretation of Melville's *Billy Budd* by decrying "this gay thing pervading our society" ("Eliose"). And don't forget Junior's concern that his expertise at oral sex be kept a secret lest his sexual orientation be called into question ("Boca"). So, for better or worse, on at least one point the boys seem to be in agreement with Church doctrine.

Level Three: Fraud and Deception

Although constituting only two of the nine circles of Hell, the discussion of the sins of fraud comprises nearly half of *Inferno*. This is surely an indication of the seriousness that Dante attached to these transgressions. We might initially be inclined to perceive Dante's rating fraud as morally worse than murder to be a medieval relic. But rather than trying to correct Dante's ranking of sins, I believe we can learn from it. Indeed, if Enron and the other corporate accounting scandals have shown us anything, it is that those who use their wile and cunning to take advantage of others can have a much more destructive influence on society than those who commit an isolated murder. Hence, the suggestion at several points in the series that there exists a moral parity between mob maneuvers and so-called legitimate business practices may in fact find a sympathetic ear in Dante. As a dinner guest of the Cusamanos confesses: "Some of the things I see in the boardroom, I don't know if I'd make a distinction" ("A Hit Is a Hit"). And when Dr. Melfi confronts Tony about his involvement with illegal activities he responds, "What about chemical companies? Dumping all this shit into the rivers and they got all these deformed babies popping up all over the place" ("Down Neck"). But suggesting that there exists a moral equivalency between mob activities and some contemporary corporate behavior does not, of course, let Tony and company off the hook. Rather, the moral to be derived from such observations is that perhaps we should take corporate fraud and deception more seriously than we currently do. Indeed, a little of the Dantean spirit might be just what our justice system needs.

The Eighth Circle of Hell contains the souls of those guilty of what Dante dubs "simple fraud," deception against those with whom one has no special relationship. This region is composed of ten ditches. Here, we only have time to briefly point out a few highlights. In the first ditch are the pimps and panderers, those who take advantage of women. Ironically Dante—Silvio Dante—the manager of the Bada Bing!, the strip club frequented by various gang members, would more than likely be found here among the pimps, running from one demon's whip to another (just as they traded women from one man to another). The list of Janice Soprano's transgressions make it difficult to know exactly what to do with her. Janice's sins run the entire gamut from taking credit for a pan of lasagna she didn't bake in order to help her woo a bereaved Bobby Bacala to shooting her fiancé, and include such high points as a fraudulent disability claim, the theft of a prosthetic leg and, perhaps most unforgivably, naming her son Harpo. But it seems her true gift is to profess or to do one thing while believing something entirely different. Carmela points out the contradiction between her claiming to be a feminist while allowing Richie to hold a gun to her head; her own mother calls her "a real snake in the grass" for pretending to want to care for her but in reality coveting her money; and she even feigns finding Jesus and latches onto a narcoleptic born-again boyfriend in order to break into the Christian contemporary music scene. For this talent, Dante might deservedly place her in the sixth level of the Eighth Circle among the hypocrites who wear dazzling cloaks lined with lead. In the seventh ditch of the Eighth Circle, where thieves undergo a gradual and bizarre transformation into snakes, we will doubtless discover Hesh, Tony's Jewish friend and counselor. As a record producer in the 1960s, Hesh routinely took credit for songs that he did not write and as a result received royalties that rightly belonged to others.

The eighth ditch of the Eighth Circle holds the false counselors, those who gave untrue and deceptive advice to others, and provides the material for a consideration of one of the most complicated moral issues on the show: the status of Tony's therapist, Dr. Jennifer Melfi. In his condemnation of Guido da Montefeltro to the realm of false counselors, Dante has provided us with an important moral lesson to keep in mind on this point. An ex-soldier who late in life joined a monastery, Guido is called out of retirement by Pope Boniface VIII. In return for absolution, Guido advises the Pope on an underhanded but ultimately successful method of capturing the city of Palestrina. Despite his being declared free from moral taint by Boniface, Guido is condemned to Hell. The message is clear: vindication from the relevant authority does not absolve one from moral culpability.

This is precisely the message that Melfi's ex-husband delivers when he warns her of the "cheesy moral relativism" of their shared profession ("The Legend of Tennessee Moltisanti"). Melfi's own therapist questions her motivation for continuing to treat Tony, speculating that it may be more for the thrill than for anything else ("Big Girls Don't Cry"). And though one cannot doubt her sincere commitment to Tony's mental health, in the end any moral assessment of Dr. Melfi will have to answer the question of whether she is doing anything more than aiding Tony in becoming a better mob boss. As he abandons his therapy at the end of season four, Tony informs Melfi that what he has derived from "all that fucking self-knowledge" is "maybe, at the beginning, some strategy" ("Eloise"). To be sure, this single statement is hardly the final word on four years of treatment, and the issue is too complicated to decide here. All I wish to suggest is that in Dante's world, as in any serious moral scheme, judgment will fall on Melfi regardless of the level of Tony's personal growth and regardless of whether she receives the imprimatur of her peers.

In the pit of Hell, the Ninth Circle, are those who have committed complex fraud against individuals with whom they had a special relationship—relatives, country, guests, and superiors. At the absolute bottom, we find a three-headed Lucifer munching on individuals who betrayed their lords and masters. In the center mouth is the greatest traitor of them all, Judas, while stuck in the side orifices are Cassius and Brutus, the assassins of Caesar. With this powerful image, Dante draws together two of the central themes of *The Divine Comedy*, the authority of Church and of State. To usurp these fundamental underpinnings of human

life, the sources of earthly and heavenly order, is in Dante's eyes
to commit the ultimate crime against humanity.

Likewise, the crime family and the nuclear family provide
order and authority in the universe of *The Sopranos*. Indeed,
Tony's troublesome relations with each of these are central
themes. His nuclear family is breaking up—the ducks are leaving home—and he feels like he "came in at the end" with his
crime family. Just so, the attempted assassination of Tony by his
mother and his uncle is an effort to undermine and usurp this
authority: Livia clearly wishes to get rid of Tony as head of the
nuclear family while Junior wants to remove Tony from his leadership role in the crime family. For their efforts at subversion of
the given order (and even though they are not successful) we
must, I think, assign these two to the depths of Soprano Hell.

There is of course one piece of the puzzle still missing: What
about Tony? Where does the leader of it all wind up? We know
that Tony himself does not believe he is going to Hell. Instead,
Tony asserts that Hell will be populated by "the worst people."
Who are the worst? "The twisted and demented psychos who
kill people for pleasure...the degenerate bastards who molest
and torture little kids . . . the Hitlers, the Pol Pots." But not Tony.
He is a soldier. "Soldiers don't go to hell . . . Soldiers kill other
soldiers . . . It's business" ("From Where To Eternity").

Is he correct? Alas, dear reader, I fear that after four seasons
I have grown quite fond of him and cannot quite bring myself
to condemn him to eternal damnation. At this point, you have
all the information you require to pass judgment. Good luck.
And be merciful—but just!

17

"What Kind of God Does This . . . ?"

PETER H. HARE

If God is all-good and all-powerful, why is there evil in the world? Why is there all "this shit," Tony asks Dr. Melfi? Why did God allow Tony's beloved horse Pie-O-My to be horribly burned to death? If God is unlimited in power, he should be able to remove the evil, and if he is unlimited in goodness, he should want to remove it—but he does not. Apparently he is limited in power or goodness, or does not exist at all. This is "the problem of evil" that many have considered a good reason to reject theistic belief in God.

The problem has been formulated in many ways. A basic division exists between those who consider it a *logical* problem and those who consider it an *evidential* problem. The former group thinks that the question is whether logical inconsistency can be found in a set of statements such as: God exists; God is almighty; God is infinitely good; God is all-knowing; evil exists. Theists and atheists alike have increasingly recognized that the logical formulation of the problem is inadequate and that the problem is fundamentally evidential. It is agreed that the existence of *some* evil (the whacking of those who have flipped?) is logically consistent with—even required by—the existence of an all-powerful, all-good God. The crucial question is whether the available evidence shows that some evil (an arrow's brain damage to a 13-year-old boy?) is probably unnecessary. Does this gratuitous (pointless) evil make improbable, though not logically impossible, the existence of a theistic God? Can Father Phil—with the help of his more intellectually gifted brethren—prove to Carmela that *all* the evil in the world is probably necessary?

But how is *evil* to be defined? While it is controversial how evil is to be defined, atheists ("brights," as they prefer to be called today) invite the most gifted theologians to define evil any way they like but argue that some of *that* sort of evil is gratuitous. They argue that there is pointless evil in the world according to any conception of evil that has been proposed.

Irrespective of definitions of evil, both theists and atheists have found it useful to distinguish between *physical* evil and *moral* evil. Physical evil is, for example, the suffering of Jackie Aprile and Uncle Junior from their cancers. Moral evil is such wrongdoing as lying, stealing, torture, and murder. An especially graphic example is Tony's garroting of Fabian Petrulio, former mobster turned informant. Other moral evils are the character traits of deceitfulness, selfishness, and cruelty—and the consequences of such traits. Livia has these character traits in such quirky abundance that it is amusing. Tony is also amply endowed with them (for example his philandering with *goomahs*), but most viewers think he has more redeeming qualities than his mother does. Some evils are not clearly classifiable as solely physical or solely moral. The brain damage done to a child by an arrow seems to be both types of evil. Was the boy's father culpably negligent in not supervising play with bows and arrows, or was this a terrible accident for which no one is responsible?

Any systematic attempt to show that all evil is necessary or justified is traditionally called a theodicy. Although over the centuries a vast theodicist literature has been produced, the basic arguments tend to recur with small variations. The following are some of the arguments designed chiefly to explain physical evil.

By-product of Natural Laws.

Evil is thought to be an unavoidable by-product of natural laws that produce beneficial results overall. God, for example, created laws of human physiology that have the evil effect of Uncle Junior's cancer, but it would be irrational to expect God to suspend these physiological laws by miraculous intervention since intervention would jeopardize our moral fiber and render nature so irregular as to make impossible the use of our reason. A mobster would be at a loss to figure out when to come heavy because of the unpredictability of the behavior of his potential enemies. Critics of this argument point out, however, that God could have created a world with *modified* laws of human physiology that would have produced similar goods (Uncle Junior's skillful practice of cunnilingus) while avoiding many of the evils of this world (making possible Jackie Aprile's recovery from cancer). Even Tony's favorite natural law, "shit runs downhill," could be altered so sewage ran more swiftly downhill and backed up less often.

Punishment for Sin

When Carmela mistakenly believes that she has ovarian cancer, she tells a priest that this disease is God's punishment for the sin of colluding with her husband's corruption. However, it seems highly improbable that all those suffering from ovarian cancer—any more than all those who die in a massive earthquake—have committed sins that merit such punishment. This explanation has fallen out of favor among more sophisticated theists because it requires belief in an outrageous number of sins unknown to everyone except God. Moreover, this explanation conflicts with the belief that God is merciful. "My son's lying in the hospital, hooked up to a machine," Ralph tells Father Phil. "He never did nothin' to nobody . . . I've done things in my life that I shouldn't have done. He's making my son pay for it. That's how he's punishing me." To which Father Phil replies: "God is merciful. He doesn't punish people" ("Whoever Did This"). This is the priest's feeble attempt to undermine Ralph's claim that God is committing the awful injustice of punishing an innocent child for crimes committed by his parent.

A Warning

Men need to be shocked, so the argument goes, into an awareness of God's presence by an awesome display of power. However, painful warnings are often misinterpreted. When Christopher is handcuffed, beaten, and subjected to a mock execution, he "makes number two in his pants" (as Adriana describes it) at the thought that Tony has found out about his supplying Meadow with drugs, when actually it is Junior, not Tony, who is trying to warn him to stay in line. No less are natural calamities like tidal waves a grossly ineffective and callous way for a powerful being to make his presence known. Surely a being both all-good and all-powerful could design a more reliable—and more humane—way to communicate with human beings.

All's Well in God's View

In God's higher morality evil is an illusion, according to this attempted solution. Just as a musical chord heard in isolation may sound dissonant but when heard in context sounds harmonious, so it is with evil. This is the gist of Carmela's remark to Janice about the death of Bobby Bacala's wife: "Karen was a wonderful person. I'm sure God must have his reasons. But sometimes you have to wonder" ("Calling All Cars"). An event seen in isolation is called evil by human beings but seen in relation to all other events is called good by God. Whenever a person judges that "X is evil," she is mistaken. Whatever human beings ordinarily call evil is not evil after all but good according to God's higher morality.

This sort of argument has probably outraged critics more than any other. The reaction of critics is not unlike Tony's reaction to psychiatry: "This psychiatry shit. Apparently what you're feeling is not what you're feeling. And what you're not feeling is your real agenda" ("Pax Soprana"). Doubletalk and more doubletalk. If there really is no evil in the world, then any efforts to remove what we existentially encounter as evil are necessarily morally wrong. Also, the fact that God would allow human beings to be completely deceived about the nature of evil would itself be the most terrible evil He could have permitted. It would be as if in the final episode of the final season of *The Sopranos* it were revealed that from the beginning Tony had secretly rejected *omertà* (the Mafia code of silence) as a value. But the most fundamental objection to this argument is that the concept of God's higher morality has no meaning whatever. If God's higher morality is completely different from our ordinary notions, then this higher morality is completely meaningless, since we have no other notions of good and evil except the ordinary ones. It is as if Tony were to proclaim with great fanfare that he had established a Mafia family without the vow of *omertà*—or a mathematician were to announce to his colleagues that he had drawn a triangle with four sides.

All's Well that Ends Well

Human beings, seeing only short-run consequences, fail to understand that such evils as famines eventually lead to important goods. God, however, seeing long-run consequences, understands that they are good enough to compensate for the evils along the way. For Artie, whose restaurant is burned down by Tony's order, the fire is a disastrous evil, but Tony sees the short-term evil as leading to the greater long-term good of a new and improved restaurant built with the insurance money. This argument does not claim that evil is an illusion; it claims that evil is justified by the long run, not that our ordinary concept of evil disappears because of it. Numerous objections to this type of theodicy have been presented. Even if it should be true that all short-run evils produce long-run goods, all this would prove is that the world is less evil than it would be if short-run evils always produced long-run evils. It would not explain why God permits short-run evils to exist. Could he not have produced the same results with less ghastly short-run evils? If Tony were the *capo d'tutti capi* instead of a simple captain, he could certainly have found another way to prevent a Mafia hit in the restaurant. Surely an all-powerful God could eliminate lots of short-run evils. In using this argument the theist has another difficulty. He or she thinks that if it is *possible* that God arranged the world so that evil always results in long-run good, it is *probable* that he did. Ordinarily, however, we do not consider it legitimate to go from possibility to probability without evidence to bridge the gap, and the evidence we have points in the opposite direction—toward belief that present evils will have predominantly evil long-term results—that organized crime will in the long-term hopelessly corrupt law enforcement agencies. And wouldn't it be just as legitimate to go from the mere possibility that short-run *goods* will result in long-term *evils* to the probability that short-term goods will bring long-term evils in the long run, from the possibility that Carmela's efforts to get Meadow accepted by a top college will lead to long-term evils, to the probability that it will eventually have dire consequences?

Sometimes a sweeping version of the all's-well-that-ends-well explanation of evil is proposed. According to this view, immortality compensates for whatever evil happens to a person in this life. Eternal bliss is thought capable of making worthwhile any amount of suffering along the route to that goal. However, the afterlife argument is far from convincing. It is as if Ralphie, while beating to death the topless dancer pregnant with his own child, had told her that her entrance to heaven was guaranteed. Tracee would have been delighted to hear that she had such a glorious future ahead of her, but she wouldn't have understood why she needed to be beaten so brutally in order to get there.

Character Building

According to this view, the rough edges of the world are necessary for producing spiritually significant beings. In a world without tears there would be no occasion for the production of courage, endurance, charity, and sympathy. But such a world would not miss them since it would have no need for them. Such a world might seem good in prospect but in fact would be very bland—much less desirable than a world that had both evil and the greatness of spiritual growth. Dr. Melfi bluntly rejects this theodicy when she rhetorically asks Tony: "How many people have to die for your personal growth?" ("Guy Walks into a Psychiatrist's Office"). This attempted solution is simply inapplicable to some physical evils, insanity being the most convincing example. At best, it can account only for a small amount of evil and cannot account at all for the maiming of character, which too much evil often produces, or the mass annihilation of people in natural disasters. Moreover, as Melfi suggests, the price paid for spiritual growth even when it does occur is often too high to be justly exacted. The life of even one of her other patients seems an unfair price to pay for Tony's spiritual growth—if we make the dubious assumption that Tony has achieved genuine spiritual growth as her patient. And it is not clear why God, if he is all-powerful, could not have created spiritually significant people in the first place. It is just as logically impossible, so the answer goes, for God to create a spiritually significant being who never experienced suffering as it is for him to create a relaxing form of *agita* or a tender whacking. This answer is plausible as far as certain virtues are concerned. It would be absurd to expect a mobster to develop courage in a world without competing Mafia families and without the FBI. But these negative virtues do not exhaust the spiritual realm. Love, for example Tony's love for Meadow, does not depend for its possibility on the existence and consequences of evil. Finally, if courage, endurance, charity, sympathy, and the like are so spiritually significant, then the evil conditions which foster them should not be mitigated by social, political and legal reforms. RICO should be immediately repealed. Even Dr. Melfi, whose own psychiatrist tells her that she gets a "vicarious thrill" from her mobster patient, does not endorse such justification of suffering, at least not when the pain is visited on her own patients. She thereby reflects the fact that we all have spiritual values we place above the negative ones fostered by extremely trying conditions.

Inherent Depravity

Having considered the more significant proposed solutions of the problem of physical evil, we must now consider explanations of *moral* evil. Moral evil, as has been indicated, entails both debasement of character and the infliction of suffering on fellow creatures. Why does God permit self-damaging and other-damaging behavior? Theists have two major solutions of the problem. One depends upon the specific concepts of an historical religion, namely Christianity, and the other, the free-will solution, is endorsed universally by any believer in God.

According to one version of the Christian tradition, human beings are sinful by nature and deserve eternal punishment. "Our Lord gave his only begotten son to suffer" and die on the cross in order to atone for man's sinfulness and to redeem him for his justly deserved punishment. This is the counsel that Father Phil gives Ralph. The dubiousness of this view is suggested by Livia's behavior after she tried unsuccessfully to have her own son murdered. Tearfully, she says to Junior, "He's my only son" ("Isabella"). Whether done by a Mafia mother or by God, the basic idea of sacrificing a son as good is absurd. Indeed, the difficulties with this view are so numerous that it has ceased being a dominant tradition, though it is sometimes mouthed as a routine piety by less intellectually scrupulous (and more focused on lonely women and food) clergy such as Father

Phil. The first point to notice is that the doctrines of incarnation, atonement, and redemption, even if true, have no value whatever in solving the problem of evil. They would at most provide a grateful release from suffering but would not begin to explain the need for it in the first place. Further, we have already seen the deficiencies in the view that evil is punishment for sins. Lastly, critics point out that it throws serious doubt on the unlimited goodness of God to say he created finite beings that are evil by nature and reap eternal punishment. If human beings are evil by nature—that is, have no chance of choosing between good and evil—then it makes no sense to say they *deserve* punishment. If Tony is correct in saying, "You're born to this shit. You are what you are" ("Down Neck"), then he is powerless to act in ways other than he does, and no one—not even God—is morally justified in punishing him for his acts.

Free Will

Most theologians have recognized that the difficulties of an appeal to the inherent depravity of human beings are so great that they must rely on some version of the free-will solution to the problem of evil. One version is this: God, being omniscient, knew that human beings would willfully choose the wrong sometimes if they had free will, but God granted them free will because not to do so would have produced greater evil. A world with only robots in it would be less good than a world with freely choosing people who sometimes rebel against morality. When Tony wonders whether his life would have been different if his father hadn't been a mobster and consequently whether A.J. is also fated to be a mobster, Dr. Melfi insists that he and A.J. have genuine choices—in America they are free to choose among a wide range of lifestyles despite their family heritage. Clearly Melfi does not believe that the inevitability of evils such as those involved in organized crime means that a mobless world of robots would be preferable.

There are, however, several serious problems for this version of the free-will solution. (1) God could have created a world in the first place where free will, when misused, would not produce such disastrous consequences as in the present one. Couldn't God have created a world in which it was more difficult to choke a person to death? (2) Although it would have been logically impossible for God to *guarantee* the consistently good-and-free acts of human beings, he could have avoided the more ghastly consequences of misused freedom by creating people with a *disposition* to act rightly even though they might choose sometimes to do evil. The latter is all that would be required for the possibility of human freedom and moral rebellion. Though her parents worry about the trouble Meadow gets into (her father teasingly calls her "the Bride of Frankenstein"), they would acknowledge that Meadow's disposition to get into trouble is much weaker than the disposition of lots of young people they know (for instance Jackie). Couldn't God have created more people with Meadow-like dispositions? Yet God did not do so. Such behavior seems to argue against either all-powerfulness or all-goodness. It is insufficient for the theist to reply that God did not create people with a tendency to act rightly because this would preclude the moral growth attendant upon struggle in the face of great odds. This reply misses the point that great evil, rather than causing growth, often stunts and destroys the human soul. Certainly, for example, the evils of the mob environment have had stunting effects on the souls of Sean Gismonte and Matt Bevilaqua (aka Chip and Dale). God, in this view, is doing dreadful things apparently: He creates human beings with free will, some of whom will grow spiritually through great evil, and some of whom will be destroyed completely. How can the former justify God's way in view of the latter? The price is too high to pay. We would consider it immoral to tempt a recovering alcoholic by getting drunk in his presence or to dare a person known to be reckless to do some impossible feat. If Tony and Carmela acted in that way toward their children, it would be considered morally irresponsible, if not insane—if God acts that way, why should we call him moral and omniscient? (3) God could mitigate a particularly terrible result in a stopgap fashion by miraculous intervention. He could have, for example, seen to it that the man who gruesomely raped Dr. Melfi suffered a cerebral accident as he was making plans to rape her. It is not sufficient for the theist to reply that it is likely that God *does* interfere often to prevent terrible consequences (for example, responding to Carmela's prayers by bringing Christopher back from the brink of death) without our knowing it. This reply only terrifies us by suggesting how bad the universe might have been, but helps in no way to explain why it is not better than it is. (4) It is logically possible that human beings having free will should always choose to do wrong, and that even so, a universe of thoroughly evil people with free will (for instance, a world entirely populated with free mobsters or, even worse, a world entirely populated with free Nazis) would be intrinsically better than one of saintly robots. The absurdity of this consequence suggests the falsity of the premises.

Inconclusive?

It is sometimes objected that all any critic can hope to show is that no theodicy has yet successfully solved the problem of evil, not that the problem is insoluble or that all modified theisms are destined to fail. It is always logically possible that a new solution or a new modification of theism will arise that will be successful. This objection has little force. No one denies that success always remains a logical possibility for the religious cosmologist. The question is rather what likelihood is there, in view of the present state of evidence, that success will eventually occur? The answer is that there is not only no evidence for the likelihood of such success but that repeated failures, the recurrence and clustering of criticisms, the permutations of basic moves that have been found wanting, and the slight variations of old solutions count heavily against the likelihood of what no one denies is a logical possibility.

A demand for definitiveness or finality based on exhaustive knowledge is misplaced. If such a demand for exhaustive knowledge is made, no deliberation (such as that in a court of law) would ever arrive at a reasonable conclusion, that is, a conclusion justified beyond a reasonable doubt. To demand finality is to abdicate one's responsibility to make decisions based on a clear preponderance of evidence. Having long suspected that Pussy had turned FBI informant but reluctant to take action because of their special relationship, Tony painstakingly gathers evidence for his guilt. It is not until he finds the wire equipment in a cigar box that he concludes that Pussy has indeed betrayed him. Suspecting Tony of being unfaithful, Carmela finds more and more incriminating signs, but it is not until she gets a phone call from one of Tony's former mistresses that she concludes that he is guilty. These are both reasonable conclusions based on a clear preponderance of evidence, but in neither case is there absolute certainty.

To be sure, there is no *logical* point at which failure to find convincing explanations of evil requires abandonment of belief in God. This is not an all-or-nothing affair. But it does not follow from the fact that the force of such failures is not an all-or-nothing affair that they have only *psychological*, not *evidential*, force. What critics of theodicies have shown is not that some magical point has been passed in the accumulation of explanatory failures, but instead that the failures are so extensive that the likelihood of eventual success is dim. Indeed, atheists can accept a broad notion of confirmation such that some evidence (as in religious experience or in the reports of psychics about the activities of Pussy and Tony) confirms theism as an empirical hypothesis. But if one finds, as critics have, that no solution of the problem of evil is successful, one may fairly conclude that theism is *more* disconfirmed than confirmed by the facts of the world. A broad notion of confirmation, while it makes theism confirmable, also makes the disconfirming evidence of evil that much more obviously overwhelming as compared to the feeble confirming evidence.

Yahweh

Sometimes it supposed that the problem of evil can be solved by adopting one of an indefinitely large number of clearly non-theistic beliefs. Manicheanism, for example, is a religious view almost as old as Christianity according to which two forces, one good and the other evil, battle for control of the world. Satanism is even farther from theism; it explains evil by supposing that an evil being has power over the world—a cosmic Livia perhaps, who exercises "power through powerlessness." Although it is unquestionably possible to believe in evil deities, "solutions" of this type are unsuccessful because they abandon one of the essential tenets of theism, namely, the belief that there is only one deity and that that deity is wholly good. Believing in another non-theism, Gloria tells Tony that "the Buddha preached joyful participation in the sorrows of the world" ("The Telltale Moozadell"). Janice samples lots of non-theistic religions before she hooks up with a man who ponderously repeats "He is risen," when he is not asleep.

Other pseudo-solutions include those in which there is only one God, a deity considered all-good and all-knowing but drastically limited in power. If the deity is sufficiently weak, obviously the problem of evil does not arise—a helpless deity cannot be blamed. To solve the problem in this way is analogous to Carmela "solving" the problem of her husband's infidelity by adopting a radically new definition of 'infidelity'.

In the context of the Sopranos' world there is, however, one form of theism (mistakenly so classified?) that is important to consider as a way of solving the problem of evil—Judaism. According to some interpretations of Jewish theology, the deity is *both* good and evil morally, and, furthermore, much less than omnipotent. Though the existence of a deity with those traits presents numerous other evidential and logical challenges, none of those challenges would correspond to what I have discussed above as the problem of evil. Yet the deity of the Old Testament resonates powerfully with the events and characters of *The Sopranos*. I am not the first to point out that Tony is in many ways the Old Testament deity writ small. Like Tony, Yahweh is a jealous, vengeful ruler who brutally punishes those who betray Him. He has the divine analogue of the "mood swings" that Carmela worries about. The moral justification (or lack thereof) of "smiting" is often little different from the moral status of "whacking." And the Old Testament deity tests and warns his creatures with every bit as much vicious alacrity as Mob bosses test and warn the denizens of their world. Recall how Yahweh ordered Abraham to kill his firstborn son Isaac. How morally different is that procedure from Junior's mock execution of Christopher? And Hebrew patriarchs like Abraham enjoyed concubines with as little moral compunction as Mob bosses have *goomahs*. The similarities between Tony's *admirable* traits and those of the Old Testament deity are equally striking. Both are impressively loving and loyal to the members of their favored tribe or family. Some media commentators are puzzled by how someone as violence-prone as Tony can have such wide and long lasting appeal to audiences—can indeed be *loved*. Is this appeal any more mysterious than the appeal of Yahweh to countless millions for thousands of years?

I look forward to a future episode whose plot is loosely based on the Book of Job—with a tragicomical twist.

Episode Guide

Season One

Season Two

2/7	"D-Girl"
2/8	"Full Leather Jacket"
2/9	"From Where to Eternity"
2/10	"Bust Out"
2/11	"House Arrest"
2/12	"The Knight in White Satin Armor"
2/13	"Funhouse"

Season Three

3/1	"Mr. Ruggerio's Neighborhood"
3/2	"Proshai, Livushka"
3/3	"Fortunate Son"
3/4	"Employee of the Month"
3/5	"Another Toothpick"
3/6	"University"
3/7	"Second Opinion"
3/8	"He Is Risen"
3/9	"The Telltale Moozadell"
3/10	"To Save Us All from Satan's Power"
3/11	"Pine Barrens"
3/12	"Amour Fou"
3/13	"Army of One"

Season Four

4/1	"For All Debts Public and Private"
4/2	"No Show"
4/3	"Christopher"
4/4	"The Weight"
4/5	"Pie-O-My"
4/6	"Everybody Hurts"
4/7	"Watching Too Much Television"
4/8	"Mergers and Acquisitions"
4/9	"Whoever Did This"
4/10	"The Strong, Silent Type"
4/11	"Calling All Cars"
4/12	"Eloise"
4/13	"Whitecaps"

The Family

Jennifer Baker has taught philosophy at Duke University and at UNC—Chapel Hill. She works on ancient eudaimonist theory, arguing that its account of morality is better than that of contemporary ethical theories. Prior to entering academia, Jennifer was a "hostess" at the Bing!

Noël Carroll is a former don of the American Society for Aesthetics. Presently he is in the witness protection program in the philosophy department of the University of Wisconsin—Madison. Yale University Press has a contract out on his forthcoming *Engaging the Moving Image*.

Lisa Cassidy is a Jersey Girl and an Assistant Professor of Philosophy at Ramapo College of New Jersey. Her research interests are ethics and feminist theory. She wrote her dissertation on feminism, responsibility, and embodiment at the University of Connecticut. Like Adrianna, Lisa shops at Bebe's, but she's still waiting for a garbage bag full of size 7 Jimmy Choo shoes to fall off the back of a truck.

Steven C. Combs is an Associate Professor in the communication studies department at Loyola Marymount University. He is the author of a forthcoming book, *The Dao of Rhetoric*. Steve has started his own unsuccessful crime family and lives in a chronic state of anxiety after accidentally putting out a hit on himself.

Michael E. Gettings is an Assistant Professor of Philosophy at Hollins University, a career he fell back on after losing his shirt on Webistics stock and betting against Pie-O-My at the track. His research interests include philosophy of fiction and ontological arguments for God's existence. He's still looking to get invited to the executive game.

AL GINI is a Professor of Philosophy at Loyola University Chicago and co-founder and Associate Editor of the journal *Business Ethics Quarterly*. He's also a regular commentator on Chicago's NPR affiliate, WBEZ. His most recent books include: *My Job My Self: Work and the Creation of the Modern Individual* (2000) and *The Importance of Being Lazy: In Praise of Play, Leisure, and Vacations* (2003). Oh yeah, in case you haven't figured it out, he's Italian.

RONALD M. GREEN directs the Ethics Institute at Dartmouth College where he also serves as chair of the Department of Religion. His books include *The Ethical Manager* (Macmillan, 1994). He consults for many business organizations. He has taught business ethics at Dartmouth's Amos Tuck School of Business. He's currently thinking of introducing a new business ethics course entitled "Whacking Stakeholders."

RICHARD GREENE is an Assistant Professor of Philosophy at Weber State University. He received his Ph.D. in Philosophy from the University of California, Santa Barbara. He has published papers in epistemology, metaphysics, and ethics. While Richard enjoys working with students, he is often relieved that they don't use Brylcreem.

DAVID HAHN is a former Graduate Student from Buffalo, N.Y. He now resides in Toledo, Ohio, where he continues reading Prince Matchabelli, Sun Z, and other peaceful thoughts. He is waiting for the books to open so that he, too, can get his button.

PETER H. HARE is State University of New York Distinguished Service Professor of Philosophy Emeritus at the University at Buffalo. He has published books in the history of American philosophy and philosophy of religion, as well as a biography of an anthropologist. His chief labor of love for more than thirty years has been editing *The Transactions of the C.S. Peirce Society: A Quarterly Journal in American Philosophy*. In their disputes with Tony he would like to see Meadow and A.J. use Job's arguments in the Old Testament—lamentations with "fuck" screamed at regular intervals.

JAMES HAROLD is an Assistant Professor of Philosophy at Mt. Holyoke College. His areas of interest include the philosophy of art, ethics, and medical ethics. His work has been published in *Philosophy, Psychiatry, and Psychology*, *The Journal of Aesthetics and Art Criticism*, and *The British Journal of Aesthetics*, among other places. He's currently working on a comprehensive treatise which will discuss the complex and exciting ontological relationships between quarterbacks, halfbacks, hunchbacks, Quasimodo, Nostradamus, and Notre Dame.

SHEILA LINTOTT is an Assistant Professor of Philosophy at Appalachian State University. She works in the areas of aesthetics, feminist philosophy, and ethics. The academic journals publishing her work include the *British Journal of Aesthetics*, *Hypatia: A Journal of Feminist Philosophy*, and the *Journal of Aesthetic Education*. Unlike Carmela Soprano, Sheila *graduated* from Montclair State University.

MIKE LIPPMAN is a graduate student at Duke University who should be finishing up his dissertation on the connections between feminine religious ritual and Ancient Greek Comedy (catchy title forthcoming). He splits his time between teaching in Durham, N.C. and writing and researching at the American School of Classical Studies in Athens, Greece. Mike thinks it's all a big nothing and demands to know what makes you think you're so special.

H. PETER STEEVES is f#@%ing Associate Professor of f#@%ing Philosophy at DePaul f#@%ing University where he specializes in ethics, social and political philosophy, and f#@%ing phenomenology.* His f#@%ing books include *The Things Themselves* (State University of New York Press, 2004), *Founding Community* (Kluwer, 1998), and f#@%ing *Animal Others* (State University of New York Press, 1999).* Madonn!* What a load of sh*t!*

KEVIN STOEHR teaches philosophy in the College of General Studies at Boston University. He wrote his dissertation on Hegel's *Logic*. He has edited and published a volume of essays on the philosophies of religion and art, a collection of articles on film and epistemology, and a dialogue on Jungian psychology. He attended Bowdoin College as an undergraduate, continues to live in Maine, and kindly asks all mob informants to refrain from hiding out in that state, especially close to college communities.

PETER J. VERNEZZE is an Associate Professor of Philosophy at Weber State University in Ogden, Utah. He received his Ph.D. from the University of Washington (under an assumed name), and is most recently the author of the Stoic self-help manual *Don't Worry, Be Stoic: Ancient Wisdom for Troubled Times* (University Press, 2004). He really does have a relative named Rico.

SCOTT D. WILSON is an Assistant Professor at Wright State University in Dayton, Ohio (the *true* birthplace of aviation). He received his Ph.D.

from the University of California, Santa Barbara in 2002. His research focuses mostly on applied ethics, and he has published papers on the moral status of animals. Late at night, when no one is watching, he likes to have a little gabagool.

Index